# IN THE SHADOW OF CHINA

D1795223

曾銳生編

在中共的投影下

一九四九年以來的台灣政治發展

金庸題

# In the Shadow of China

## Political Developments in Taiwan since 1949

*edited by*
STEVE TSANG

Hong Kong University Press
香港大學出版社

**Hong Kong University Press**
139 Pokfulam Road, Hong Kong
© Steve Tsang, 1993

This edition first published 1993

ISBN 962 209 341 8

Originating publisher: C. Hurst & Co., London

This soft cover edition published by Hong Kong
University Press is available in Asia, Australia
and New Zealand.

Printed in Hong Kong by Hing Yip Printing Company Limited

# CONTENTS

v

# TABLES

# PREFACE

The idea for this volume grew out of recognition of how widespread in the Western World is unfamiliarity with what has happened in Taiwan since 1949. The exciting developments there, particularly in the political arena since the middle of the 1980s, are not generally recognised. When conversations in senior common rooms and among other generally well-informed people touch upon political developments in Taiwan, they often reflect remarkable ignorance. Until recently what interest the academic community has shown in Taiwan has usually focused on its economic successes. Politically Taiwan is still seen by many as an oriental military dictatorship, tainted by the imposition of a Kuomintang party-state which lost the civil war to the Communists in China in 1949. Politics there are all too frequently dismissed as a peripheral subject in the study of modern China. This volume, I hope, will serve to disperse much of this out-of-date conception, and highlight the important fact that Taiwan has emerged politically from the military dictatorship of Chiang Kai-shek in the 1950s to become an increasingly democratically oriented state in the early 1990s.

The transformation still underway in Taiwan today is, or should be, a matter of great interest and concern to all scholars working on modern China. The Kuomintang, which under Chiang Kai-shek retreated from the Chinese mainland to Taiwan in 1949, was a Confucian-oriented Leninist-style party apparatus of a dictatorship. Since the late 1950s, as it settled down in Taiwan under Chiang and accepted the improbability of its forcible recovery of the mainland, it has gradually evolved into what political scientists call "soft authoritarianism". The quantum leap from the road to authoritarianism in whatever form to a road leading towards some kind of a multi-party democracy happened in 1986. Chiang Ching-kuo, then President and a former chief of the security apparatus, made the fateful decision to end the long-standing ban on an effective opposition party. Taiwan has not yet become a genuine liberal democracy in the Western sense. It still has a long way to go. However, the general elections of December 1992 have, in the view of the editor, taken Taiwan past the point of no return on the way to develop into a kind of democracy, one recognisable as such in the West. This extraordinary transformation challenges earlier assumptions that liberal democracy and the Chinese culture are mutually incompatible. It also raises the intriguing question of whether the Kuomintang party-state's experience of accommodating socio-economic changes in Taiwan holds any lesson for the Communist party-state across the Straits. In an important sense, the existence of Taiwan as a polity functions, however imperfectly, rather like the control in an experiment for all who seriously try to understand the forces of change in China.

The development of politics in Taiwan since 1949 has occurred in the shadow of China, as regards both its cultural and political heritage and the rival regime in Peking. In many ways Chiang Kai-shek's government in Taiwan was what he would have wished to create on the Chinese mainland, had his nation-building efforts of the 1920s and 1930s not been derailed by the Japanese invasion and the Communist insurgency. Chiang's methods stayed basically the same, and the ideology of the Kuomintang remained unchanged although the ethos of the party-state did undergo some modifications when most of its corrupt elements had been eliminated. There was, nevertheless, one vital difference between the former Kuomintang regime on the mainland and that in Taiwan. The former believed it held its mandate from heaven, whereas the latter had continuously to justify its existence in the face of a powerful rival with a legitimate claim to the government of China, constantly working or waiting for its demise. This awareness on the part of the Kuomintang leadership in Taiwan was not in itself enough to cause the great transformation that has taken place; the socio-economic changes since 1949 have also played a vital part. However, this awareness is a crucial factor that keeps the Kuomintang leadership on the alert. It is therefore an important subject, which is addressed in this volume.

By implication, Taiwan's successful move towards a prosperous, stable and increasingly liberal democratic political system under ethnic Chinese rule must present a challenge to the Communist Party leadership on the mainland, and serve as a model for many people there. As Taiwan under the Kuomintang emerged from defeat in the civil war in the shadow of China, the time has now come when China in turn must find a way to modernise itself in the shadow of Taiwan. Whether or not it will achieve this is not dealt with in this volume, but the question none the less highlights the need for closer scholarly study of Taiwan which, needless to say, is in itself an important subject for research.

In an attempt to redress this neglect, the Centre for Modern Chinese Studies at Oxford organised a series of eight lecture-seminars on this subject in late 1991. The participants included the world's leading authorities on various aspects of political development in Taiwan, based in the United States, Taiwan, Germany and Britain. This volume, which had its origin in papers presented at Oxford, represents an international collaborative effort to promote better understanding of the dynamism of political development in Taiwan. This will, I hope, stimulate interest in Taiwan and help to encourage others to look at Chinese politics in a new light.

In organising the series of lecture-seminars mentioned above and turning the papers into a book, I have received generous assistance from colleagues and friends. I am most grateful to all who participated in the seminars for their thoughts, and to my colleagues at the Centre for Modern Chinese Studies, especially Professor Glen Dudbridge and Dr Cyril Lin, for their encouragement. I am also indebted to Miss Naomi Brown, Professor Chu Hong-yuan, Professor Chen Yung-fa, Professor Chang Yu-fa and Mrs Rosanne Richardson for help in different ways. I would also like to thank Professor Jason Hu, Mr Raymond Tai, Mr David Liu and Mr Ging-lin Chung for seeking and securing the necessary financial support, without which the series of seminars could not have been organised.

Last but certainly not least, Professor Louis Cha, the great master of novels in the tradition of *The Water Margin*, deserves special gratitude for writing in calligraphy the Chinese title of this work for the front of the book.

*St Antony's College, Oxford*                   STEVE TSANG
*Spring 1993*

# NOTES ON THE CO-AUTHORS

HUNGDAH CHIU is a Professor of Law at the University of Maryland, and Director of its East Asian Legal Studies Programme. He was a participant of the National Affairs Conference held in Taipei in 1990 and has been a Research Member of the National Unification Council of the Republic of China since 1991.

JÜRGEN DOMES is a Professor of Political Science, Chairman of the Political Science section, and concurrently Director of the Research Unit on Chinese and East Asian Politics at the Saar University, Saarbrücken, Germany. He has published many books and articles in academic journals on the PRC and the ROC in the last thirty years.

THOMAS B. GOLD is Chairman of the Centre for Chinese Studies and an Associate Professor in Sociology, University of California at Berkeley. He is author of *State and Society in the Taiwan Miracle* (Armonk, NY, 1986).

HERMANN HALBEISEN teaches East Asian politics at the Department of East Asian Studies, Ruhr University, Bochum, Germany. His research interests focus on political thought in modern China and the political development of Taiwan.

FU HU is Lien Chen-tong Professor of Law and Political Science at the National Taiwan University. An expert in constitutional law, he has inspired many discussions of constitutionalism in Taiwan. His more recent research projects focus on the study of political behaviour and political changes, laying special emphasis on the relations between political culture, political participation, electoral behaviour, and the process of democratisation. He is a pioneer of empirical research in political science in Taiwan.

YING-JEOU MA is Vice Chairman and spokesman of the Mainland Affairs Council in Taiwan (since 1981). He served as President Chiang Ching-kuo's secretary and the KMT's deputy secretary-general in charge of democratic reforms during 1982–8. He joined the Cabinet in 1988.

HUNG-MAO TIEN is a Professor of Chinese Politics at the University of Wisconsin–Milwaukee and a Senior Fellow of the East Asian Legal Centre at the University of Wisconsin Law School. He is also Director of the Institute for National Policy Research. His many publications include *The Great Transition: Political and Social Change in the Republic of China* (Stanford, CA: Hoover Institution Press, 1989) and *Government and Politics in Kuomintang China, 1927–1937* (Stanford University Press, 1972).

STEVE TSANG is a Research Fellow at the Centre for Modern Chinese Studies and at St Antony's College, Oxford. He is author of *Democracy Shelved: Great Britain, China and Attempts at Constitutional Reform in Hong Kong* (Oxford University Press, 1988).

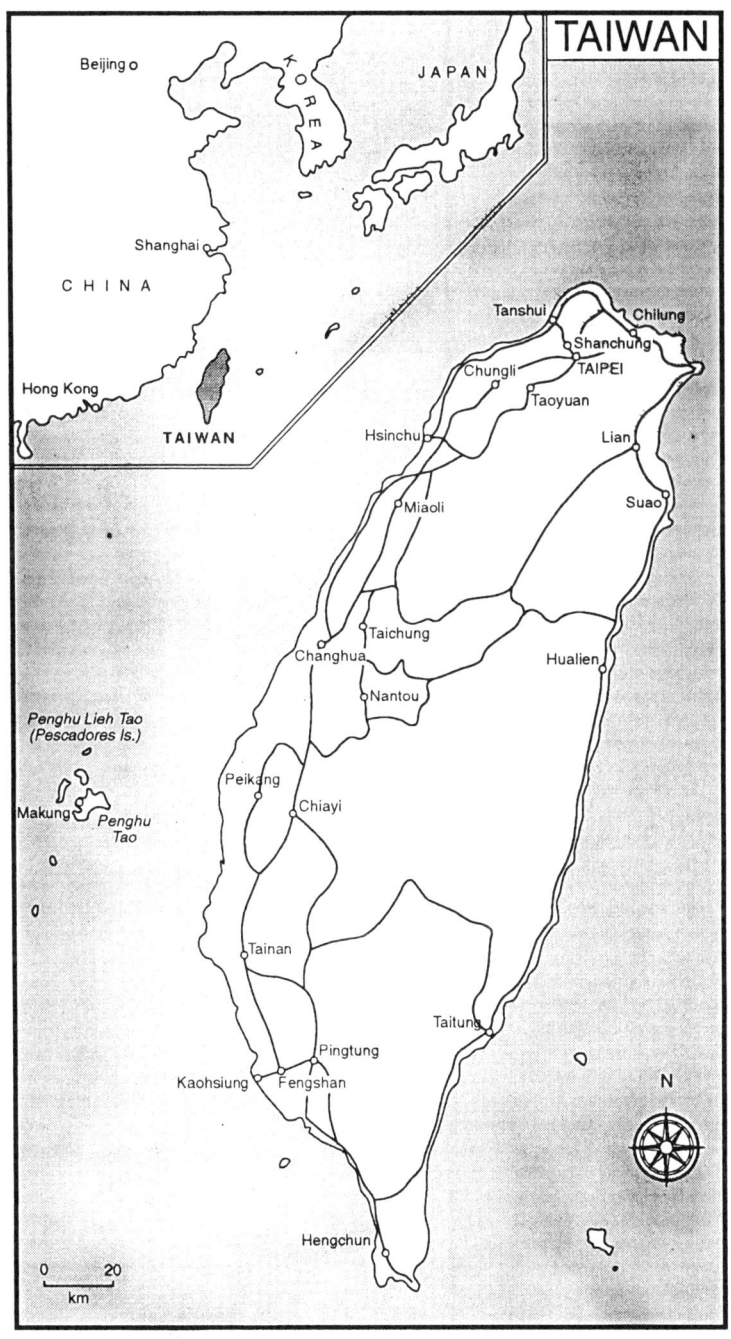

# TAIWAN

Beijing o

KOREA

JAPAN

Shanghai o

CHINA

Hong Kong

TAIWAN

Tanshui    Chilung
Shanchung
Chungli    TAIPEI
Taoyuan
Hsinchu    Lian

Miaoli    Suao

Taichung
Changhua    Hualien
Nantou

Penghu Lieh Tao
(Pescadores Is.)

Peikang
Makung  Penghu    Chiayi
Tao

Tainan

Taitung
Pingtung
Kaohsiung  Fengshan    N

Hengchun

0    20
km

# INTRODUCTION

The history of Taiwan since 1949 is a paradox. For all practical purposes, it is an independent state. However, its government has most vehemently held that an independent state of Taiwan does not exist. In the days when its government still held a seat in the United Nations, it strove to maintain that it and it alone represented China. Although the realm of the government in Taipei was limited to Taiwan, Penghu (the Pescadores) and a number of small islands off the coast of the Chinese mainland and in the South China Sea, it claimed to represent the government of all China and was recognised as such by a majority of the nations in the world.[1] This picture changed in 1971 when Richard Nixon, then President of the United States, decided to improve relations with the People's Republic of China (PRC) on the Chinese mainland, and ended the American effort to sustain the Taipei government's claim to be the sole legitimate government of China in the United Nations. Adhering to the instructions of its President, Chiang Kai-shek, the Taipei government continued, outside the United Nations and most international bodies which accepted the PRC government as that of China, to maintain its identity as the government of the Republic of China (ROC). Realism gradually gained ground, however, and by the late 1980s the Taipei government began to seek an international identity as the ROC in Taiwan and to press for re-admission to international bodies, usually under the name of Chinese Taipei. This new position does not represent an acceptance of Taiwan as an independent state. Nor does it imply giving up Taiwan's claim to be part of China, and that there is but one China. What it does mean is that although the ROC in Taiwan is not part of the PRC, it is still part of China and is a *de facto* actor in the international community. This anomaly is an important factor determining the scope of political developments in Taiwan, and is likely to continue as long as Taiwan exists in the shadow of China.

## The Chinese shadow

There are three aspects to the Chinese shadow. First, there is the question of survival, as the PRC repeatedly tried to relegate the ROC to the

---

1. The first time the Taipei government received fewer votes than the Peking government at the United Nations was in 1970, by a margin of two votes.

1

dustbin of history and bring the unfinished civil war to an end. Secondly, there are questions of *fa-t'ung* (legitimacy) and the identity of the people living in the Taiwan area. This is, in a sense, a legacy of history. And finally, the ROC in Taiwan is a continuation and a derivative of Chiang Kai-shek's Nationalist government on the Chinese mainland before 1950. While it is possible, for analytical purposes, to separate these three points, they are in fact closely intertwined, and their constant interaction since 1949 has fundamentally shaped political developments in Taiwan.

The issue of survival defines the limits of political change in Taiwan. Admittedly the actual danger of a PRC military take-over was removed by the interposing of the American Seventh Fleet in the Taiwan Straits as long ago as the summer of 1950 on the outbreak of the Korean War. Taiwan's security was later guaranteed by the 1954 Mutual Defence Treaty with the United States. The abrogation of this treaty, which resulted from the normalisation of relations between the United States and the PRC in 1979, in principle nullified this guarantee but did not in fact lead to an increase in the military threat from the PRC. Indeed, in the Taiwan Relations Act (1979) the United States continued to express strong interest in Taiwan's security. It has pledged itself to maintain the capabilities "to resist any resort to force or other forms of coercion that would jeopardise the security, or the social or economic system, of the people on Taiwan."[2] Nevertheless, the reality remains that the PRC has consistently reserved the right, and demonstrated its intention and willingness, to use force against Taiwan if the latter were to go down the road to independence. In other words, given the military disparity across the Taiwan Straits, the limit for political change in Taiwan in the last four decades has been set so as to exclude independence or freedom of determination for the residents of the island state; and this will remain the case in the foreseeable future.

From 1950 to 1975, during the rule of Chiang Kai-shek, this limitation was academic since he adamantly ruled out independence in any form or guise. This policy was continued by his successors as President of the ROC, Yen Chia-kan and Chiang Ching-kuo, until 1986. Indeed, they withdrew the ROC from all major international organisations (except the Asian Development Bank) which recognised the PRC as the official representative of China. They permitted no flexibility in

2. Quoted in Richard Bush, "Helping the Republic of China to Defend Itself", in Ramon Myers (ed.), *A Unique Relationship: The United States and the Republic of China under the Taiwan Relations Act* (Stanford, CA: Hoover Institution Press, 1989) p. 83.

upholding the myth that there was but one China. In those days, the advocacy of Taiwanese independence was one of the two most heinous crimes conceivable; the other was support of the rival Communist regime.

But all this changed in 1986 as Taiwan under Chiang Ching-kuo, Chiang Kai-shek's son, gingerly embarked on the road towards developing a more democratic political system, less than two years before his death. In April 1986 Chiang appointed a twelve-member task force within the Kuomintang Central Standing Committee to study political reform. This was followed by his tacit acceptance of the formation of an opposition party (the Democratic Progressive Party or the DPP), in violation of the law at the time. It was no coincidence that it was also in this year that Chiang's government agreed for the first time to use the name "Chinese Taipei" when it participated in the Women's World Cup baseball championships in Moscow, and to rejoin the Olympic Council of Asia. Taiwan's policies towards the mainland and towards domestic political development are intertwined.

If the lock on the door to democracy in Taiwan was unlocked by the events of 1986, the door itself was opened as martial law was lifted in July 1987. This was partly the result of a long process of economic progress and social development, which had gradually but steadily undercut the foundations of authoritarianism and brought in a demand for pluralism and democratic practices. Chiang Ching-kuo must also be given credit for steering the course of this remarkable transformation. Despite the presence of a strong undercurrent favouring political change, when Chiang decided in favour of liberalisation in 1986 he still had the party-state, the security apparatus and the armed forces firmly under his control. Since the undercurrent was only beginning to surface, a lesser leader would, and no doubt could, have ignored it or tried to resist change by clamping down. However Chiang, hardly a democrat by conviction, had the vision and wisdom to see and recognise the need for change in order to meet the challenges posed by both domestic and external developments.

The very presence of the PRC as a potential threat to the survival of Taiwan was the single most important external factor in the decision of Kuomintang (KMT) leaders, including Chiang Ching-kuo, to introduce democratic reform in the latter half of the 1980s. Paradoxically, the economic reform of Teng Hsiao-ping on the Chinese mainland, which till 1989 looked promising despite facing numerous difficulties, was potentially as much a threat to KMT rule as any military threat. Despite the KMT leaders' own long-standing rhetoric stressing the goal of unification, they knew that the disparity in power, size, population and resources would make the KMT a junior partner in a unified China. They had no intention of allowing modern Taiwan — very much their creation, as they saw it — to be swallowed up in a China dominated by the Communists, with their party relegated to a minor role of peripheral or merely regional importance. As the results of opinion surveys in Ying-jeou Ma's chapter show, a large majority of the people of Taiwan would be in favour of unification with the mainland if the Chinese Communists were to practise democracy and freedom. If Taiwan were to remain stagnant politically, successful economic reform in the PRC could narrow the gap between the two territories and encourage more Taiwanese to demand a new Kuomintang–Communist partnership. To avoid this eventuality, a step-by-step reform programme from above would be essential. This would widen the gap between Taiwan and mainland residents in their political expectations and definitions of freedom and democracy, thus forestalling a unification with the Communist Party as the senior partner, yet it would still be subject to the general direction of the KMT and would not abandon the idea of of unification.

There has been an upsurge in the activities of opposition political leaders and parties since the late 1980s, with their increasing demands for more democratic changes, and this has undoubtedly influenced the agenda for reform and forced the pace of political change. However, Taiwan's moves towards democracy have largely remained under the direction of the ruling KMT. The KMT's political reform "from above" has proved successful because the party has largely been able to make way for younger, more broad-minded and more dynamic leaders to take the party a small step ahead of public opinion most of the time. This, in turn, was possible because public opinion in Taiwan was, like the KMT, constrained by its perception of political changes. The genie of democracy, once released from the bottle in Taiwan, emerged with the knowlege of just how far its magic could be employed. Pushing for political change in Taiwan itself is one thing, but clamouring for the right to self-determination, including the right to independence, as a logical step on the road to democracy is another. Any serious move towards independence is seen by the majority of people in Taiwan as likely to provoke a much-feared hostile reaction from the PRC, which could threaten Taiwan's survival. Hence, the DPP's inclusion in its parliamentary election campaign of late 1991 of a provision to set up a Republic of Taiwan to replace the ROC proved to be an electoral liability rather than an asset. The people of Taiwan know that they have to approach the question of democracy with some circumspection.

The second element of the Chinese shadow on Taiwanese politics is a legacy of history, which raises questions about *fa-t'ung*, the identity of the people and the Chinese people's historical aspiration for a united country. The source of legitimacy, or *fa-t'ung*, for the ROC government in Taipei is the ROC Constitution of 1947. This was drawn up on the basis of Dr Sun Yat-sen's Three Principles of the People for the whole of China, including Taiwan as a province, rather than for the territories under the ROC's control after its retreat to Taipei in 1949. The political system which has existed in Taiwan is, therefore, still a four-tier one. At the apex is the central or national government, ostensibly for all China. Below that is the Taiwan provincial government, to which the special municipalities of Taipei and, more recently, Kao-hsiung are to be added. Below that again is the city/county level of government, with the town/borough level of local administration at the bottom. Administratively such a structure is superfluous, since the span of control of the ROC government coincides with that of the province of Taiwan, except for a few islands off the coast of the Chinese mainland and in the South China Sea. It is difficult to conceive that a constitution drawn up specifically with the geographical reality of the present-day ROC in mind would provide for such a structure. However, if the ROC government were to reduce this structure by one tier, at either the provincial or national level, it would become increasingly a government of Taiwan alone and would imply giving up its claim to being the government of China. This will require amending the 1947 Constitution or the drawing up of a new one, raising questions about the *fa-t'ung* of the ROC government. This has been an important consideration, during the political debates of the early 1990s, in the KMT's resistance to replacing the existing constitution by a new one.

The same need and desire to uphold the *fa-t'ung* created another notable anomaly in the ROC: namely "ten thousand years parliament", which continued to exist until the end of 1991. After 1949 the ROC government could not hold elections on the mainland to replace those members of the National Assembly, the Legislative Yuan and the Control Yuan, who had been returned from mainland constituencies in the elections of 1947, when their terms expired. If the Taipei government had reconstituted these bodies by holding elections only in territories under its control, it would have lost its claim to represent

China. In order to maintain the myth that the ROC government was the government of all China, over most of which it had had no control since 1949, it chose to regard these ageing members as representatives of the Chinese nation. This continued till January 1989, when a law was passed to pension them off and requiring all of them to retire by the end of 1991. This change reflected the ROC government's search for a new international personality, embodied in ideas such as "one country, two governments" or "one country, two realities."

With this new development, the KMT government could not resist, and had indeed decided in favour of, a review of the Constitution. The question of the ROC's *fa-t'ung* needs to be addressed in the 1990s, as it moves increasingly towards democracy. However, this is likely to remain a thorny issue as it is intertwined with other sensitive political matters, particularly those relating to the identity of the residents of Taiwan and the historical aspiration of the Chinese people to unification.

National identity is a crucial factor in constitutional reform. There exists in Taiwan a very strong *T'ai-wan i-shih*, or Taiwanese consciousness—a concept still subject to debate among the Taiwanese themselves. *T'ai-wan i-shih* can be taken in its narrower sense to imply Taiwan for the Taiwanese (*pen-sheng-jen*), or, in its broader and more widely accepted meaning, a common identity for all residents who identify with Taiwan. Either way it poses the question of whether being Taiwanese is the same as being Chinese. If a new *fa-t'ung* were to be erected on the foundation of democracy and self-determination, the need to uphold the one-China principle would lose its relevance. However, for the existing *fa-t'ung* to continue in any meaningful way, it is essential that the people of Taiwan do not consider being Taiwanese as so distinct an identity that it amounts to belonging to a nation separate from China.

An important aspect of the identity problem is the rift between the Taiwanese and the mainlanders (*wai-sheng-jen*), which was torn asunder in the *erh-erh-pa shih-chien* or the 28 February Incident of 1947. Although they have been improving in recent years, the delicate relations between the two groups remain a cloud hanging over political life in Taiwan. Whatever the truth of the matter, whatever the number of people of both Taiwanese and non-Taiwanese origins killed in the course of the whole incident, and whatever the degree of justification for the scale of military force used, this tragic event came to symbolise the mainlander-dominated KMT's oppression of the Taiwanese in the early post-war period. Taiwan could not come to terms with it fully until 1992, when President Li Teng-hui[3] formally apologised to families of the victims and his government published a credible official report. In an effort to reduce distinctions between these two groups, Li's government also ended the the former practice of asking for one's ancestral home (*chi-kuan*) on official forms. These and other government efforts, such as accelerating localisation of the public service, will help to reduce tension and differences between the two groups but will not remove them overnight. Nevertheless, the shared experiences and the common pride in Taiwan's successes in the last few decades, as well as the general acceptance that a new way of life has emerged, will help eventually to disperse this cloud. Till then, the rift will remain an important factor in politics in Taiwan.

The other aspect of the identity problem is the presence of a strong potential demand for self-determination. The emergence of a way of life distinct from that on the mainland of China has given rise to a Taiwan identity which has little, if any, room for incorporating or being incorporated into the PRC. However, in the early 1990s this identity does not preclude those who share it from being Chinese at the same time. It has not resulted in a general outcry or support for independence, as demonstrated in the DPP's failure to win widespread backing for its independence platform in the 1991 elections.

This phenomenon is due mainly to the presence of a strong counter-vailing force — the so-called historical aspiration of the Chinese people for a united country. In spite of the fact that throughout its long history China has been divided longer than it has been united as a single political entity, most Chinese are unaware of this; and they believe that normality implies unification. Opinion surveys in Taiwan in the early 1990s continue to indicate that the overwhelming majority of the people of Taiwan would wish to see unification, though (except for a small minority) not with the Communists as the dominating force. The people of Taiwan on the whole are proud of the cultural heritage of China. Most think of themselves as both Taiwanese and Chinese, and live happily in the shade of China's history. Whether or not this is living under "the tyranny of history",[4] it is a powerful factor which conditions political changes in Taiwan.

The third element of China's shadow on political life in Taiwan is

---

3. The President spells his name Lee. For consistency, the Wade-Giles spelling, Li, is used throughout this volume.

4. A phase borrowed from W.J.E. Jenner's work *The Tyranny of History: The Roots of China's Crisis* (London: Allen Lane, 1992).

the fact that its government is a continuation and a derivative of Chiang Kai-shek's nationalist regime in Nanking. Chiang took with him to Taiwan in 1949 a determination to erect a Confucian-oriented Leninist-style party-state, and a public commitment to re-conquer the mainland lost to the Communists. These considerations formed the political foundation upon which present day Taiwan was built.

After his defeat on the mainland in 1949, Chiang Kai-shek's priorities in Taiwan were to prevent this island redoubt from falling to the Communists and to turn it into his new revolutionary base. He reflected on his regime's failures in the previous two decades, and tried to erect in Taiwan what he wanted to create for China. In Chiang's mind, what China needed was a modernised Confucian benevolent dictatorship, buttressed by the triumvirate of armed forces, security apparatus and the KMT, and masked as a democracy under tutelage in the name of Dr Sun Yat-sen's Three Principles of the People. This was what he established in Taiwan, except that democracy was suspended under siege by authority of the "Temporary Provisions Effective during the Period of Communist Rebellion" (1948). He combined in his regime elements of Confucianism, Leninist tactics in party organisation and Sun's brand of tutelage democracy temporarily held in abeyance. Chiang was a dictator but he was also in his own mind a revolutionary. He was power-hungry, yet he wanted power not only for the sake of it but also in order to promote his revolutionary goals. His vision for China, and hence for Taiwan since 1949, was to establish a powerful, stable and united country — one which would provide the conditions for economic development, for cultural and moral rejuvenation, and for restoring China to its rightful place in the world. His tactics were the elimination of his opponents, the use of his subordinates to check and balance each other, the education and indoctrination of his subjects, the strengthening of social control, and a strong dictatorial leadership. Apart from bracing his forces for defence against a Communist onslaught, which would have occurred in the autumn of 1950 but for the Korean War, Chiang embarked on a purge and reorganisation of the KMT, which was officially completed at the Seventh Party Congress in 1952. He also rebuilt the security apparatus from the ground up, entrusting this mission to his son, Chiang Ching-kuo. The younger Chiang was also given the tasks of reintroducing a Soviet style political commissar system to the armed forces and of directing the younger generations towards the right thoughts through the Anti-Communist

National Salvation Youth Corps—a derivative of the Communist Youth League. On the island of Taiwan Chiang Kai-shek imposed his revolutionary vision as a political model, and no major deviation from this was possible during his lifetime.

Chiang's public commitment first to reconquer, then to recover, the mainland also had deep implications for political developments in Taiwan. On the one hand, his constant reiteration of this theme, the reverse of which would be a Communist invasion or take-over, served to remind the people of Taiwan how vulnerable their island was. The setting up of a police state and the substitution of martial law for constitutional rule were less objectionable in a time of exigency. Local Taiwanese aspirations could also be ignored more than would otherwise have been the case, in the name of the wider national good, without provoking major local disturbances. In short, it made the imposition of his benevolent dictatorship more readily acceptable.

On the other hand, this had the effect of reminding the KMT party-state that it too was vulnerable. To survive, it would not only have to buttress its defence and security forces and strengthen its party apparatus; it would also have to win popular support. As Chiang and his regime ruled out participatory democracy at the national level as a means to achieve this, they opted to provide an efficient, effective and paternalistic government, which would improve the standard of living. Chiang knew that he could by and large steam-roller through virtually any aspect of life in Taiwan, but he also understood that he had to be selective and circumspect in doing so, providing justifiable grounds for his heavy-handedness. Otherwise he might provoke an uprising or produce a situation conducive to a Communist invasion. Hence, Chiang's dictatorship was one with an "inhibited centre"— an important factor which faciliated its subsequent transformation into a more democratically oriented state.

Chiang's instinct as a Chinese nationalist and his steadfast refusal to give up his avowed object of recovering the mainland closed the door to one direction of political development, namely the possibility of Taiwan becoming an independent state in its own right. After the outbreak of the Korean War, both the United States and leading members of the British Commonwealth had seriously contemplated supporting Taiwanese efforts to develop into an independent state within the framework of the United Nations, should there be such an attempt. In 1953 the American Secretary of State, John Foster Dulles, "devised a preliminary scheme to allow both China and Taiwan into the General Assembly when the U.N. charter was revised in 1955".[5] Although this proposal failed, and American documents of the time do not explicitly advocate a "two-China" policy, it was what the U.S. President, Dwight D. Eisenhower, and Dulles were prepared to support.[6] Indeed, as the 1950s unfolded, the United States "nudged the ruling KMT along a path consistent with a two-China policy".[7]

Even the British, who were reluctant to risk being sucked into the Chinese civil war, worked on the basis that Taiwan's status was not settled. They took the legalistic view that while the Cairo Declaration (1943) expressed a common objective among the Allies to restore Taiwan (among other territories) to China after the defeat of Japan, the Chinese occupation of the island under general orders of the Allied Powers in 1945 did not amount to a transfer of sovereignty—a matter which would need to be addressed and formalised in a peace treaty. This position was not, in the British view, rectified by the peace treaty signed between the ROC and Japan in 1952, since it merely provided for the termination of Japanese sovereignty.[8] Taiwan's sovereignty was not formally transferred to either the ROC or the PRC, though the ROC exercised *de facto* control over it. The British recognised that there would be many thorny complications in any course leading to the independence of Taiwan, either directly or through the medium of a United Nations trusteeship in the first instance, and were not keen to get involved. However, they were prepared to support such a course, in order to prevent the tension in the Taiwan Straits from destabilising the region. A prime example of this was "Operation Oracle", a joint British–New Zealand effort to defuse the First Taiwan Straits Crisis (1954–55) by taking the matter to the Security Council as a situation likely to endanger peace.[9] From Chiang's point of view, Britain and New Zealand were attempting to clear the ground for the PRC to enter the United Nations,[10] which would be the thin end of the wedge

5. Gordon H. Chang, *Friends and Enemies: The United States, China, and the Soviet Union, 1948–1972* (Stanford University Press, 1990), p. 146.

6. *Ibid.*, p. 145.

7. *Ibid.*, p. 160.

8. British Foreign Office archives at the Public Record Office (Kew), "Future of Taiwan", FC10210/2, *FO371/105216*.

9. "Chinese Off-shore Islands", January 1955 , File PM264/3/2 Part 2, *Department of External Affairs Series 2619* (National Archives of New Zealand).

10. President to Ambassador in Washington (for Foreign Minister), telegram, 27 January 1955, File B.13.1(e) (Ceasefire Agreement), Box 145, *Papers of Wellington Koo* (New York: Butler Library at Columbia University).

leading eventually to either a "two-China" scenario or a United Nations trusteeship over Taiwan. Chiang worked vehemently against this. Whether or not the Americans or British could ever have enabled a Taiwan desiring its independence to achieve this goal in the 1950s and 1960s, particularly in the light of the PRC's objections, Chiang's emotional commitment to a united China made this a purely academic exercise and blocked the road to self-determination for the people of Taiwan.

## Organisation of the book

The central theme of this volume is the development and transformation of a Leninist-style authoritarian party-state into an increasingly democratically oriented state in Taiwan, happening as it did in the shadow of China. Each chapter addresses an aspect of this change from a different angle and not all contributors are in full agreement over the dynamics behind this transformation. While the chapters, having been originated as independent papers, can be read on their own, readers are encouraged to follow the structure of this volume.

In Chapter 1, Hungdah Chiu begins by setting out the constitutional framework for political changes. He explains in some detail, from a legal scholar's point of view, the provisions of the ROC's Constitution, which came into force in December 1947, and the "Temporary Provisions Effective during the Period of Communist Rebellion", which became effective in May 1948 and were not terminated until May 1991. The latter were adopted in response to the rise of the Chinese Communist challenge on the mainland, and provided President Chiang Kai-shek with power to assume many functions originally envisaged in the Constitution for the Executive Yuan. Two of the particularly powerful instruments in this connection are the National Security Council and the Central Personnel Administration. Having outlined the constitutional framework, Chiu gives an account of how the Presidents of the ROC first built up their power and authority and then took the initiative to give them up, in the light of (in President Li Teng-hui's words) "the changing domestic and international situation and the increasingly ardent desire of the people for democratic rule of law". The rest of the chapter examines the problems in constitutional reform since the National Affairs Conference of 1990. The dilemma is that a meaningful constitutional reform must tackle the question of Taiwan's relations with the rest of China, but no practical solution for this problem acceptable to both the KMT and the DPP can be found.

Even after the KMT's landslide victory in the National Assembly elections of December 1991, in which the DPP campaigned on (among other things) a platform for an independent Taiwan and lost, the problem refuses to fade away.

Chapter 2 takes a historical approach. Steve Tsang addresses the question of whether Taiwan in fact attempted to reconquer the Mainland in the 1950s, and examines critically the ramifications of following such a policy. He argues that despite Chiang Kai-shek's strong emotional commitment to recover the mainland, Chiang realised that he did not have the resources to do so. Chiang the nationalist and the revolutionary could not give up this goal, but Chiang the realist accepted the reality throughout the 1950s. The maintenance of a huge military establishment, the tremendous investments in the armed forces, and the associated reforms of the military, the KMT and the security apparatus appear at first sight to indicate Chiang's intention to retake the Mainland. In fact they were all needed for Taiwan's defence and for the kind of political system which Chiang envisaged for Taiwan. This creation of a powerful party-state invested dictatorial powers in Chiang. Yet his constant reference to the presence of a threat from across the Straits reminded the ruling KMT and the people of the regime's inherent vulnerability. This resulted, paradoxically, in the emergence of an "inhibited centre" in an otherwise mighty authoritarian state. In the long term, this proved a crucial factor which led the KMT under Chiang Ching-kuo to embark on the road to democratisation a slight step ahead of mainstream public opinion.

In Chapter 3, Hermann Halbeisen argues that the question of *fa-t'ung* was the central issue for debates on political reform after 1949. He points out that the KMT regime did have to face criticisms even in the 1950s. The use of emergency power to enhance the power of the executive at the expense of the legislative branch, and the reinterpretation of the Constitution to legitimise Chiang Kai-shek's hold on the presidency beyond two terms, were the main issues. They were about *fa-t'ung*. But the related question of national identity was not tackled, as the principal opposition leaders then were predominantly liberals from the mainland, and identified themselves with China. The issue finally emerged as a major topic for debate within the mainstream opposition in the 1970s. With the rise of a Taiwanese identity, the legitimacy of a mainlander-dominated government came into question. In Halbeisen's view, the KMT decided on political reform in the 1980s because it saw a rising public demand for the policy. Its first step, taken in 1986, was to remove some of the strict limitations on personal liberties, the media and organised political activities. As Taiwan has advanced closer to democracy the question of national identity has become even more important. The DPP moved the issue of the establishment of a new state with an identity of its own further and further up its list of priorities, until it reached the top of the list in late 1991. The KMT as a whole has preferred to avoid the issue and to emphasise democratisation within a framework of stability. The two parties' differences on this matter also affect their approaches to reform as a whole. This is reflected in the KMT's support for amending the Constitution and the DPP's demand for replacing the constitution with a new one, for a Republic of Taiwan. Halbeisen concludes that the KMT will continue to be the main force in shaping the direction and content of political reform, particularly after it gained a mandate in its resounding victory in the 1991 elections.

Hung-mao Tien explores the dynamics behind reform from a different angle in Chapter 4. He stresses that socio-economic developments, the demand for changes by opposition forces and the ruling elite's decision to respond by pursuing democracy interacted to form the driving force for behind Taiwan's democratic transition. It happened in two stages. As Taiwan developed, the old "hard authoritarian" regime under Chiang Kai-shek evolved into a pluralistic "soft authoritarian" regime under Chiang Ching-kuo in the 1970s and 1980s. The political domination of the mainlanders, a hallmark of the regime in the 1950s and 1960s, gradually weakened as the Taiwanese were admitted in increasing numbers to the ruling élite. The Taiwanese component of the KMT's Central Committee increased from a token share in the 1950s and 1960s to 17 per cent in 1984, and 40 per cent in 1988. The second stage began in 1988 as democracy flourished within the KMT, following the death of its last strongman, Chiang Ching-kuo. The recognition that the party must change to win electoral support increasingly became a force behind democracy. In the meantime rapid economic developments since the 1950s led to a proliferation of secondary associations, which increased from a little over 2,500 in 1952 to almost 14,000 in 1990. Once the KMT party-state began to let its control over these organisations weaken, many of them transformed themselves into issue-oriented interest groups. This assisted the emergence of a civic society, an important development in the process of democratisation. But further institutional changes need to take place before Taiwan becomes a democracy. This will continue to be, in Tien's view, a painful process, since it involves the transformation of an authoritarian corporatist party-state into a democracy and the simultaneous tackling of the question of national identity.

Jürgen Domes traces, in Chapter 5, the development of opposition politics in Taiwan. He identifies the Taiwanisation of decision-making and pluralisation of the political system under Chiang Ching-kuo since 1972 as the starting point for the reform process. This process picked up momentum in 1977. On the one hand, Chiang commissioned a group of Western-trained social scientists to make confidential recommendations on matters relating, *inter alia*, to the end of martial law and press censorship, the legalisation of new political parties, and the reconstitution of the central parliamentary bodies whose members dated from the 1940s. On the other hand various opposition groups, which had forged a close alliance after 1975, achieved a breakthrough in the elections of 1977 by gaining one third of the votes and 27 per cent of the seats in the Taiwan Provincial Assembly. The process was temporarily halted in 1979, as stability appeared under threat following derecognition by the United States and the Kao-hsiung Incident. However, the trend could not be reversed. As the American-trained technocrats within the KMT grew in importance in the 1980s they advocated, in contrast to the old guard, carefully orchestrated political relaxation from above as the best guarantee of national security and social stability. The opposition forces, for their part, continued their struggle in elections and moved towards forming a party in all but name. The eventual peaceful birth of the DPP in 1986, before new parties were legalised, was a culmination of this process and the result of tolerance being exercised by Chiang Ching-kuo himself. Domes sees that the KMT is responsible for this transformation is at least as much as the opposition forces have been. After the breakthrough of 1986 opposition politics entered a new phase. As Taiwan moved at a quickening pace from an authoritarian state to a pluralistic representative one, the questions of the direction of political reform and the national identity emerged as key issues and became intertwined.

In Chapter 6 Fu Hu scrutinises the notion that elections were the major force for political changes in Taiwan. He points out that elections had been an important element of political life since the early 1950s. In those days the KMT successfully used elections, which it could and did manipulate and control, to recruit a limited number of Taiwanese into the political system up to the provincial level in order to ameliorate its authoritarian rule. This was necessary because in the aftermath of the tragic events of February and March 1947 the KMT government was seen by many Taiwanese as a kind of colonial regime. Periodic elections also willy-nilly performed what Hu calls the "circumvolving function", and became a social catalyst and a socialisation agent for the electorate. Elections became the institution whereby the local political elite found their identity and upon which the local power structure rested. This process gradually developed into a driving force for democratic transformation, and assisted the rise of the DPP. While empirical data for the earlier period are unavailable, Hu supports his interpretation by the results of surveys he and his colleagues conducted in 1984, 1987 and 1990. Employing log-linear analysis, he also assesses the nature of electoral competition in Taiwan in recent years. His findings suggest that underlying political cleavages over legitimacy based on popular mandate and national identity are as important as social distinctions along the sub-ethnic and socio-economic class lines.

Thomas Gold takes a sociological approach in Chapter 7. He goes behind the question of political development and investigates the ingredients and the rise of the Taiwan identity. Developed as it was in the triple shadow of China—which, in Gold's analysis, consisted of geography, history, and the presence of the PRC regime on the mainland—the KMT government tried to impose a Chinese identity on all the residents of Taiwan. However, national identity is not a matter which can be settled by administrative orders even when backed up by a powerful party-state. An identity of its own gradually emerged in Taiwan as a result of the interaction of several forces. Rapid economic growth brought in its wake fundamental social changes, including the spread of literacy and Western culture, the emergence of a middle class, and the rise of social movements. The KMT itself underwent important changes, not least the localisation of its membership. Internationally, the US–PRC rapprochement of 1971, which led to the ROC's diplomatic isolation, greatly weakened its legitimacy. The end of US recognition in 1979 further raised questions about the legitimacy of this mainlander-dominated regime's near monopoly over politics in Taiwan. In the mean time, the PRC's pursuit of a policy of reform under Teng Hsiao-ping in the 1980s encouraged the people of Taiwan to reflect on their own experiences. Gold also examines the environments of literary, scholarly and popular culture to find the ingredients of a Taiwan identity and the process for its development. In this continuing process the related consciousness of *Chung-kuo i-shih* and *T'ai-wan i-shih* constantly interact with each other.

In Chapter 8, Ying-jeou Ma provides an insider's view of the ROC's policy towards the Chinese mainland, where the presence of a Communist regime is a major element in the Chinese shadow. He begins by giving a brief review of the relations between Taiwan and the mainland since 1949, and then provides a summary of the PRC's current policy towards Taiwan. The main thrust of this chapter is, however, to explain the content and mechanics in the formulation of the ROC's policy towards the Mainland, since its historic decision in November 1987 to allow Taiwanese residents to visit the mainland. Ma, a leading light in the making of the ROC's policy in this matter, clearly states Taipei's position towards the mainland. Taipei supports the goal of unification, but only if it will result in "a free, democratic and equitably prosperous country", and only if it can be achieved on the basis of "reason, peace, parity, and reciprocity". In this chapter, Ma also provides the results of recent opinion polls held in Taiwan on various aspects of the island's relations with the Mainland, and other illuminating statistics on various forms of contacts between the two territories which have been taking place.

Finally, I put forward in the Epilogue my reflections on whether the experiences of political developments in Taiwan in the shadow of China have any relevance for China. I suggest that the most important lesson the PRC can usefully learn from Taiwan is that forces for political changes towards greater freedom, democracy and respect for human rights will follow successful economic development. Taiwan has proved that even a quasi-Leninist party-state can adapt successfully to such changes, albeit only slowly, and go on to win genuine popular support. The volume concludes on the note that Taiwan's very existence will provide a living alternative model of what the Chinese people can do politically, economically, socially and in any other field.

# 1

## CONSTITUTIONAL DEVELOPMENT IN THE REPUBLIC OF CHINA IN TAIWAN

### *Hungdah Chiu*

When the Constitution of the Republic of China (ROC) was adopted by the National Assembly held in Nanking on 25 December 1946, the ROC government was fighting a civil war with the Chinese Communists on the mainland; therefore, the National Assembly also adopted at the same time the "Temporary Provisions Effective during the Period of Mobilisation for the Suppression of the Communist Rebellion", which granted extraordinary power to the President. After its defeat by the Chinese Communist forces on the mainland, the ROC government moved to Taiwan on 8 December 1949. Because the Chinese Communists threatened to take over Taiwan by military force, Taiwan was placed under martial law by the ROC government on 20 May 1949. The elections of the National Assembly, the Legislative Yuan and the Control Yuan were also suspended and those members who had been elected in the mainland in 1947 continued to serve indefinitely.

With the reduction of tension in the Taiwan Straits during the 1980s, President Chiang Ching-kuo decided on 15 July 1987 to lift martial law, which also ended the ban on organising new political parties. At the same time, the ROC announced the termination of foreign exchange controls, so that anyone could remit up to a total of US$5 million abroad in a year without any questions asked. Thus the ROC took an historic step in the direction of greater political and economic liberalisation and political democratisation in Taiwan.

On 25 December 1987, President Chiang announced a plan to reform the ROC's parliamentary bodies at the annual meeting of the National Assembly. Unfortunately, Chiang died on 13 January 1988 before he could implement this reform. Dr Li Tenghui, who succeeded to the presidency on the same day, pledged to carry out Chiang's policy. Under Li's leadership, the policy of democratisation and the liberalisation process in politics and the economy continued. The purpose of this chapter is to review the constitutional development in the ROC since

17

its removal to Taiwan in late 1949. It begins with a summary of the main features of the Constitution adopted in 1946.

## The main features of the 1946 Constitution

After the end of World War II in September 1945, the national government convened a Political Consultative Conference, composed of twenty-nine delegates representing different political parties and non-partisan groups, from 10 to 30 January 1946.[1]

The National Assembly was convened on 5 November 1946; and on 25 December, primarily based on the consensus reached at the Political Consultative Conference, it adopted the Constitution of the Republic of China, which came into force on 25 December 1947. The main contents of this Constitution[2] are summarised below:

1. *Preamble.* The Constitution is enacted in accordance with the teachings bequeathed by Dr Sun Yat-sen.
2. *Chapter I. General Provisions.* The Republic of China shall be a democratic republic of the people, to be governed by the people and for the people (Article 1), sovereignty shall reside in the whole body of citizens (Article 2) and there shall be equality among the various racial groups in the Republic of China (Article 5).
3. *Chapter II. Rights and Duties of the People.* All citizens are equal before the law (Article 7), and personal freedoms are guaranteed by a system similar to *habeas corpus* (Article 8).[3] No person shall be subjected to trial by a military tribunal except for those in military service (Article 9). The people shall have freedoms of residence, change of residence (Article 10), speech, teaching, writing, publication (Article

1. For the complete text on the constitutional issue decided by the Conference, see Chin Hsiao-yi (ed.), *Chung-hua Min-kuo chung-yao shih-liao ch'u-pien — Tui-jih k'an-chan shih-ch'i, Ti-ch'i-pien, Chan-hou Chung-kuo* (Preliminary Compilation of Important Historical Materials of the Republic of China — The Period of War Resisting Japanese [Aggression], Part VII, Post-war China), vol. II, (Taipei: distributed by Chung-yang Wen-wu kung-yin-she, 1981 [actual year of publication is 1984]), pp. 240–2. For a summary of this issue, see Chien Tuan-sheng, *The Government and Politics of China* (Cambridge, MA: Harvard University Press, 1950, reprinted in 1967), pp. 317–18.

2. English translation in *Republic of China Yearbook 1990–91* (Taipei: Kwang Hwa Publishing Co., 1990), pp. 712–21. For an analysis of the structure of this Constitution, see Tsao Wen-yen, *The Constitutional Structure of Modern China* (Melbourne: Melbourne University Press, 1947).

3. Complete text of Article 8 is:

11), privacy of correspondence (Article 12), religious belief (Article 13), assembly and association (Article 14). The people shall have the right of existence, work, property (Article 15), presenting petitions, lodging complaints, instituting legal proceedings (Article 16), election, recall, initiative, referendum (Article 17), taking public examinations and holding public offices (Article 18). With respect to duties, the people shall pay taxes (Article 19) and perform military service in accordance with the law. In view of the Chinese tradition emphasising education, the Constitution provides that the people have not only the right but also the duty to receive education (Article 21). There is also a provision guaranteeing those freedoms and rights not provided in the Constitution as long as they "are not detrimental to social order or public welfare" (Article 22). The freedom and rights enumerated in the above articles "shall not be restricted by law except by such as may be necessary to prevent infringement upon the freedoms of other persons, to avert an imminent crisis, to maintain social order, or to advance public welfare" (Article 23). Article 24 establishes the state compensation system for damage done by a public functionary who, in violation of the law, infringes upon the freedom or right of any person.

4. *Chapter III. The National Assembly.* The National Assembly is retained despite the fact that the 1946 Political Consultative Conference

---

Personal freedom shall be guaranteed to the people. Except in cases of *flagrante delicto* as provided by law, no person shall be arrested or detained otherwise than by a judicial or a police organ in accordance with the procedure prescribed by law. No person shall be tried or punished otherwise than by a law court in accordance with the procedure prescribed by law. Any arrest, detention, trial, or punishment which is not in accordance with the procedure prescribed by law may be resisted.

When a person is arrested or detained on suspicion of having committed a crime, the organ making the arrest or detention shall in writing inform the said person, and his designated relative or friend, of the grounds for his arrest or detention, and shall, within 24 hours, turn him over to a competent court for trial. The said person, or any other person, may petition the competent court that a writ be served within 24 hours on the organ making the arrest for the surrender of the said person for trial.

The court shall not reject the petition mentioned in the preceding paragraph, nor shall it order the organ concerned to make an investigation and report first. The organ concerned shall not refuse to execute, or delay in executing, the writ of the court for the surrender of the said person for trial.

When a person is unlawfully arrested or detained by any organ, he or any other person may petition the court for an investigation. The court shall not reject such a petition, and shall, within 24 hours, investigate the action of the organ concerned and deal with the matter in accordance with law.

suggested its abolition, but the Assembly's power is now limited to the election and recall of the President and the Vice-President, amending the Constitution and voting on proposed constitutional amendments submitted by the Legislative Yuan by way of referendum (Article 27).

5. *Chapter IV. The President.* The President is the head of state (Article 35) and supreme commander of the land, sea and air forces (Article 36). The President shall appoint and remove civil and military officials (Article 41) and exercise other powers; he shall promulgate laws and issue mandates only with the counter-signature of the Premier of the Executive Yuan or ministers concerned (Article 37). This makes the President's position similar to that of Western democracies with a cabinet system where the real power is vested in the Premier, a leader of the majority party or a coalition. However, the President still has some real powers under this Constitution. He may, in accordance with the law, declare martial law with the approval of, or subject to confirmation by, the Legislative Yuan (Article 39). He can also exercise emergency powers. In case of a natural calamity, an epidemic or a national financial or economic crisis that calls for emergency measures, the President, during the recess of the Legislative Yuan, may, by resolution of the Executive Yuan Council and in accordance with the Law on Emergency Orders, issue emergency orders proclaiming such measures as may be necessary to cope with the situation. Such an order, however, shall, within one month after issuance, be presented by the Legislative Yuan for confirmation; if the Legislative Yuan withholds confirmation, the said order shall forthwith cease to be valid (Article 43). Moreover, in case of disputes between two or more Yuans other than those for which there exist relevant provisions in the Constitution, the President may call a meeting of the Premier or Presidents of the Yuans concerned for consultation with a view to reaching a solution (Article 44). Finally, the President may approve the request of the Premier of the Executive Yuan to veto a bill passed by the Legislative Yuan, which the latter can override only by a two-thirds majority (Article 57, paragraph 2).

6. *Chapter V. Administration.* The Executive Yuan is the highest administrative organ of the state (Article 53). The Premier (President) of the Executive Yuan is appointed by the President with the approval of the Legislative Yuan (Article 55, paragraph 1) and is responsible to the latter (Article 57). The Legislative Yuan may by resolution request the Executive Yuan to change any important policy, but the latter may, with the approval of the President, petition the Legislative Yuan for reconsideration. If a two-thirds majority of the Legislative Yuan

upholds the original resolution, the Premier shall either accept the resolution or resign from office (Article 57, paragraph 2). As stated earlier, the Premier may seek the approval of the President to veto a bill adopted by the Legislative Yuan, which can only be overridden by a two-thirds majority of the Legislative Yuan (Article 57, paragraph 3).

7. *Chapter VI. Legislation.* The Legislative Yuan is comprised of members directly elected by the people, occupational groups and overseas Chinese, and is the highest legislative organ of the state (Articles 62 and 64). Members of the Legislative Yuan may not concurrently hold any governmental post (Article 75) and this makes the Chinese system different from other cabinet systems. While the Legislative Yuan has extensive legislative and budgetary powers, it shall not make proposals for an increase in the expenditures in the budgetary bill presented by the Executive Yuan (Article 70). The Legislative Yuan may also propose constitutional amendments and submit the same to the National Assembly for referendum (Article 174, paragraph 2).

8. *Chapter VII. Judiciary.* The Judicial Yuan is in charge of civil, criminal and administrative cases, and disciplinary measures against public functionaries (Article 77). Its Grand Justices, who are appointed by the President of the Republic with the consent of the Control Yuan, are in charge of interpreting the Constitution and unifying the interpretation of laws and orders (Articles 78 and 79). Judges shall hold office for life (Article 81), shall be above partisanship and shall, in accordance with the law, hold trials independently, free from any interference (Article 80).

9. *Chapter VIII. Examination.* The Examination Yuan is in charge of matters relating to examination, employment, registration, service rating, scales of salaries, promotions and transfers, security of tenure, commendation, pecuniary aid in case of death, retirement, and old age pensions (Article 83). Its President, Vice-President and members are appointed by the President of the Republic with the consent of the Control Yuan (Article 84).

10. *Chapter IX. Control Yuan.* The Control Yuan consists of members elected by Councils of Provinces or their equivalents (big cities) and overseas Chinese; it exercises powers of consent, impeachment, censure and auditing (Articles 90 and 91).

11. *Chapter X. Power of Central and Local Government.* The powers of central, provincial and city or county governments are specified in the Constitution (Articles 107 to 110). However, any matter not enumerated in the Constitution shall fall within the jurisdiction of the

central government, if it is national in nature; of the province, if it is provincial in nature; and the county or city, if it concerns the county or city. The Legislative Yuan shall settle any dispute (Article 111).

12. *Chapter XI. System of Local Government.* The self-government of provinces and counties or cities is assured in the Constitution, and the provincial governors, county magistrates and city mayors shall be elected directly by the people (Articles 112–28).

13. *Chapter XII. Election, Recall, Initiative and Referendum.* Except for those prescribed by the Constitution, all kinds of elections shall be held by universal, equal and direct suffrage and by secret ballots (Article 129). All candidates are required to campaign openly for their election (Article 131). In various kinds of elections, the number of women to be elected shall be fixed by law (Article 134).

14. *Chapter XIII. Fundamental National Policies.* The land, sea and air forces shall be above personal, regional or party affiliations — and they shall be loyal to the state and shall protect the people (Article 138). Neither political party nor any individual shall make use of the armed forces as an instrument in a struggle for political power (Article 139), and no military man in active service may concurrently hold a civil office (Article 140). The national economy shall seek to effect equalisation of land ownership and the restriction of private capital in order to attain a well-balanced sufficiency in national wealth and people's livelihood (Article 142); but private citizens' productive enterprises and foreign trade shall receive encouragement, guidance and protection from the state (Article 145). Within the territory of the Republic, all goods shall be permitted to move freely from place to place (Article 148). In order to promote social welfare, the state shall establish a social insurance system (Article 155) and a system of public medical services (Article 157). All children of school age from six to twelve years shall receive free primary education and all citizens above school age who have not received primary education shall receive supplementary education free of charge (Article 160).

15. *Chapter XIV. Enforcement and Amendment of the Constitution.* Laws that are in conflict with the Constitution shall be null and void, and the Judicial Yuan shall decide whether there is a conflict (Article 171). Ordinances that are in conflict with the Constitution or with the laws shall be null and void (Article 172). The Constitution may be amended upon the proposal of one-quarter of the members of the National Assembly and by a resolution of three-quarters of the delegates present at a meeting having a quorum of two-thirds of the entire Assembly

(Article 174). As stated earlier, the Legislative Yuan may propose an amendment and submit the same to the Assembly for referendum.

A general election for delegates to the first National Assembly, and for members of the Legislative Yuan and Control Yuan in areas under the control of the national government, held in 1947 and 1948 in accordance with the Constitution. The President and Vice-President were elected by the National Assembly and took office on 20 May 1948. A constitutional government had finally come into effect in China.

The defeat of the Republican forces by the Chinese Communist forces in the 1946–9 civil war and the removal of the Republican government to Taiwan in late 1949 ended the operation of this Constitution on the mainland, but in Taiwan it has been in force since its passage on 25 December 1947.

*Temporary provisions of the Constitution and the President's emergency power*

When the first National Assembly met at Nanking in March–April 1948, full-scale civil war between government forces and Chinese Communist forces had been continuing for some time; therefore, the National Assembly, through the constitutional amendment procedure, adopted the "Temporary Provisions Effective during the Period of Communist Rebellion" on 18 April 1948; these became effective on 10 May 1948.[4]

According to these provisions, the President may, for the period in question, by resolution of the Executive Yuan (cabinet) Council, take any emergency measure necessary to prevent the state or the people from facing immediate danger or to cope with serious financial or economic crises without being subject to the procedural restrictions as prescribed in Articles 39 and 43 of the Constitution of the Legislative Yuan. These two articles provide the first of the President's emergency powers. Article 39 provides that the President may declare the institution of martial law (which in Taiwan is similar to a state of siege in other constitutions) but must secure prior or subsequent approval from the Legislative Yuan. Article 43 provides that during a natural calamity, epidemic or serious financial or economic crisis, when the Legislative Yuan is in recess, the

---

4. See *Kuo-chia chien-she ts'ung-k'an, Ti-i-ts'e, Tsung-lun* (National Reconstruction Series, vol. 1: *General Discussion*) (Taipei: Cheng-chung Book Co., 1971), pp. 224–6.

President may issue emergency orders by resolution of the Executive Yuan Council and in accordance with the Law on Emergency Orders,[5] but those orders will lapse unless they are confirmed by the Legislative Yuan within one month. Under the Temporary Provisions, this procedural requirement of confirmation by the Legislative Yuan was removed, the term "orders" was replaced by the term "measures" and the description of a situation that would authorise the President to take such measures was changed to "immediate danger" rather than the narrowly defined "natural calamity" or "epidemic." However, under Article 57 of the Constitution the Legislative Yuan can still modify or annul presidential emergency measures by a resolution. Such a resolution, however, is subject to presidential veto, which in turn can only be overridden by a two-thirds majority of the Legislative Yuan—an unlikely event.

Despite the extent of the President's emergency power, the experience since 1949 has unequivocally demonstrated that the President has used maximum restraint in exercising this power. In fact, presidents have invoked their emergency powers on only four occasions. The first was to declare the application of martial law in civil war areas in 1948–9, the second to announce monetary reforms during the same critical stage of the civil war. The third instance enabled the President to deal with serious floods that occurred in the central and southern parts of Taiwan in 1958. The last occasion, announced by the President on 16 December 1978, was to put the armed forces on full alert, to take necessary measures to maintain economic stability and development, and to suspend the pending election of national elective bodies when the United States abruptly announced its decision on 16 December 1978 to terminate diplomatic relations with the ROC on 1 January 1979 and to abrogate the US–ROC mutual defence treaty a year later.

On 19 March 1966 the National Assembly amended the Temporary Provisions and gave the President additional powers:

1. The President is authorised to establish, in accordance with the constitutional system, an organ for making major policy decisions concerned with the national mobilisation and suppression of the Communist rebellion and for assuming administrative control in war zones; and
2. To meet the requirements of national mobilisation and the suppression of the Communist rebellion, the President may make adjustments in the administrative and personnel organs of the central government, as well as their organisations.[6]

5. This law has not yet been enacted.
6. National Reconstruction Series, vol. 1, *General Discussion*, p. 27.

Under these provisions, two agencies established by the Temporary Provisions have had considerable impact on the form of government. The National Security Council, which is chaired by the President, has in several cases decided major national policies and then instructed the Executive Yuan to implement or enforce them. The extension of compulsory education from six to nine years, the extension of the territorial sea limit from 3 to 12 miles, and the establishment of a 200-mile economic zone are well-known examples. Therefore, with the establishment of the National Security Council, the President can, if he wants, play a leading role in the national decision-making process. In addition, the Central Personnel Administration of the Executive Yuan, established by the President in accordance with the Temporary Provisions, has assumed many functions previously held by the Ministry of Personnel of the Examination Yuan. It thus changes the relationship between these two Yuans.

On 1 May 1991 the Temporary Provisions were terminated, but the President's emergency power is retained in modified and more restricted form in Article 7 of the Additional Articles of the ROC Constitution,[7] which came into force on the same day. A President's emergency order shall be submitted to the Legislative Yuan for confirmation within ten days of its issuance. Should the Legislative Yuan withhold confirmation, the said emergency orders shall forthwith cease to be valid.

The National Security Council and the Central Personnel Administration of the Executive Yuan are also retained in Article 9 of the Additional Articles, but their organic laws are to be enacted by the Legislative Yuan by 31 December 1993.[8]

## Martial law and military trial of civilians

Because of the Chinese Communists' threat to take over Taiwan by force, martial law was declared on 20 May 1949.[9] The state of "martial law" in the ROC is, in fact, similar to a "state of siege" in civil law countries and is different from the concept of martial law in common law countries. This point needs further explanation.

The difference lies essentially in the divergent attitudes between the common and civil law systems towards the origin of this emergency

---

7. English transl. in *Free China Journal (FCJ)*, vol. VIII, no. 32 (2 May 1991), p. 8.
8. *Ibid*.
9. Tuan Shao-yen (compiler), *Liu-fa pan chieh hui-pien* (Collection of Precedents and Interpretations on Six Codes) (Taipei: San Min Book Co., 1963), p. 1788.

measure. "Martial law" emphasises the suspension of certain normal rules of law, whereas "state of siege" emphasises the emergency as an effective threat against public safety and order. Thus, the prerequisite for martial rule in the United States is either that the civilian courts are closed or they can no longer perform their functions properly.[10] This condition does not apply to the civil law state of siege, under which the civilian courts may still function and only those crimes against national security, the Constitution and public safety and order are under the jurisdiction of military courts. The civil and military powers within the government work side by side in a spirit of cooperation and do not have to be substituted one for the other, as is the case in a common law country.[11] Another major difference should not be overlooked. The executive and/or the legislature in civil law countries has the final word as to whether an emergency has arisen; the courts assume this function under the common law.

All these features of the state of siege existed in the Republic of China between 1949 and 1987. The President had the power to initiate the application of martial law, i.e. state of siege, although this power was subject to confirmation by the Legislative Yuan. Under Article 39 of the Constitution, the latter, by resolution, might have asked the President to terminate the application of martial law. As a practical matter, the structure and functions of government and the way of life of the people in the ROC were virtually unaffected by the imposition of martial law between these dates.

Under martial law, non-military personnel in the ROC were subject to a military trial if they had committed one of four types of crimes: (1) sedition, (2) espionage, (3) theft, or (4) unauthorised sale or purchase of military equipment and supplies, or theft or damage of public communication equipment and facilities.[12] In response to popular demand

10. Traditionally, the fact that civil courts are open has precluded the use of martial law. However, the doctrine has undergone a revision, because the nature of modern war has changed; it is still possible for the civil courts to be open even in an actual fighting zone. Therefore, whether the function of the courts is obstructed or not should not be the real criterion. See Charles Warren, "Spies, and the Power of Congress to Subject Certain Classes of Civilians to Trial by Military Tribunal", *American Law Review*, vol. 53 (1919), p. 201. Robert S. Rankin also cited a list of supporting articles on this point; see his *When Civil Law Falls* (Durham, NC: Duke University Press, 1939).

11. For details, see Clinton L. Rossiter, *Constitutional Dictatorship*: (Princeton University Press, 1948), pp. 86–87.

12. "Measures of Dividing Cases to be Tried by the Military Law Organs Themselves and Those to be Tried by Courts during the Period of Martial Law in the Taiwan Area", promulgated by the Executive Yuan on 10 May 1952. Tao Pai-chuan (ed.), *Tsui-hsin liu-fa ch'uan-shu* (Latest Edition of Six Codes) (Taipei: San Min Book Co., 1976), p. 350.

for swift and severe punishment against a rising trend of violent crime, in 1976 the government expanded the scope of military trials to include nine serious offences such as homicide, robbery, intentionally killing the victim after a rape or robbery, and kidnapping. However, not all these types of cases were automatically placed under military jurisdiction; a decision by the Executive Yuan was required on a case-by-case basis before such crimes were referred to the military courts.[13] After the imposition of military trials for these offences, the number of robbery and snatching cases dropped from 833 in 1975 to 494 in 1976.[14] The deterrent effect no doubt has been realised and, consequently, between 1976 and 1980 there were almost no military trials for robbery or snatching.[15]

Trials in the military courts generally follow the model of the civilian courts. The most controversial aspect is that a judgement must be approved by a commanding officer before delivery.[16] However, this is not only a general practice of military trials in other countries but, contrary to the American practice that no limitation be imposed,[17] the commanding officer in the ROC may express his disapproval only once.[18] Another problem related to military trials is that a defendant may be sent to reformatory education because of mitigating circumstances, or because he surrendered himself to the authorities.[19] The maximum period for reformatory education is three years and may not be extended. Upon the expiration of the term, he must be released immediately, although two guarantees may be required to assure his later good behaviour.[20]

How the military trial of civilians not in active service during the martial law period could be reconciled with Article 9 of the Constitution, which prohibits military trial of civilians, was a question which

13. *Chung-yang jih-pao (Central Daily News)*, 25 January 1976.

14. Research Centre of Crime, Ministry of Justice, *Fan-tsui chuang-k'uang chi ch'i fen-hsi* (The Condition and Analysis of Crimes) (Taipei: Ministry of Justice, 1979), pp. 108–9.

15. *Central Daily News*, 8 January 1980.

16. Article 133, para. 1 of the Military Trial Law, *Latest Edition of Six Codes*, p. 557.

17. See *Manual for Courts-Martial, US*, 1967 revision, para. 88.

18. Article 133, paragraph 3 of the Military Trial Law, *Latest Edition of Six Codes*, p. 557.

19. Article 8 of the Statute for the Finding and Purging of Spies during the Period of Communist Rebellion, promulgated on 13 June 1950 and amended on 28 December 1954, *Latest Edition of Six Codes*, p. 301.

20. Article 9 of the Statute for Punishment of Rebellion, promulgated on 21 June 1949 and last amended on 26 July 1958, *Latest Edition of Six Codes*, p. 301.

was never submitted to the Council of Grand Justices of the Judicial Yuan for an authoritative interpretation.

Another restriction on the people during the martial law period was the prohibition on organising new political parties, though existing parties were allowed to continue to operate. This is contrary to Article 14 of the Constitution which guarantees people's freedom of assembly and association. A plausible justification might be based on Article 23 of the Constitution, which authorises the restriction of the freedoms and rights of the people by law if it is necessary "to avert an imminent crisis, to maintain social order, or to advance public welfare". This issue of prohibiting new political parties was also not submitted to the Council of Grand Justice for an authoritative interpretation.

On 15 July 1987, martial law in Taiwan was lifted by President Chiang Ching-kuo;[21] since then no civilians have been subject to a military trial, and the people's freedom to organise new political parties has also been restored.

*Local self-government and the question of the election of national elective bodies*

Local self-government began in Taiwan in 1951. All mayors, county magistrates, city or county councils and the Taiwan Provincial Assembly have since then been periodically elected by the people. However, the Governor of Taiwan and the mayors of Taipei and Kao-hsiung, after the mid-1960s when both became special municipalities, have been appointed by the central government and not elected by the people, despite the constitutional provisions to the contrary.

In 1951, the three-year term for members of the Legislative Yuan expired and all members were due for re-election. However, at that time the Chinese Communists already controlled the mainland, so no elections could be held there. Therefore, by resolution of the Legislative Yuan, the members' terms were extended until a new election could be held. In 1954 the members of the Control Yuan were also due for a new election. Again, because the Chinese Communists controlled the

---

21. "Taiwan Ends 4 Decades of Martial Law", *The New York Times*, 15 July 1987, p. 4. For an analysis of the martial law in Taiwan, see Tao-tai Hsia with Wendy Zeldin, "Laws on Emergency Powers in Taiwan", in Shao-chuan Leng (ed.), *Coping with Crises, How Governments Deal with Emergencies* (Lanham, NY and London: University Press of America, 1990), pp. 173–208.

mainland no re-election was possible. Therefore the question was submitted to the Council of Grand Justices of the Judicial Yuan for
guidance. In its Interpretation Shih Tzu no. 31 rendered on 29 January
1954,[22] the Council of Grand Justices stated that pending a new election, members of the Legislative Yuan and Control Yuan elected in
1948 could continue to serve. In 1954 the delegates to the National
Assembly were also due for an election, but it was not possible to hold
an election because of the Communist control of the mainland.
However, Article 28, paragraph 2 of the Constitution provides that
"the term of office of the delegates to each National Assembly shall
terminate on the day on which the next National Assembly convenes."
Because it was not possible to hold an election for the next National
Assembly, those delegates elected in 1948 continued to serve.

While, through the above constitutional interpretation, the three
elective bodies—the National Assembly, the Legislative Yuan and the
Control Yuan—could continue to function, this situation in fact
prevented the people in Taiwan from moving to a leadership role in
the national elective bodies. It therefore came under increasing public
criticism.

In 1966, a provision was added to the Temporary Provisions of the
Constitution authorising the President to

initiate and promulgate for enforcement regulations providing for elections to
fill, according to law, those elective offices at the central government level
which have become vacant for legitimate reasons, or for which additional
representation is called for because of population increases, in areas that are
free and/or newly recovered.[23]

In 1969, a supplementary national election was held to elect fifteen
members to the National Assembly and eleven members to the
Legislative Yuan. The Taiwan Provincial Assembly also elected two
members to the Control Yuan. These new members were to serve
"indefinitely"; that is, they enjoyed life-time tenure.

The above measure was hardly a reasonable response to the popular
demand for more democracy in Taiwan. Therefore, on 17 March 1972,
the National Assembly again added another provision to the Temporary
Provisions as follows:

22. *Shih-fa Yuan Ta-fa-kuan hui-i jie-shih hui-pien* (Collection of Interpretations of the
Council of Grand Justices of the Judicial Yuan) (Taipei: Secretariat of the Judicial Yuan,
1974), p. 53.
23. *China Yearbook, 1970–71* (Taipei: China Publishing Co., n.d.), pp. 720–1.

6. During the period of national mobilisation and the suppression of Communist rebellion, the President may, in accordance with the following stipula-
tions, initiate and promulgate for enforcement regulations providing for
elections to strengthen elective offices at the central government level without
being subject to the restrictions prescribed in Article 26, Article 64 or Article
91 of the Constitution.

(1) In free areas, additional members of representatives may be elected
to all elective offices at the central government level by elections to be held
at established times. The President may initiate regulations for the selection
of members of the Legislative Yuan and the Control Yuan who were to
have been elected from among Chinese nationals residing overseas but whose
election could not be carried out because of the actual situation . . .

(3) Representatives additionally elected to the elective offices at the central
government level shall carry out the same functions as those elected previously. The new delegates to the National Assembly elected for additional representation shall stand for re-election every six years; those of the
Legislative Yuan, every three years; and those of the Control Yuan, every
six years.[24]

In the same year, an election was held and fifty-three delegates to the
National Assembly, thirty-one members (plus fifteen appointed seats for
overseas Chinese) of the Legislative Yuan, and ten members (plus five
appointed members from overseas Chinese) of the Control Yuan were
elected. They were subject to re-election every six years (National
Assembly and Control Yuan) or every three years (Legislative Yuan).
These elections came to be known as "supplementary elections". In
1986, eight-four new delegates were elected to the National Assembly;
and in 1989, seventy-two new members (plus twenty-nine appointed
seats from overseas Chinese) were elected to the Legislative Yuan; and
in 1987, twenty-two new members (plus ten appointed seats from
overseas Chinese) were elected to the Control Yuan by the Taiwan
Provincial Assembly and Taipei and Kao-hsiung city councils.

On 3 February 1989 the President promulgated a law adopted by the
Legislative Yuan for voluntary retirement of those members of three
elective bodies who were formerly elected in the Chinese mainland in
1948 and in Taiwan in 1969.[25] On 21 June 1990 the Council of Grand
Justices rendered Interpretation Shih-Tzu no. 261, which states that all
members of the three elective bodies who were elected in 1948 and 1969

24. *China Yearbook, 1972–73* (Taipei: China Publishing Co., n.d.), pp. 747–8.
25. Text in *Fa-wu-pu kung-pao* (*Gazette of the Ministry of Legal Affairs*), no. 104 (28
February 1989), pp. 15–17.

must resign from their offices by 31 December 1991 and that new elections should be held for these bodies.[26] Thus, from 1 January 1992 all members of the National Assembly, the Legislative Yuan and the Control Yuan were to be periodically elected in Taiwan.

## Reduction of tensions in the Taiwan Straits and constitutional reform

Before early 1980, the policy of the Chinese Communist government towards Taiwan was that it would use force to "liberate Taiwan" at an appropriate time. This policy was even explicitly stated in the Preamble to the Constitution of the People's Republic of China, adopted on 5 March 1978.[27] Under such a constant military threat, the ROC government considered it necessary to restrict people's freedoms for national security reasons. However, since the early 1980s mainland–Taiwan relations have significantly changed.

On 1 January 1979, when diplomatic relations were established between the United States and the People's Republic of China (PRC), the Standing Committee of the PRC's National People's Congress sent a "Message to Compatriots in Taiwan"[28] calling for "unification" of Taiwan with the mainland. It said that the PRC leaders would take present realities in Taiwan into account in accomplishing the "great cause of reunifying the motherland", would respect the status quo in Taiwan and the opinions of the people in all walks of life there, and would adopt reasonable policies and measures in settling the question of reunification so as to avoid causing any loss to the people of Taiwan. It also called for establishing "three links" (mail, trade, and air and shipping services) and "four exchanges" — relatives and tourists, academic groups, cultural groups and sports representatives — with Taiwan, as a first step towards the ultimate goal of reunification.

Marshal Yeh Chien-ying, then Chairman of the Standing Committee of the National People's Congress and *de facto* head of state of the PRC, made a specific nine-point proposal to Taiwan on unification on 30

26. Text in *Fa-ling yueh-k'an* (*Law Monthly*), vol. 41, no. 9 (1 September 1990), pp. 21–4.

27. Teaching and Research Office of Constitutional Law and Office of [Research] Materials of the Department of Law of Beijing University (eds), *Hsien-fa tsu-liao hsuan-pien* (Selected Materials on Constitutional Law), vol. 1 (Peking University Press, 1982), p. 305.

28. "NPC Standing Committee Message to Compatriots in Taiwan", *Beijing Review*, vol. 22, no. 1 (5 January 1979), pp. 16–17.

September 1981. The proposal offered Taiwan "a high degree of autonomy as a special administrative region" after unification with the PRC. Taiwan could also retain its armed forces. The PRC also renewed its 1979 call for establishing "three links" and "four exchanges" with Taiwan.[29] This proposal set forth the basic principles of the Chinese Communists' unification policy towards Taiwan. While the PRC has not to date ruled out the use of force against Taiwan, the increased contacts through trade, investment and travel have greatly reduced the tension in the Taiwan Straits. Under this more relaxed atmosphere, it was only natural for the general public in Taiwan to demand the full implementation of the Constitution of the Republic of China and further demand that the ROC government make necessary amendments to the Constitution for its application to the Taiwan area.

On 15 July 1987 President Chiang Ching-kuo decided to lift martial law, which also ended the ban on organising new political parties. At the same time, the ROC also announced the termination of foreign exchange controls, so that anyone could remit up to a total of US$5 million abroad in a year. On 25 December of the same year, President Chiang announced a plan to reform parliamentary bodies at the annual meeting of the National Assembly. Under that plan, all members of parliamentary bodies would be periodically elected in Taiwan within a few years.

Chiang died on 13 January 1988 before he could implement this reform. Dr Li Teng-hui, who succeeded to the presidency on the same day, pledged to carry out Chiang's policy. Under Li's leadership, the Central Standing Committee of the ruling Chinese Nationalist Party approved the reform plan on 3 February 1988. At the Thirteenth National Congress of the party held in July 1988, Li was elected party Chairman. The new party platform, which would serve as the government's policy guidelines for the next four years, stressed the continuation of the democratisation and liberalisation process in politics and the economy.

On 23 January 1989 the President promulgated the Civic Organisations Law adopted by the Legislative Yuan, which, among other items, set rules for the formation of new political parties.[30] Thus it marked a

29. "Chairman Yeh Jianying's Elaboration on Policy Concerning Return of Taiwan to Motherland and Peaceful Reunification", *Beijing Review*, vol. 24, no. 40 (5 October 1981), p. 10.

30. *Gazette of the Ministry of Legal Affairs*, no. 104 (28 February 1989), pp. 6–10.

transition of the ROC's political system from an essentially authoritarian one-party state to a democratic, competitive, multi-party system. Eleven days later the Election and Recall Law[31] was also revised to lift many restrictions on campaign activities. On the question of reform of the Legislative Yuan, the Control Yuan and the National Assembly, a voluntary retirement law was adopted for those members who were formerly elected in the Chinese mainland in 1948 and in Taiwan in 1969.

On 21 March 1990, after learning he was elected to a six-year term by the National Assembly, President Li Teng-hui said that the government would hold a National Affairs Conference and would invite legislators, scholars, experts, industrial and business leaders and journalists to attend in order to develop a consensus on such major issues as constitutional reform and the policy towards the mainland.

In his inaugural address entitled "Opening a New Era for the Chinese People", delivered on 20 May,[32] President Li announced that, "with the changing domestic and international situation and the increasingly ardent desire of the people for democratic rule of law", he hoped that "a termination of the period of mobilization for the suppression of the Communist rebellion" could be declared in the shortest possible period of time. In other words, he was willing to give up the extraordinary power granted to the President under the Temporary Provisions and return to normal constitutional rule. Moreover, Li also indicated his willingness to make necessary revisions to the Constitution to strengthen democracy in the ROC. He stated:

[B]ased on the many years of experience we have accumulated in implementing our Constitution and on the needs arising from the current national environment, forward-looking and necessary revisions will be made to portions of the Constitution concerning such matters as the parliamentary organs of the central government, the system of local government, and government organization to provide the Chinese people with a legal code that is in accord with the trends of our times, and to establish a great model of political democracy for all times.

In order to show his sincere commitment to carry out these reforms, the President specifically stated that he hoped the reform could be completed within a period of two years.

31. Text of the revised provisions in *ibid.*, pp. 10–15. The law was revised again on 2 August 1991 to further liberalise restrictions on campaigning. For text, see *Law Monthly*, vol. 41, no. 10 (1 October 1991), pp. 18–23.
32. Text in *Republic of China Yearbook, 1990–1991*, pp. 722–4.

*The National Affairs Conference*

The National Affairs Conference (NAC) was held from 28 June to 4 July 1990 in Taipei.[33] It was unprecedented in the political history of the ROC because its participants included people holding divergent political views, ranging from those who advocated Taiwan's independence to those in favour of unification with the Communist-controlled mainland.

As only a limited number of people could be invited to attend the NAC, the ROC government consulted a wide range of people to seek their opinions before the conference was held. A total of 119 discussion meetings were held in Taiwan and abroad, with more than 13,000 people attending.[34] A National Affairs Box was set up at a Taipei post office and received 2,187 letters, while a National Affairs Hotline received 1,180 telephone calls.[35] Two public opinion polls were conducted to identify the attitudes of social élites and the general public toward constitutional reform. The results were released on 24 June 1990, a few days before the conference.[36]

The social élites poll, conducted between 17 May and 15 June 1990, involved interviewing 284 college professors, 35 people's representatives, 156 entrepreneurs, 54 mass media workers and 54 responsible officers of civic organisations relating to social movements. Of the élites polled, 86.4 per cent considered that there was a constitutional crisis in Taiwan, while only 8.9 per cent did not think so, with 2.6 per cent expressing other opinions and 2.1 per cent expressing no opinion. On the question of how to strengthen the constitutional system, 54 per cent expressed the view that this should be done through amending the Constitution, 19 per cent considered that full implementation of the Constitution should be sufficient, 12.2 per cent were in favour of enacting a Basic Law to replace the present Constitution, 11.1 per cent were in favour of enacting a new Constitution, and 2.7 per cent expressed other opinions and 1 per cent no opinion. With respect to the question of who should exercise the power of amending the Constitution, 70.3 per cent thought that it should be the National Assembly after the resignation of all life-tenure members who were elected in 1947 and the re-election

---

33. For details, see *Kuo-shih hui-i shih-lu* (Faithful Record of the National Affairs Conference), 3 vols (Taipei: Secretariat of the National Affairs Conference, 1990).
34. *Ibid.*, vol. I, pp. 9–10.
35. *Ibid.*, p. 8.
36. *Ibid.*, vol. 3, pp. 3007–62.

of its other members in Taiwan, while only 9.6 per cent considered that the National Assembly in its existing composition (i.e. with at least 80 per cent comprising life-tenure members elected in 1947) should exercise the power of amending the Constitution. On the question of possible Chinese Communists' response to the constitutional reform, the interviewed élites believed that full implementation of the Constitution would do the least to raise the suspicion of the Chinese Communists, followed by amending the Constitution or enacting a Basic Law, while enacting a new Constitution would cause high suspicion among the Chinese Communists. An interesting question relating to constitutional reform was the effect on social stability as a result of choosing different methods of constitutional reform. The social élites interviewed considered that amending the Constitution would have the least effect on social stability, followed by full implementation of the Constitution and enacting a Basic Law. Enacting a new Constitution would have a high cost in terms of social stability. They also considered that amending the Constitution would be most appropriate in mitigating the dispute over unification and independence, while enacting a new Constitution would be the least appropriate one.

The poll of the general public was conducted through telephone interviews of 1,068 people. In sharp contrast to the social élites' opinion, 45 per cent considered that there was no constitutional crisis in Taiwan, while 43.7 per cent thought that there was such a crisis. On the question of which problems the government should pay special attention to in carrying out the constitutional reform, 93.1 per cent designated the reform's impact on social stability as the most important one, followed by 83.1 per cent on the timetable for reform, 67.2 per cent on achieving a consensus and compromise with the Democratic Progressive Party, and 52.6 per cent on taking into consideration the response of the Chinese Communists. Similar to the social élites' opinion, 57.8 per cent of the people interviewed considered that constitutional reform should be carried out by amendment, followed by 15.6 per cent who advocated full implementation of the Constitution and 11.7 per cent who wanted to enact a new Constitution.

On 21 June 1990, a week before the opening of the NAC, the Council of Grand Justices of the Judicial Yuan rendered its Interpretation No. 261, stating that all life-tenure representatives in the parliamentary bodies—the National Assembly, the Legislative Yuan and the Control Yuan—should resign by 31 December 1991.[37] This view was accepted

---

37. See note 26 above.

by the majority of the participants in the NAC, though some would have preferred an earlier resignation date. There was also a general consensus on favouring the direct election of the Governor of Taiwan Province and the mayors of Taipei and Kao-hsiung municipalities. As a matter of fact, the Constitution already provided for such an election.

A high degree of consensus was reached on the ROC's policy towards the mainland and the need to enact a law to regulate relations between Taiwan and the mainland in such areas as trade, investment, travel and culture. Most considered that the ROC government should clarify its present seemingly inconsistent mainland policy and liberalise functional exchanges with the mainland. The government should also consider beginning functional and non-political negotiations with the Chinese Communists through an "intermediate body" with authority delegated by the government.

On the constitutional reform issue, all participants agreed that the Temporary Provisions Effective during the Period of Mobilisation for the Suppression of the Communist Rebellion, which granted extraordinary power to the President and were annexed to the Constitution, should be terminated as soon as possible. They were divided, however, on the issue of how to achieve constitutional reform. A majority considered that reform should be carried out by amending the Constitution through the procedure provided in the Constitution. A minority would have liked to enact a new Constitution. The difficulty in accepting this view is that the President does not have the constitutional power to abrogate the present Constitution and pass a new one. Moreover, the ROC Constitution, enacted in 1947 when the ROC government was on the mainland, is the symbol of the "one-China" principle. To enact a new Constitution applicable to Taiwan alone would undermine that principle and imply that Taiwan is independent. Because the Chinese Communists have repeatedly warned that they will not tolerate Taiwan's independence and will use force to suppress independence, passing a new Constitution would increase tensions in the Taiwan Straits.

The majority of participants considered that the present form of electing the President — i.e. the National Assembly may elect anyone it likes to serve as President without consulting the people's opinion — should be reformed. Almost all participants agreed that the President should be "elected by the people", but they were divided on whether he or she should be directly elected by the people or by a system similar to that of the United States, where voters cast ballots for electoral college delegates representing the electorate's views as proxies. Supporters of this view pointed out that the direct election of the President in Taiwan might give people the impression that the President is elected only by the people of Taiwan, thus implying Taiwan's independence. An electoral college system could include some national and overseas Chinese seats apportioned according to the party preference of Taiwan voters.

## *Process and problems in implementing constitutional reform*

The participants in the NAC generally agreed that the Constitution should be amended by an organ with a basis in public opinion, i.e. one whose members are elected by the people for a fixed term. Therefore the National Assembly under its then composition, with more than 80 per cent life-tenure members elected in 1947, was inappropriate for exercising the function of amending the Constitution. Only when all members of the National Assembly were elected in Taiwan for a fixed term should the Assembly begin to amend the Constitution. This, however, was not scheduled to happen until late 1992 when the Assembly came up for re-election. The complicated legal problems involved need explanation.

The National Assembly, in addition to the life-tenure members, included eighty members elected for six-year terms in Taiwan; their terms were not due to expire till December 1992. However, according to Interpretation Shih Tzu no. 261 of the Council of Grand Justices of the Judicial Yuan, all life-tenure members of the Assembly were to resign by 31 December 1991. Therefore 1992 was to see only eighty members in the National Assembly. Legally, they would have authority to amend the Constitution; however, politically, they should not do so because when they were elected in 1986, the people did not give the members the mandate to amend the Constitution. In view of this, the government considered holding an election in 1991 to elect 291 new members to the Assembly, to begin to serve on 1 January 1992. Under that arrangement, in 1992 a rejuvenated National Assembly would have had 375 members[38] to amend the Constitution, all of them elected in Taiwan. This sounds like a logical solution, but the problem centred

---

38. The ROC National Security Council proposes that in the future the total number of representatives of the National Assembly should be 375, all of them serving six-year terms.

on whether the President had the legal authority to move the election date from December 1992 to December 1991 or even earlier, thus shortening the term of eighty members of the Assembly who were elected in 1986. A possible flimsy legal basis for taking this action would have been to invoke the emergency power under Article 1 of the Temporary Provisions. However, the Temporary Provisions were abolished on 1 May 1991, so this approach would not have been possible.[39]

Moreover, some of the members of the National Assembly, the Legislative Yuan and the Control Yuan were elected for a fixed term under Article 6 of the Temporary Provisions.[40] The termination of the Temporary Provisions was regarded as possibly undermining the legal basis for those members to continue to serve their terms until December 1992. If an election was to have been held according to the provisions of the ROC Constitution, and not under the Temporary Provisions,

---

39. Even if it were not abolished, both the Legislative Yuan and the National Assembly may rescind an emergency measure taken by the President.

40. See note 26 above and accompanying text. Article 6 of the Temporary Provisions provides:

> During the period of national mobilisation and the suppression of the Communist rebellion, the President may, in accordance with the following stipulations, initiate and promulgate for enforcement regulations providing for elections to strengthen elective offices at the central government level without being subject to the restrictions prescribed in Article 26, Article 64, or Article 91 of the Constitution:
>
> (1) In free areas, additional members of the National Assembly, the Legislative Yuan, and the Control Yuan may be added through regular elections. Members of the Legislative Yuan and Control Yuan that must be elected by Chinese citizens living abroad who are unable to hold elections shall be chosen according to regulations established by the President of the Republic.
>
> (2) Representatives elected to the National Assembly, Legislative Yuan and Control Yuan in the first elections were chosen through popular vote by the people of the entire nation. These representatives exercise their powers of office in accordance with law; the same principle applies to the representatives elected to fill vacancies or provide additional representation.
>
> Elections for the National Assembly, Legislative Yuan and Control Yuan shall be held on the Chinese mainland one by one, as each area is recovered.
>
> (3) Additional members elected to serve in the National Assembly, Legislative Yuan and Control Yuan shall exercise the same powers of office in accordance with law as the members elected in the first elections.
>
> Additional members of the National Assembly shall stand for re-election every six years; members of the Legislative Yuan, every three years; and members of the Control Yuan, every six years.

only thirty-nine members could have been elected to the National Assembly[41] and twenty-seven to the Legislative Yuan.[42]

Another possibility floated was to adopt a two-stage constitutional reform, i.e. to convene, immediately prior to the termination of the Temporary Provisions, an extraordinary session of the National Assembly to amend only those provisions in the Constitution relating to elections and those Temporary Provisions relating to the President's emergency power and the National Security Council. Additional constitutional reform could then be left for the next session of the National Assembly, to be composed of members entirely elected in Taiwan. This was the approach later adopted by the ruling Nationalist Party and implemented in April 1991.

On 23 April 1991 the extraordinary session of the National Assembly adopted Additional Articles. Seven days later, President Li announced the entry into force of these Additional Articles and the termination of the Period of Mobilisation for the Suppression of Communist Rebellion, beginning on 1 May 1991.

## *The Additional Articles of the Constitution of the Republic of China*

The Additional Articles of the Constitution of the Republic of China[43] number only ten and their contents are summarised here:

---

41. Article 26 of the Constitution provides:

The National Assembly shall be composed of the following delegates:
(1) One delegate shall be elected from each hsien, municipality, or area of equivalent status. In case its population exceeds 500,000, one additional delegate shall be elected for each additional 500,000. Areas equivalent to hsien or municipalities shall be prescribed by law . . .

42. Article 64 of the Constitution provides:

Members of the Legislative Yuan shall be elected in accordance with the following provisions:
(1) Those to be elected from the provinces and by the municipalities under the direct jurisdiction of the Executive Yuan shall be five for each province or municipality with a population of not more than 3,000,000; one additional member shall be elected for each additional 1,000,000 where the population exceeds 3,000,000 . . .

43. English translation in source cited in note 7 above.

(1) *Membership in the National Assembly, the Legislative Yuan and the Control Yuan*: According to Articles 1 to 3, the seats of the three elective bodies are allocated as follows:

*(National Assembly)*
1. Two members shall be elected from each special municipality, each county or city in the free area. However, where the population exceeds 100,000 persons, one member shall be added for each additional 100,000 persons.
2. Three members each shall be elected from lowland and highland aborigines in the free area.
3. Twenty members shall be elected from Chinese citizens living abroad.
4. Eighty members shall be elected from one nationwide constituency.

*(Legislative Yuan)*
1. Two members shall be elected from each province and each special municipality in the free area. Where the population exceeds 200,000 persons, however, one member will be added for each additional 100,000 persons; and where the population exceeds 1 million persons, one member will be added for each additional 200,000 persons.
2. Three members each shall be elected from lowland and highland aborigines in the free area.
3. Six members shall be elected from Chinese citizens living abroad.
4. Thirty members shall be elected from one nationwide constituency.

*(Control Yuan)*
1. Twenty-five members shall be elected from Taiwan Province in the free area.
2. Ten members shall be elected from each special municipality in the free area.
3. Two members shall be elected from Chinese citizens living abroad.
4. Five members shall be elected from one nationwide constituency.

However, if an election district has between five and ten seats, one seat must be reserved for a woman. The same rule is applied to a party winning between five and ten seats representing overseas Chinese or one nationwide constituency. Where the number exceeds ten, one seat out of each additional ten must be reserved for a woman.

Elections for members of the National Assembly and Legislative Yuan shall be conducted by direct popular votes, but members representing Chinese citizens living abroad and one nationwide constituency shall be elected by party-list proportional representation (Article 4). Under the above stated amendment to the Constitution, there will be approximately 327 members of the National Assembly, 161 of the Legislative Yuan and 52 of the Control Yuan.

2. *Transitional Arrangement.* Articles 5 and 6 set the date for new elections. The National Assembly election shall be held before 31 December 1991 and the elections for the Legislative Yuan and Control Yuan shall be held before 31 January 1993. The President should convene an extraordinary session of the newly elected National Assembly within three months after the election. Those members of the National Assembly who were elected in Taiwan for a six-year term in 1986 may continue to serve until 31 January 1993. If the revision of laws originally in effect solely during the Period of National Mobilisation for Suppression of the Communist Rebellion is not completed by the termination of the Period of National Mobilization for Suppression of the Communist Rebellion, these laws shall remain in effect until 31 July 1992 (Article 8).

3. *President's Emergency Power, National Security Council and Central Personnel Administration.* These topics have been discussed in the earlier parts of this chapter[44].

4. *Mainland–Taiwan Relations.* The relationship of rights and obligations between the people of the mainland China area and those of the free area, and the disposition of other affairs, shall be specially regulated by law (Article 10).

## The 21 December 1991 second National Assembly elections

On 1 May 1991, President Li announced the termination of the Period of Mobilisation for the Suppression of Communist Rebellion and the Temporary Provisions of the Constitution. At the same time, he announced the passage of the Additional Articles to the Constitution adopted by the extraordinary session of the National Assembly. According to the first of these Articles, 225 members were to be elected to the Assembly and an additional 80 nationwide members and 20 overseas members were to be allocated according to the percentage of popular votes received by political parties which constituted at least 5 per cent of all popular votes. Articles 5 and 6 set the date for the new election to the Assembly for not later than 31 December 1991, and the President was instructed to convene an extraordinary session of the newly elected National Assembly within three months after the election in order to revise the Constitution. The election date was later set for 21 December 1991.

During the campaign for the National Assembly elections, the Democratic Progressive Party (DPP) advocated Taiwan's independence

---

44. See notes 7 and 8 above and accompanying text.

while the Kuomintang (KMT) called for "reform, stability and prosperity" and ultimate unification with the Chinese mainland. It also warned the public that supporting the DPP's cause could but lead Taiwan on a confrontation course with the Chinese Communists, which would only bring disaster to all the people of Taiwan. The result of the elections was a disaster for the DPP. Nearly 9 million voters went to the polls in fifty-eight election districts. The KMT received 71.17 per cent of the popular votes and 179 seats. The DPP received only 23.94 per cent and forty-one seats. With sixty nationwide and fifteen overseas seats to be allocated according to the popular votes received, the KMT had a total of 254 seats, while the DPP had twenty nationwide and five overseas seats, for a total of sixty-six seats. Because there were seventy-eight members of the National Assembly (the KMT had 64, the DPP 9 and other parties 5) who had been elected in 1986 and who were also to join the Second National Assembly to amend the Constitution, the total membership of the National Assembly was to be 403. The KMT had 318 members, that is 78.91 per cent of the total membership.[45] According to Article 174 of the Constitution, an amendment to the Constitution must be adopted by a resolution of three-quarters of the members of the National Assembly at a meeting having a quorum of two-thirds of the entire Assembly. The KMT thus had more than three-quarters of the votes in the National Assembly to amend the Constitution.

However, things did not go so well for the KMT in the Second National Assembly convened by the President on 20 March 1992, because of the KMT's internal dispute over the issue of how the President should be elected by the people — whether by direct election or by proxy vote.

### The issue of how to elect the President

As stated earlier, during the 1990 National Affairs Conference the participants were divided over the issue of how to elect the President. During the December 1991 election campaign, the majority of the KMT candidates campaigned on a platform supporting an electoral college system, where voters cast ballots for electoral college delegates representing the electorate's view as proxies. On 15 February 1992 the KMT

45. Susan Yu, "ROC Voters give KMT Whopping Mandate", *FCJ*, vol. VIII, no. 98 (24 December 1991), p. 1.

Constitutional Amendment Group, after several hundred consultative meetings, made a preliminary decision to propose the adoption of the electoral college system to the KMT Central Standing Committee, scheduled to be held in early March 1992. If approved, the proposal was to be submitted to the Third Plenum of the Central Committee to be held in mid-March 1992.[46]

All appeared to go well up to this moment. However, at the KMT Central Standing Committee meeting held on 9 March 1992, instead of only the proposal for an electoral college system to elect the President, a proposal for direct election was also presented to the meeting, thus triggering a sharp debate among the participants.[47] The Central Standing Committee could not reach an absolute majority on this issue, so it decided to present both proposals to the Third Plenum of the thirteenth Central Committee meeting for a final decision.

At the Central Committee meetings held on 14–16 March 1992, marathon debates took place. Those in favour of an electoral college system, usually referred to as the "direct election by delegation" faction, argued that a President elected by a direct popular vote in Taiwan could give the impression of being a "President of Taiwan", thus implying independence. Moreover, a system based on direct popular votes would exclude overseas Chinese participation in the election process. Some KMT members opposed this method of electing the President because the opposition DPP had been on record as favouring such a constitutional change. Those in favour of direct election of the President pointed out that such a system would be in keeping with recent popular trends demonstrating the people's desire to have more participation in the government.[48]

The debate became so divisive that the Central Committee halted the debate and decided to adopt a compromise formula to defer the issue. The final proposal approved by the Central Committee provides that the President and Vice-President will be elected by residents of free areas of the Republic of China in such a way as to reflect the public will.[49] In fact, it makes no decision on the method of electing the President.

46. *Chung-yang jih-pao* (*Central Daily News*), international edition, 17 February 1992, p. 1.

47. See *Shih-jie jih-pao* (*World Journal*), New York, 10 March 1992, p. 28.

48. Susan Yu, "No Decision on Electing ROC President", *Free China Journal*, vol. IX, no. 18 (17 March 1992), p. 1.

49. *Ibid.*

*The adoption of additional amendments to the constitution of the Republic of China*

On 20 March 1992, the extraordinary session of the Second National Assembly was convened by President Li Teng-hui. Because the question of how to elect the President was so divisive, the President, who is also Chairman of the KMT, decided to postpone the resolution of this issue. In a speech to 318 KMT members of the National Assembly on 25 March, Li said that he would call an extraordinary session of the National Assembly before 20 May 1995, for a final decision on this issue.[50]

On 27 May 1992, the extraordinary session of the Second National Assembly adopted eight additional articles (Articles 11 to 18) to amend the Constitution of the Republic of China which will be applicable to the Taiwan area before national unification. The contents of these articles are summarised below:[51]

1. *President and Vice-President*: According to Article 12, both the President and the Vice-President shall be elected by the entire electorate in the free area of the Republic of China; the method of election shall be decided by an extraordinary session of the National Assembly to be convoked by the President before 20 May 1995. Their terms in office are shortened to four years, and they may be re-elected for a second term. With respect to the question of participation of overseas Chinese in the election of the President and the Vice-President, Article 18, paragraph 7, vaguely provides that the state "shall accord to Chinese nationals residing overseas protection of their rights to political participation".

2. *The National Assembly*: According to Article 11, the terms of delegates to the National Assembly shall be shortened to four years. The President shall convoke an extraordinary session of the National Assembly annually. When the Assembly is in session, it shall hear a report on the state of the nation by the President, discuss national affairs and offer counsel.

3. *The Control Yuan*: Members of the Control Yuan were formerly elected by the Taiwan Provincial Assembly and Taipei and Kao-hsiung city councils. There were strong criticisms of the bribery scandals surrounding those elections. Therefore, Article 15 abolished the election for members of the Control Yuan and converted this Yuan into a semi-judicial organ. From

50. Tammy C. Peng, "3-Year Delay in Vote on Electing President", *FCJ*, vol. IX, no. 21 (27 March 1992), p. 1.

51. For translation of the text of these articles, see *FCJ*, vol. IX, no. 44 (23 June 1992), p. 7.

1993 on, members will be appointed by the President with the consent of the National Assembly. Members of the Control Yuan must be beyond party affiliation and independently exercise their powers, discharging their responsibilities in accordance with the law.

4. *Judicial Yuan and the dissolution of unconstitutional parties*: Article 13 makes some minor revisions to the organisation and function of the Judicial Yuan. The President, Vice-President and the Grand Justices of the Judicial Yuan shall be appointed by the ROC President with the consent of the National Assembly. Formerly, members of the Judicial Yuan were appointed with the consent of the Control Yuan, which was indirectly elected by the people through their Provincial Assemblies or Councils of cities under direct administration of the Executive Yuan. Because the Control Yuan now is no longer a people's representative organ, but rather a semi-judicial organ, there is no reason for the Control Yuan to retain the power of consent to the appointment of judicial officials.

A new function is entrusted to the Grand Justices: the adjudication of issues involving unconstitutional political parties. Under the existing Civic Organisation Law, the Party Review Committee of the Executive Yuan may decide to dissolve a political party if said party advocates Communism or splitting national territory. This part of the law was criticised by some commentators as unconstitutional, because it appears to infringe without due process upon the people's right to association. Article 13, therefore, shifted this power to dissolve political parties to the Grand Justices of the Judicial Yuan. They will form a Constitutional Tribunal to adjudicate matters relating to the dissolution of unconstitutional political parties. A political party is defined as unconstitutional "if its goals or activities jeopardise the existence of the Republic of China as free, democratic constitutional order".

5. *Examination Yuan*: Because the Control Yuan is no longer a people's representative organ, its power to give consent to the ROC President's appointment of the President, Vice-President and members of the Examination Yuan is shifted to the National Assembly, as provided in Article 14. Moreover, in the first stage of constitutional reform, Article 9, paragraph 2, of the Additional Articles authorised the Executive Yuan to establish the Personnel Administration therefore, the Examination Yuan's function is now limited to "all legal matters relating to the employment, discharge, performance evaluation, scale of salaries, promotion, transfer, commendation and award for civil servants". In other words, the execution and implementation of these functions are now transferred to the Personnel Administration of the Executive Yuan.

6. *Local self-government*: Article 17 provides a legal basis for the Legislative Yuan to enact a law permitting the direct election of the Governor of a province, i.e. the Taiwan Province. At present, the Governor of Taiwan is appointed by the President with the consent of the Taiwan Provincial Assembly.

7. *Fundamental national policy*: Article 18 adds certain items to fundamental national policy, which is the subject of Chapter XIII (Articles 137–69) of the Constitution. Among these items are environmental protection, the elimination of sexual discrimination, safeguarding personal safety for women, the right of handicapped and disabled persons to insurance, and legal protection for aborigines and other groups.

## Future prospects

The second stage of constitutional amendments, while making the ROC's government system more democratic (e.g. the direct election of the Governor of Taiwan) and simplifying the parliamentary procedure by removing the Control Yuan from people's representative organs, has also raised several important issues regarding the operation of the Republic of China's governmental system. The first issue is if the extraordinary session of the National Assembly to be convoked by the President before 20 May 1995 cannot reach an agreement on the method of electing the President (either by electoral college or by direct election), then how will the next President of the Republic be elected? This deadlock is possible because, according to Article 174 of the Constitution, any constitutional amendment can only be adopted by a resolution of three-quarters of the members of the National Assembly at a meeting having a quorum of two-thirds of the entire Assembly. If this happens, the logical solution to this issue is to refer the question to the Council of Grand Justices of the Judicial Yuan for an authoritative interpretation. However, the Council may also deadlock on this issue, because any constitutional interpretation from the Council is required to be adopted by a resolution of three-quarters of the members of the entire Council.[52]

Second, assuming that the 1995 extraordinary session adopts the method of direct election of the President, there remains the question of whether the President should be elected by absolute majority or by simple majority. In a report submitted to the KMT Central Standing Committee on the election of the President, the proposal for an electoral college and the proposal for direct election both adopt the simple majority rule. Therefore, in the future, there is a possibility that a minority President will be elected in the Republic of China, thus undermining the political stability of the country.

52. See Article 13 of the Law on the Council of Grand Justices of the Republic of China, promulgated on 21 July 1958. *Latest Edition of Six Codes*, p. 15.

Third, according to Article 11 of the Additional Articles, the National Assembly is given the authority, at its annual meeting, to hear a report on the state of the nation by the President, to discuss national affairs and to offer counsel. Since the Assembly has the power to amend the Constitution, whether it may use that power to expand its role in the future is a question that remains to be answered. If so, whether such an unprecedented bi-cameral parliamentary system will work is at least questionable.

In view of the above analysis, although the future of constitutionalism in the Republic of China appears largely positive, there exist some important questions and areas of potential conflict involving the implementation of the new constitutional amendments. Be that as it may, looking back at constitutional development in China, never before in China's history have the Chinese people paid so much attention to constitutional issues as the Chinese people in Taiwan do today. Constitutionalism, which was introduced to China early in the twentieth century, appears now to be an integral part of the political process in the Republic of China in Taiwan. If this trend continues, which is quite likely, it will have a significant impact on constitutional development on the Chinese mainland.

# 2

# CHIANG KAI-SHEK AND THE KUOMINTANG'S POLICY TO RECONQUER THE CHINESE MAINLAND, 1949–1958[*]

## Steve Tsang

In January 1949, as the tide of the Chinese civil war was turning decisively against the Kuomintang, Chiang Kai-shek formally retired from the presidency of the Republic of China. At the same time, he prepared to turn Taiwan into his new "revolutionary base" in his long-standing struggle against the Communists. In the following year the Kuomintang lost the Chinese mainland to the Communists and retreated to the island redoubt of Taiwan. In March 1950, Chiang Kai-shek resumed the Presidency and declared that his aims were to "restore the Republic of China, and to destroy international communism".[1] In other words, his regime's ultimate objective was to recover by force the mainland lost to the Communists, as crystallised in the slogan "*Fan-kung ta-lu*" or "Reconquer the mainland". In October 1958, as the Second Taiwan Straits Crisis drew to a close, Chiang openly retreated from this position. In a joint communiqué with the United States, he declared that while his government considered "the restoration of freedom to its people on the mainland . . . its sacred mission", it regarded "the implementation of Dr Sun Yat-sen's three people's principles . . . and not the use of force" as "the principal means of successfully achieving its mission".[2]

[*] The author wishes to thank the Centre of Asian Studies, University of Hong Kong; the Institute for Modern History, Academia Sinica (Taipei); the Hoover Institute (Stanford); the Butler Library, Columbia University; the Eisenhower Library (Abilene); the Truman Library (Independence); the MacArthur Memorial Library (Norfolk); the Institute of International Relations (Taipei); and the Public Record Office (Kew) for providing facilities for research for this chapter, and for giving permission to quote or refer to archival materials in their custody.

1. Ch'in Hsiao-i (comp.), *Tsung-t'ung Chiang Kung ssu-hsiang yen-lun tsung-chi: yen-chiang*, vol. 23 (Taipei: Chung-kuo Kuo-min-tang tang-shih wei-yuan-wei, 1984) (hereafter *Chiang Kai-shek: Tsung-chi*), p. 137.

2. Report on NSC5723, 15 April 1959, Annex B, NSC5523 – Taiwan, White House Office: Special Assistant to NSC: Policy Papers Box 22, *Papers of Dwight D. Eisenhower*, Eisenhower Library, Abilene (hereafter *Eisenhower Papers*).

This chapter will reconstruct the truth behind this development as far as is possible, from 1949 to 1958. The following questions will be addressed. What was Chiang Kai-shek's thinking behind his policy to reconquer the mainland? Did the Kuomintang under Chiang have the military and the political means to put this policy into effect? What preparations, if any, had they made to implement this policy? Did Chiang and his party actually make any serious attempt to reconquer the mainland? Did Chiang's October 1958 announcement represent a genuine new departure in policy? Finally, it will also highlight the implications for Taiwan of following this policy in the 1950s.

## Chiang Kai-shek's strategy

When Chiang retired from the presidency of the ROC in early 1949, he had no intention of fading into political oblivion. Instead, he reflected on the Kuomintang's failures and prepared to turn Taiwan into a new base for his campaign against the Communists. Taiwan was favoured because it was separated from the mainland by sea and was therefore less susceptible to Communist infiltration.[3] As Taiwan's main value to Chiang in 1949 and early 1950 was as his new revolutionary base, political as well as other developments in the island were subject to this primary concern.

Chiang's grand strategy was predicated primarily on three factors. In the first place Chiang himself genuinely believed that he was a revolutionary, and the successor to Sun Yat-sen. He was motivated not only by a hunger for power but also by a sense of mission. He wanted to make China into a powerful modern state along the lines of the Three People's Principles as he understood them. To him, fighting the Communists and international Communism was not only a struggle for power but also a revolutionary and a nationalistic mission. Thus, as Kuomintang power collapsed on the mainland in late 1949, Chiang would not give up hope of retaking the lost territory, even though he found himself preoccupied with massing sufficient forces merely to defend Taiwan. In 1950 the President was prepared to make a last stand in Taiwan and perish with it, if necessary, rather than entertaining the idea of giving up his mission in return for an international or an

---

3. Chiang Ching-kuo, *Feng yu chung te ning-ching* (Taipei: Cheng Chung shu-chu, 1978), p. 216; Tung Hsien-kuang, *Chiang Tsung-tung chuan* (Taipei: Chung-hua wen-hua ch'u-pan shih-yeh wei-yuan-hui, 1952), p. 526.

American guarantee of Taiwan's security. To give up hope of recovering the mainland would deprive him of the meaning of life. However, whatever his personal feelings, in formulating his policy towards the mainland he had to take other factors into account too.

The second factor which greatly influenced Chiang's plans was the painful lessons which he had learned from the defeats his forces and his party had suffered from the Communists. In his own assessment, the Kuomintang forces had a weak organisation, poor discipline, low fighting spirit, little fighting capability and no commitment to their ideology.[4] He criticised senior military officers for being pompous, arrogant, unprepared to study problems seriously, unwilling to listen to staff officers and ignorant of modern military knowledge, particularly that relating to combined operations.[5] He attributed the Kuomintang's failures to internal division, corruption, the lack of a tight organisation and an effective apparatus to safeguard confidential information, and the disloyalty of some senior Party members, as well as to Comintern plotting.[6] Chiang did try to rectify these problems by reforming the armed forces and the Kuomintang in the 1950s, relating these reforms to his policy of recovering the mainland by force.

Last but not least, there were geographical and practical difficulties which Chiang had to face as he worked out his grand strategy. While the Taiwan Straits had made the island relatively easy to defend against an invasion from the Chinese mainland, it also prevented the Taiwan-based Kuomintang forces, which had few amphibian capabilities, from counter-attacking. The other major practical difficulties for Chiang were the shortage of military equipment, the poor state of morale and general preparedness of his recently defeated troops, and the inability of the Kuomintang to function as an effective political force. In early 1950, although Chiang's forces numbered about 600,000, they had little, if any, hope of successfully defending Taiwan against an all-out attack by the Chinese Communist forces. The American Central Intelligence Agency (CIA) and the State Department intelligence section concluded that the Kuomintang could not "effect political and military adjustments sufficiently realistic to make possible a successful defense of Taiwan".[7] Even General Ch'en Ch'eng, one of Chiang's

4. *Chiang Kai-shek: Tsung-chi*, vol. 23, pp. 38–40, 84.
5. *Ibid.*, pp. 46–7.
6. *Ibid.*, pp. 83–4.
7. CIA report ORE 7–50, 20 March 50, f.1, President's Secretary's Files, Box 257, *Papers of Harry S. Truman*, Truman Library, Independence, Missouri (hereafter *Truman Papers*).

main lieutenants, admitted that Taiwan's defence was "barely adequate", and that there was "no prospect for counterattack on mainland in foreseeable future".[8] The enemy which Chiang's forces faced was the 3.7 million strong People's Liberation Army (PLA)[9] which, in mid-1950, had the ability to transport by sea 200,000 troops for an assault on Taiwan.[10]

In other words, in the spring and early summer of 1950 the real burning issue for Chiang's government was not to reconquer the mainland but to prevent the collapse of resistance in Taiwan against a possible onslaught by the Communists. Chiang's government in fact expected the Communists to invade Taiwan between July and late September.[11] Thus, despite the President's emotional commitment to retake the mainland, and the rhetoric that a military counter-attack would begin in a year's time, he frantically withdrew from Hainan and Chu-shan to reduce his defence perimeter.

The outbreak of the Korean War in June 1950 changed the situation dramatically for Chiang and his government. In response to the Communist North Korean regime's attack on South Korea, United States President Harry Truman reversed American policy towards the defence of Taiwan and "ordered the [American] Seventh Fleet to prevent any attack on Formosa [Taiwan].[12] By a stroke of good fortune, Chiang and his government were saved from an impending invasion by the Communists, to be spearheaded by General Ch'en Yi's Third Field Army, which was deployed along the East China coast opposite

8. Taipei to Secretary of State, telegram 249, 14 August 1950, "Neutralisation of Formosa", Records relating to the Korean War, Box 6, *Truman Papers*.

9. Of the 3.7 million regular troops, 2.3 million belonged to the field armies and 1.5 million to regional armies. They were further supported by a militia of almost 2 million. According to Nieh Jung-chen, the total number was 5.4 million in June 1950; *Nieh Jung-chen hui-i lu* (Hong Kong: Ming Pao Ch'u-pan-she, 1991), p. 645. For details of the PLA's capabilities, see Miscellaneous Reports — "Estimate of the Situation of the Chinese Communist Forces as of June 15, 1950", Box 29, *Papers of Admiral C.M. Cooke*, Hoover Archives, Stanford (hereafter *Cooke Papers*).

10. *Foreign Relations of the United States* 1950, vol. VI, (Washington: Government Printing Office, 1976) (hereafter: *FRUS*), pp. 395, 401; David Muller Jr, *China as a Maritime Power* (Boulder, CO: Westview Press, 1983), pp. 16–17.

11. Waichiapu telegram to Washington Embassy 357, 19 July 1950, File B.13(1)b, Box 145, *Papers of Wellington Koo*, Butler Library, New York (hereafter *Koo Papers*).

12. Hungdah Chiu (ed.), *China and the Taiwan Issue* (New York: Praeger, 1979), p. 221; Nancy Tucker, *Patterns in the Dust* (New York: Columbia University Press, 1983), pp. 57–8.

Taiwan.[13] This respite gave Chiang the opportunity to put substance to his policy of reconquering the mainland at a later stage, if that indeed was his real intention.

As the decade went on, Chiang Kai-shek fine-tuned his grand strategy. While he consolidated his power in Taiwan and reformed the Kuomintang and the armed forces, Chiang kept up his public rhetoric of recovering the mainland by force and of liberating his compatriots from the tyranny of what he called the "Communist bandits". The resumption of American aid, including both the supply of military hardware and the provision of training and military advisors, which followed the outbreak of the Korean War, transformed his forces into an effective war machine by 1958. Nevertheless Chiang was realistic enough to recognise that he was little closer to achieving his avowed objective.

Throughout the 1950s, while Chiang's rhetoric was offensive, his priority was in reality clearly defensive. This was perhaps inevitable given the disparity between the power of the Communist PRC on the mainland and Chiang's ROC in Taiwan. The Taiwan Straits Crisis of 1954–5, and that of 1958, demonstrated to Chiang and to the rest of the world that Taiwan was more likely to be invaded by than to invade the regime in control of the Chinese mainland. Chiang did not need to be reminded of this fact.

Shortly after the Korean War started, the United States was forced to engage itself in a land war in Asia against "international communism". To Chiang it must have appeared as if his prayers had been answered. After all, only a few months earlier he had stressed that the campaign to recover the mainland should be part of an international war against world communism, and that the United States would have to fight side by side with him in Asia.[14] Yet, at this particular point in history, Chiang rejected a proposal by one of his leading subordinates to start hostilities by invading the island of Hainan, on the ground that this would violate the American policy of neutralisation of the Taiwan Straits.[15] After Dwight Eisenhower succeeded

---

13. For the detailed disposition of the Third Field Army and its order of battle, see "Intelligence, Order of Battle", Communist Chinese Third Field Army, FECOM, RG-6, *Papers of General Douglas MacArthur*, MacArthur Library, Norfolk, VA (hereafter *MacArthur Papers*).

14. *Fan-kung tso-chan yung-ping ssu-hsiang yao-tse* (Taipei: Kuo-fang-pu, 1963), p. 1; *FRUS* 1950, vol. VI, pp. 281–2.

15. "Reminiscences of Dr Kuo-cheng Wu for the Years 1946–1953" (manuscript at Butler Library, New York), ff.176–7.

Harry Truman as President of the United States, he was supposed to have "unleashed" Chiang Kai-shek on the mainland in February 1953. However, Chiang in fact adhered to an unwritten understanding with the United States not to launch any large-scale military actions against the mainland without prior consultation with the Americans.[16]

In September 1954 Chiang told John Foster Dulles, the American Secretary of State, that he did not wish to drag the United States into a war with the Chinese Communists. Chiang said that he intended to reconquer the mainland with his own forces and would only ask for American arms and economic and technical support, not military assistance from any of the three services. He also stressed that he would attack only when he could be certain of success; since the Americans knew exactly what capabilities his forces had, they had no reason for concern.[17] The military reality in the Taiwan Straits area at that time was that Chiang's forces could not even defend Taiwan successfully against an all-out attack by the Chinese Communists without American air and naval support.[18] Chiang simply did not have the resources to undertake a major offensive on the mainland. Dulles aptly assessed Chiang's talk with him to mean that the President was not seriously preparing to recover the mainland by force.[19]

As Taiwan's security came under military threat from the Chinese Communists in the First Straits Crisis in late 1954 and early 1955, for the first time Chiang formally committed himself in writing to the effect that his government would neither invade nor launch large-scale attacks on the Chinese mainland without first consulting the United States.[20] Hitherto, he had only done this in the form of an unwritten understanding. Chiang made this major concession in order to secure a mutual defence pact with the United States. Since such a treaty would be defensive in nature, it would tie the Kuomintang's hands in the matter of reconquering the mainland, even though it would

16. "Record of Conversation when President Received Dulles", 9 September 1954, f.9, Folder B.212(a), Box 154, *Koo Papers*; "Notes on Talk with Rankin", 4 September 1953, FC10111/62, *FO371/105203*, Public Record Office, London.

17. "Record of Conversation when President Received Dulles", 9 September 1954, ff.9, 12, 14, File B.212(a), Box 154, *Koo Papers*.

18. "183rd Meeting of the NSC", 4 February 1954, ff.6, 8, Whitman Files: NSC Series Box 5, *Eisenhower Papers*.

19. "214th Meeting of the NSC", 12 September 1954, f.3., Whitman Files: NSC Series Box 6, *Eisenhower Papers*.

20. Chiang's telegram to Washington Embassy, 29 January 1955, File B.13.1(e), Box 145, *Koo Papers*.

also put Taiwan under American protection.

In the negotiations for the Mutual Defence Treaty, the bottom line for Chiang was that his promise not to use force without American consent should be kept secret and that he should be free to continue to preach in public the theme of a military recovery of the mainland. To Chiang, giving up the idea of recovering the mainland would have meant losing his key purpose.[21] Thus, after the crisis was over, he continued to ask his senior subordinates to prepare in general terms to retake the mainland by force, if and when general support from the people of the mainland was forthcoming.[22] While there was a contradiction between what Chiang agreed with the Americans and how he instructed his subordinates, there was probably no inconsistency in his own mind. What Chiang was prepared to do was to give up the initiative to invade, which he in any event did not have the resources to put into effect. What he refused to abandon was the hope of recovering the mainland. Equally importantly, as Chiang explained to Dulles, maintaining this position and the public façade was necessary in order to "bolster morale and keep hope alive".[23] The fact remains that from March 1955 onwards, when the US–ROC Mutual Defence Treaty came into effect, Chiang had given up the freedom to attempt a military recovery of the mainland, unless he could secure prior American consent.

In 1958, when Taiwan's security again came under threat from the Chinese Communists in the Second Straits Crisis, Chiang went one step further. On this occasion, the intensity of the Communist artillery barrage on the Kuomintang island redoubt of Quemoy was matched by the steadfastness of the Kuomintang garrison there. The Quemoy defence force stood firm against overwhelming odds, even in the early phase of the hostilities when it had little heavy artillery to mount an effective counter-attack and the enemy brought to bear its five-to-one advantage in fire-power.[24] In one place the ROC flag was blown

21. *Ibid.*

22. *Tsui-chin kuo nei wai chu-shih te t'ui-yen yu wo-men fan-kung fu-kuo chi-hua te chin-tu chih shuo-ming* Taipei: Yang-ming-shan chuang, 1955), p. 38.

23. Administration, C.-in-C., Pacific telegram to Secretary of State, 4 March 1955, ff.3–4, Formosa (China) 1952–7(4), Whitman Files: International Series Box 9, *Eisenhower Papers*; Waichiaopu to Washington Embassy telegram 367, 29 April 1955, File B.13(1)c, Box 145, *Koo Papers*.

24. *Chin-men p'ao-chan tso-chan Ta-ch'en Nan-lu ch'e-fung ching-kuo chien-t'ao* (Taipei: Kuo-fang-pu chi-hua tz'e-chang-shih, 1962), p. 39.

down seventeen times by Communist artillery fire and was promptly resurrected seventeen times.[25] Such an incident would normally not be remarked upon had it happened to a professional Western army. But it was a remarkable demonstration of the transformation which had taken place in Chiang's former rag-tag army, which had practically disintegrated in the face of the advancing Communists after the latter had crossed the Yangtze River in April 1949, less than a decade previously. The ROC Air Force, for its part, achieved professional superiority over its Communist opponent. Its fighters shot down twenty-nine Chinese Communist MIG fighters, including MIG-17s.[26] The ROC Air Force lost only one of its own fighters in combat. However, in spite of this impressive performance of his armed forces, Chiang made no attempt even to bomb mainland targets.[27] Instead, he allowed himself to be persuaded by Dulles to issue a joint communiqué, in which he declared:

The Government of the Republic of China considers the restoration of freedom to its people on the mainland its sacred mission. It believes that the foundation of this mission resides in the minds and the hearts of the Chinese people and that the principal means of successfully achieving its mission is the implementation of Dr. Sun Yat-sen's three people's principles (nationalism, democracy and social well-being) and not the use of force.[28]

This statement amounted to renouncing publicly the use of force for the recovery of the mainland. While this was a concession to the Americans on Chiang's part, it also reflected a gradual change in his attitude. Towards the latter part of the 1950s, Chiang increasingly laid greater emphasis on developing Taiwan into a model for appealing to the Chinese on the mainland. In other words, the policy to reconquer the mainland had in effect been transmuted into a policy to recover the mainland by political means, if possible.

25. *Chiang-tsung-t'ung Ching-kuo hsien-sheng yen-lun chu-shu hui pien* (Taipei: Li-ming wen-hua shih-yeh ku-fen yu-hsien-kung-ssu, 1982), vol. 4, pp. 544–5.

26. *Chin-men p'ao-chan*, p. 14. US figures suggest 31 MIGs were shot down. "Government", Taiwan, June 1960, f.6, Formosa (China) Far East Trip (5), Whitman Files: International Series Box 10, *Eisenhower Papers*.

27. "Government", Taiwan, June 1960, f.6, Formosa (China) Far East Trip (5), Whitman Files: International Series Box 10, *Eisenhower Papers*.

28. "Report on NSC 5723", 15 April 1958, annex B, NSC—5523—Taiwan, White House Office Files: Special Assistant to the NSC Box 22, *Eisenhower Papers*.

## The offshore islands

Is the above interpretation of Chiang's strategy consistent with the fact that in the 1950s Chiang progressively expanded his forces in the islands of Quemoy and Matsu, only a few miles off the coast of China? Did Chiang not say these off-shore islands would be spring-boards for a military campaign to recover the mainland? Was the heavy concentration of some of Chiang's best troops in Quemoy in the late 1950s intended to spearhead an invasion of the mainland?

While it is true that Chiang was determined to turn these offshore islands into strongholds, and that he greatly increased his military commitment to them, it does not necessarily follow that this was part of an offensive strategy. On the contrary, Chiang's main concern over these islands was also defensive in nature.

In April and May 1950, when Chiang retreated from Hainan and withdrew his forces from the Chu-shan Islands to Taiwan to strengthen the latter's defence,[29] he did not retreat from Quemoy or Matsu, which were more vulnerable. But in the overall defence of Taiwan, geography has made Quemoy and Matsu far more valuable in military terms than the other islands. Quemoy is located opposite the port of Amoy, the deepest port and potentially the best naval base along the coast of Fukien. Matsu is situated outside the estuary of the Min River, at the northern entrance to the Taiwan Straits, and commands the approaches to the port of Foochow, capital of Fukien Province. Both these islands lie on the shortest direct invasion routes between the mainland and Taiwan. Given the extremely limited capabilities of the ROC Navy in the early 1950s, and the heavy reliance of the Communists on junks and other non-amphibian vessels to transport their invasion force, holding these islands would serve several military functions. They would be the first line of defence for Taiwan, and good posts from which to observe any Communist preparation for an invasion. If their garrisons put up a good defence they could significantly delay, even to some extent disrupt an invasion of Taiwan itself. In view of the general unpreparedness of the defence forces in Taiwan, any additional advance warning, or slowing down of the invasion force, would be valuable. Neither Hainan nor Chu-shan offered these advantages.

29. Chang Ch'i-yun, *Ta-lu lun-hsien te t'ung-shih yu kuang-fu ta-lu te nu-li* (Taipei: Chung-yang wen-wu kung-ying-she, 1953), p. 54; *The Reminiscences of General Shih Chueh*, (Taipei: Academia Sinica, 1986), pp. 372-3.

At the time of the First Straits Crisis, Taiwan's own defence preparations had already been completed. Indeed, the steady reinforcement
of the Quemoy and Matsu garrisons in over the previous few years
reflected the growing capabilities of Taiwan's own defence forces.
More troops and equipment could be spared for the offshore islands and
Chiang had no intention of giving up more territory than was absolutely
necessary. In early 1955 the Communists captured Yi-kiang-shan Island
off the coast of Chekiang, and rendered the neighbouring islands of
Ta-ch'en and Nan-lu indefensible. Chiang reluctantly withdrew from
them.[30] However, for the sake of his self-esteem, the morale of the
troops and of Taiwan more generally, at that time he felt he could not
afford to lose Quemoy and Matsu as well. Not to be driven from all
the offshore islands which were not part of Taiwan Province was
also important in maintaining the myth and legitimacy of the ROC
in Taiwan in its claim to be the government of all China. Chiang's
government was mindful of the international climate. It saw the
British Commonwealth as leading a campaign in the United Nations
to separate Taiwan from China, in an attempt to settle the Taiwan
question by detaching it from China for ever.[31] If successful, such an
attempt would deprive him of any hope of recovering the mainland.
The retention of the offshore islands had by then acquired an important
political value of its own.

The massive reinforcements which Chiang sent to the offshore islands
after the First Straits Crisis was over and the Mutual Defence Treaty
with the United States was signed, were also in fact defensive in nature.
The reinforcements were primarily infantry divisions, bringing the
number of troops in the garrisons up to more than 100,000 by 1958,
a little less than one-third of Chiang's army. Their disposition was
defensive; they had few offensive capabilities across the channel. Indeed
Chiang did not deploy his potentially offensive armoured division on
these islands; he kept it in Taiwan itself. If Chiang himself believed
the offshore islands could be used as spring-boards for an invasion of
the mainland, he made no preparation for such an action. His senior
subordinates, including one-time Chief of General Staff P'eng Meng-chi,

---

30. For a ROC reappraisal of the battle for Yi-chiang-shan, see *Hai-tao kung-fang
chan-shih* (Taipei: Kuo-fang-pu shih-cheng-chu, 1959), ch. 5; for the evacuations from
Ta Ch'en and Nan-lu islands, see *Chin-men p'ao-chan*, pp. 75–154.
31. Chiang to Washington Embassy, Telegram of 30 January 1955, and Chiang
to Yeh and Koo, letter of 14 October 1954 (?), File B.13.1(e), Box 145, *Koo Papers*.

privately admitted that for such a purpose the islands were worthless.[32] No invasion of the mainland from these islands could have an element of surprise. Chiang's massive reinforcement was necessary because the 1954–5 Crisis had proved how vulnerable these islands really were, while the Americans had made it clear that they would only become involved in defending the islands as part of the defence of Taiwan. [33] The choice was between abandoning them to the Communists or entangling the Americans in their defence. By committing one-third of his best troops to these islands, the losing of which would threaten Taiwan's own survival, Chiang forestalled the American government by preventing them from letting the islands be captured by the Communists.[34] His gamble was vindicated by the American response to the Second Straits Crisis, when Quemoy was the main target of the Communists and the Americans promptly responded by coming to Chiang's aid.

## Military reforms and preparations for reconquering the mainland

In 1950 Chiang's forces were in a very sorry state indeed. A professional in-depth assessment of all three services was carried out by the American Far Eastern Command under General Douglas MacArthur in August, after the outbreak of the Korean War. As this exercise was to prepare for the resumption of American military aid, the investigating American team had no reason to underrate, or overrate, the capabilities of Chiang's forces. It concluded that the ROC Navy had few ships, which were poorly maintained, and that it could not "operate groups of ships effectively". It was deemed incapable of destroying or badly disorganising an invasion force.[35] The air force was considered neither combat-ready nor able to defend Taiwan and Penghu against the nascent Chinese Communist air force.[36] Chiang's army was in better

32. "August 23 1954", Diaries 33, Box 220, *Koo Papers*.

33. "The Taiwan Straits Situation", 3 September 1958, f.1, Formosa (1958) 2, Whitman Files: International Series Box 10, *Eisenhower Papers*.

34. "The Taiwan Straits Situation", 3 September 1958, f.6, Formosa (1958) 2, Whitman Files: International Series Box 10, *Eisenhower Papers*. Text to treaty in Chiu (ed.), *China and the Taiwan Issue*, pp. 227–30.

35. "Survey of Military Assistance Required by Chinese Nationalists Forces", 11 September 1950, f.21, FECOM Survey etc, RG-6, *MacArthur Papers*. This assessment is in line with the recollections of a former naval Commander-in-Chief. See *The Reminiscences of Admiral Ni Yue-si* (Taipei: Academia Sinica, 1991).

36. McArthur Papers, ff.23–4.

shape, but the "available equipment [was] inadequate to support protracted or severe defensive operations".[37] Before this official American assessment, an independent group of retired American officers, under the command of Admiral C.M. Cooke, operated in Taiwan to assist Chiang in defence matters. Cooke and his men arrived well before the Korean War started, at a time when the United States government had written off Chiang's regime and withdrawn all military advisors. They were very sympathetic to the ROC regime and had also made a confidential assessment of the capabilities of Chiang's forces. Their findings and the official assessments of the Far Eastern Command are generally in line with each other.[38]

The military reforms which were introduced in the 1950s represented a combination of Chiang's own thinking and American advice, which formally resumed with the establishment of the Military Assistance and Advisory Group (MAAG) in January 1951.[39] Chiang's intention was to let the Americans supply him with military hardware, train his forces in military skills, discipline and the use of equipment, and even to advise him on organisational and command structures. But he was not prepared to let his forces be turned into clones of the American forces. He engaged former Japanese (and a few German) officers to train his senior officers in order to check the American influence.[40] He kept some of his forces outrange of the MAAG's assistance and therefore its purview. Chiang had no intention of letting the control of his armed forces pass to the Americans by default. His basic military thinking also differed fundamentally from that of the Americans. The military reforms were therefore a compromise between these two differing approaches.

In the early 1950s Chiang had two main goals in military reform, other than those relating to increasing the fire-power and technical competence of his forces. He wished to instil what he called "a revolutionary spirit", or a new ethos, in his forces. He exhorted his senior officers to break down the barrier between them and the troops by

37. *Ibid.*, f.41.

38. Detailed assessments in Boxes 26–8, *Cooke Papers*. Generally speaking, Cooke's team performed the functions which were later taken over by the official MAAG.

39. *Hsien Tsung-t'ung Chiang-kung yen-lun hsuan-chi: Fan-kung fu-kuo te li-lun yu shih-chien* (Taipei: Chung-yang wen-wu kung-ying-she, 1984), p. 110; *MAAG's Decade in the Republic of China* (Taipei: Ministry of National Defence, 1961), p. 8.

40. *Reminiscences of General Shih Chueh*, pp. 403, 430; *Chiang Kai-shek: Tsung-chi*, vol. 23, pp. 255–6.

eating and living with them, by respecting the dignity of the common soldier, by allowing the management of personnel and financial matters to be inspected, by listening to junior officers, and by looking after the families of the troops.[41] This was closely related to his second goal, which was to subject the armed forces to strict party domination under his control. His principal instrument was a system of political officers under the General Political Department for the armed forces, which was revamped in April 1950.[42] He had no hesitation in borrowing from the Communist political commissar system. Indeed, he instructed his own officers to learn from the Communists, particularly in regard to organisation, security and intelligence work.[43] What Chiang aimed to achieve in this matter was to put the armed forces under the command of the party, the control of which he was progressively consolidating.

Chiang Ching-kuo, Chiang Kai-shek's eldest son and his most trusted aide since 1949, was central to the reintroduction of the political officer system. Chiang picked Ching-kuo for this task not only because he was his son but also because they shared the same views. Chiang Ching-kuo was a graduate of the Central Tolmatchev Military and Political Institute in Leningrad and had lived in the Soviet Union for almost twelve years. He understood Communism and the Soviet political commissar system better than most other generals in the ROC armed forces, and had a respect for their effectiveness that was shared by his father. The younger Chiang was not a professional soldier, but this was not a serious disadvantage since his job was not that of a field commander; Chiang Kai-shek himself had little real understanding of modern warfare in the context of the 1950s, despite his own belief to the contrary. In every other respect he was exactly what his father wanted of a revolutionary general. He was loyal, dedicated, ideologically sound and committed, courageous under fire, meticulous in handling security and intelligence matters, good at building up rapport with the common soldiers, and virtually incorruptible. Indeed, for the purposes he had in mind Chiang Kai-shek himself could not have done better than his son in indoctrinating and training a new generation of political officers loyal to himself.

At the Academy for Political Officers at Fu-hsing-kang, Chiang Ching-kuo taught his cadets that the war against the Communists was primarily a political struggle and they should therefore use

---

41. *Chiang Kai-shek: Tsung-chi*, vol. 23, pp. 40–3, 90.

42. Pai Kuang-ya (ed.), *Kuo-chun cheng-chan-shih* (Taipei: Cheng-kung kan-pu hsueh-hsiao, 1970), p. 88.

43. *Chiang Kai-shek: Tsung-chi*, vol. 23, pp. 84, 135.

Communist methods to beat them at their own game.[44] To him ideology played a role similar to that of religion, and everyone had to believe unconditionally in the Three People's Principles.[45] He taught his cadets that Chiang Kai-shek was not just the state President but the Leader, who personified China and its 5000 years of history; as such his authority was unlimited and subject to no circumscribed period of tenure.[46] They should, therefore, follow the Leader without reservation. The younger Chiang's cadets were also instructed to devote their lives to the party, always to follow the party, observe its discipline, carry out its tasks and sacrifice themselves for the party if necessary. On no account should any one of them wish to use the party for personal gain.[47] At the day-to-day level, political officers were trained to enhance the party's organisation and build up a strong core of cadres within the armed forces, to protect secrets and prevent infiltration, to establish a "revolutionary" worldview, to devise new management techniques, to prepare themselves for political warfare and to serve as civil affairs officers in the event of the successful recovery of territories by the armed forces.[48] When the newly revamped political officer system was first put to the test in the battle for Ta-ch'en during the First Straits Crisis, it proved ineffective.[49] In the 1958 battle for Quemoy, however, the political officers finally came of age and, despite a few notable failings, won the approval of Chiang Ching-kuo.[50]

In the purely military reforms of the armed forces, Chiang Kai-shek was more prepared to accept American advice and even follow the American model, particularly in technical matters. When Chiang reorganised the Ministry of Defence and the high command in 1950, he enjoyed the advice of Admiral Cooke's team of non-official advisors.[51] He also acted on American advice when he reorganised the

44. Pai Kuang-ya (ed.), *Kuo-chan cheng-chan-shih*, pp. 95–6.
45. *Chiang-tsung-t'ung Ching-kuo hsien-sheng yen-lun chu-shu hui pien*, vol. 2, pp. 41, 44; *Chiang Ching-kuo hsien-sheng Chiang-tz'u-chi* (Taipei: Kuo-fang-pu chen-chan-pu, 1955), p. 2.
46. *Chiang Ching-kuo hsien-sheng Chiang-tz'u-chi*, p. 11.
47. *Chiang-tsung-t'ung Ching-kuo hsien-sheng yen-lun chu-shu hui pien*, vol. 2, pp. 65–6.
48. *Chiang Ching-kuo hsien-sheng Chiang-tz'u-chi*, pp. 68–70; *Chiang-tsung-t'ung Ching-kuo hsien-sheng yen-lun chu-shu hui pien*, vol. 2, pp. 327–8.
49. *Chiang Ching-kuo hsien-sheng Chiang-tz'u-chi*, pp. 68–70; *Chiang-tsung'ung Ching-kuo hsien-sheng yen-lun chu-shu hui pien*, vol. 2, pp. 327–8.
50. *Ching-kuo hsien-sheng yen-lun chu-shu hui pien*, vol. 4, pp. 8–12.
51. *Ibid.*, p. 513; *Chin-men p'ao chan*, pp. 21–2, 41–2.

army into field army units along American lines in 1954.[52] But he
fiercely resisted an American proposal of the mid-1950s to consolidate
his army of twenty-eight under-strength divisions into twenty-one
full-strength divisions of 11,000 each, which would have improved their
overall fighting capabilities. Instead, he opted to maintain twenty-four
divisions, each 15 per cent under-strength.[53] Keeping the higher
number was preferred both for prestige reasons and because Chiang
believed that this would provide greater scope for expansion in the event
of an invasion of the mainland. But if such an invasion had occurred,
it would have required several times the total strength of the available
Kuomintang forces; the existence of three additional divisions in
name could only have had a nominal positive effect at best. Chiang also
organised all-officer combat regiments, which were supposed to provide
a pool of officers for an expanding invasion force.[54] But since these
officers were not regularly rotated to normal combat units for refresher
exercises, the real value of maintaining these regiments was to avoid
having to discharge them into the community, as unemployed former
officers were always a potential source of instability. While these
gestures indicate that Chiang had the aim of recovering of the mainland
at the back of his mind all the time, they do not prove that he was
seriously planning an invasion.

Between 1950 and 1958, Chiang's armed forces were gradually
transformed beyond recognition. In 1950, the armed forces were
essentially loose groupings of some effective and some ineffective
military units. In some cases the soldiers within a unit did not even
have the same calibre rifles, never mind sharing any other standard
equipment or training. Even their ability to absorb American aid was
limited, as most officers and men had neither the training nor the
technical competence to employ and maintain modern sophisticated
weapon systems, or even fairly basic equipment such as motor vehicles,
tanks, ships or aircraft.[55] However, by 1958 a unique proficient party-
army, an efficient modern defensive air force and a small defensive
coastal navy had emerged. Even though the forces were about the

---

52. Cooke to President, memo 164, 4 Nov. 1950, Technical memorandum—
Chinese Army—Report by O.T. Pfeiffer, Box 28, *Cooke Papers*.

53. *Reminiscences of General Shih Chueh*, p. 404.

54. Yeh to Radford, letter of 23 March 1954, File L.210, Box 169, Koo Papers.

55. *Chung-hua-min-kuo nien-chien 1953* (Taipei: Chung-hua-min-kuo nien-chien she,
1954), p. 343; *Chung-hua-min-kuo nien-chien 1955*, pp. 305 and 314.

same in number as they had been in 1950, they were much more formidable.

From the top down a new command structure, which permitted the rotation of senior commanders at regular intervals, was introduced. The last vestiges of warlordism were stamped out, as the forces increasingly instituted a system of promotion by merit and the allocation of resources according to need.[56] For the first time in its history the ROC forces eliminated "paper soldiers" and introduced both a modern system of conscription and a system of discharging ex-servicemen without simply turning them into bandits.[57] Ineffective career soldiers were gradually weeded out, either pensioned off or put to work on government-sponsored projects.[58] Despite initial resistance from Chiang, the American model of training steadily gained acceptance until it became standard. A system of training reserves and calling them up in emergencies was also developed.[59] A professional officer corps and an *esprit de corps* slowly emerged. Combined operations ceased being a novelty and became the norm. Notwithstanding the continued existence of many problems in the armed forces, the military reforms had made remarkable progress.

The product of the army reforms was a cross-breed: an American equipped and trained defence force, with the ethos of a Kuomintang party rather than a Chinese or Taiwanese national army. It incorporated a political officer system which in some ways resembled that of its principal opponent, the People's Liberation Army. The air force not only acquired the appearance of being the best in non-Communist Asia, excluding the American Air Force, but actually proved its professionalism in combat in the 1958 Crisis.[60] By 1957 the standard of its ground communications and electronics facilities reached such a level that some American fighter pilots on exercise admitted that "they

56. Ewing to Cooke, memo of 18 Oct. 1950, Plans and Reports of Military Manoeuvres and Exercises, Box 26, *Cooke Papers*.

57. Cooke to Chiang, memo of 3 Nov. 1950, and Severt to Cooke, memo of 31 July 1950, Technical Memoranda—Chinese Marine Corps, Box 28, *Cooke Papers*.

58. "Report on NSC 5723", 16 April 1959, Annex, f.9, NSC 5523—Taiwan—White House Office: Special Assistance to the NSC Policy Papers Box 14, *Eisenhower Papers*.

59. Nine reserve divisions were ready by 1958. "Review of US policy towards Formosa and the Government of ROC", Annex, NSC 5503—Policy towards Formosa and ROC, White House Office: Special Assistance to the NSC Policy Papers Box 4, *Eisenhower Papers*.

60. Franklin to Lloyd, dispatch of 19 Jan. 1957, FCN1193/1, FO371/127494.

were even better than ours in the US".[61] The navy remained the ROC's Achilles' heel, but it did reach a level of technical competence equal to that of the Chinese Communist navy.[62]

Despite the impressive progress which Chiang's forces had made, and their commendable performance in the 1958 Straits Crisis, they were essentially defensive forces. Their American sponsors had not provided them with much in the way of offensive capabilities. They did not have the resources to launch an amphibian operation of more than 18,000 forces against the Chinese mainland.[63] Nor did they have the bombers and naval escorts to support a major offensive operation.[64] Even the élite Marine Corps and the Armoured Force were only large enough to act as a strategic reserve in defence, rather than to spearhead an invasion of the mainland. Worse still, the Americans kept Chiang's forces on a tight leash by limiting the stockpile of war materiel in their hands. Throughout the 1950s, the ROC forces seldom if ever had more than ninety days' supply of ammunition.[65] Indeed, before the First Straits Crisis Chiang's forces had only forty-five days' supply of combat reserve ammunition.[66] The balance of military power in the Taiwan Straits remained overwhelmingly in the Communist PRC's favour. In 1958, without American support, Chiang's forces were still inadequate to defend Taiwan against an all-out attack by the Communists. Consequently, whatever Chiang's personal feelings might have been, he simply did not have the military capabilities to put into effect his avowed object of retaking the mainland.

### Political reforms and preparations for reconquering the mainland

Shortly after Chiang formally retired from the Chinese presidency in early 1949, he started the process of reorganising the Kuomintang. The first step he took was to appoint a special committee loyal to him to work out a plan. At that stage he envisaged using Taiwan and the

61. Tamsui consulate to Far Eastern Department, letter of 26 Nov. 1957, FCN1193/30, FO371/127494.

62. Muller, *op. cit.*, pp. 43 and 96–7.

63. Franklin to Mayall, letter of 18 Dec. 1957, FCN1022/8g, FO37 27494.

64. Details of ROC capabilities in "Review of US Policy towards Formosa & ROC", n.d. (?1958), Annex A, NSC5503—Policy towards Formosa and ROC, White House Office: Special Assistance to NSC Policy Papers Box 14, *Eisenhower Papers*.

65. "Review of US Policy . . .", *ibid.*

66. "Answers to Questions Raised by the Van Fleet Mission", 27 June 1954, f. VI-2-3, File of same title, Box 171A, *Koo Papers*.

East China coastal regions as the base for training new cadres and for retraining the old ones. By late summer the East China coastal regions were largely lost to the Communists. Chiang proceeded to set up the Institute for Revolutionary Practice (*Ko-ming shih-ch'ien yen-chiu-yuan*) as the principal instrument for retraining senior cadres.[67] But the reorganisation of the party really gained momentum after Chiang resumed the presidency in Taiwan in 1950. Saying that he needed to re-register all Kuomintang members, Chiang formally eliminated from the party his former opponents, those who had wavered in the face of the Communist threat and those who had failed to follow him to Taiwan.[68] To Chiang, the object of the reform was to make the Kuomintang into what he called a "democratic revolutionary party".[69]

In the 1950s, Chiang explained his concept of a "democratic revolutionary party" in the following terms:

Today, our Party is a democratic party designed to promote constitutionalism. On the other hand, however, our Party is also a revolutionary party, shouldering the responsibilities of struggling against the Communists, recovering the Mainland, and saving life and freedom for our people. As a democratic party, our Party should observe the norms of democracy and rule of law, and participate in elections as the political parties do in democracies. As a revolutionary party, however, our Party should strengthen the organisation, maintain strict discipline, arouse revolutionary spirit, and accumulate revolutionary strength in order to stage a life-and-death struggle with the Communist bandits.[70]

While Chiang was careful to appear balanced in stressing both the "democractic" and the "revolutionary" elements in his formula, he clearly laid emphasis on the latter. In practice, Chiang instructed the Kuomintang to "adopt Communist methods in order to beat the Communists" at their own game.[71]

Chiang wanted to introduce to the Kuomintang the efficiency and effectiveness of a Leninist-style party, though he did not wish to turn

67. Chiang Ching-kuo, *op. cit.*, pp. 166, 202, 229, 236; Tien Hung-mao, *The Great Transformation — Political and Social Change in the Republic of China* (Stanford, CA: Hoover Institution Press, 1989), pp. 66–7.

68. Tung Hsien-kuang, *op. cit.*, pp. 569–60 (??); Tien, *op. cit.*, p. 67.

69. English version of Chiang's programme in Milton Shieh (ed.), *The Kuomintang: Selected Historical Documents, 1894–1969* (no place: St John's University Press, 1970), pp. 207–24.

70. Hsiao-shih Cheng, *Party-Military Relations in the PRC and Taiwan: Paradoxes of Control* (Boulder, CO: Westview Press, 1990), p. 136. Cheng's translation.

71. *Chiang Kai-shek: Tsung-chi*, vol. 24, p. 33.

it into a Leninist party.[72] He wanted the Kuomintang to learn from the methods and organisation of the Chinese Communist Party. He tried to eliminate factions within his party, strengthen its organisation and centralise the training of its cadres.[73] Chiang was also adamant that the Kuomintang must continue to be guided by his interpretation of Sun Yat-sen's Three People's Principles. He clearly intended the Kuomintang to benefit from the Three People's Principles in a way that would be similar to how the Communist Party had benefited from having Communism as its ideology. But unlike Mao Tse-tung, who had developed Marxism-Leninism to suit China's conditions, Chiang had made little significant contribution to developing the Three People's Principles as an ideology. In practice, what Chiang really did in the name of ideology was to indoctrinate his followers. His intention was to create a centralised party that was even more tightly organised than the Communist Party and responsive to the command of its leader, who was himself.

The "revolutionary" tasks which Chiang set for himself and for the Kuomintang in the process of reformation were to destroy the Communist regime on the mainland, resist the Soviet Communists and restore the ROC to its former place.[74] What he did was to try to eliminate from the Kuomintang in Taiwan such ills as corruption, factionalism, empty talk, lack of revolutionary spirit, selfishness, laziness and bureaucratism, which had sapped the strength of the Kuomintang on the mainland.[75] In other words, while the long-term goal was to recover the mainland from the Chinese Communists, his immediate ambition was consolidation of power in Taiwan.

In his efforts to clean up the party and give it a new lease of life, Chiang enjoyed considerable support from the ranks.[76] He pruned the party of many inept and corrupt cadres and relegated others to lower-level tasks. Those who remained were generally relatively

72. Whether the Kuomintang in the 1950s was a Leninist-type party or not is debatable. Lu Ya-li argues that it was not. Lu Ya-li, "Political Modernization in the ROC: The Kuomintang and the Inhibited Political Centre", in Ramon Myers (ed.), *Two Societies in Opposition* (Stanford: Hoover Institution Press, 1991), pp. 111–21.

73. *Chiang Kai-shek: Tsung-chi*, vol. 24, pp. 33–4.

74. *Chiang Kai-shek: Tsung-chi*, vol. 23, pp. 433–6.

75. *Hsien Tsung-t'ung Chiang-kung yen-lun hsuan-chi*, pp. 96–122.

76. For example, the *Fan-kung pan-yueh-k'an*, published in Taipei, did put out numerous articles in support of Chiang's efforts, though it also carries many articles advocating democracy as the only real solution.

honest, dedicated and eager to serve.[77] The top officials, including Wu Kuo-cheng (Governor of Taiwan 1949–53), who openly fell out with Chiang in 1954, and General Sun Li-jen (Commander of the Army 1950–4), who was dismissed on a charge of conspiracy in 1955, were all loyal to Chiang when they were in office. On the whole they made up an experienced and relatively efficient group of cadres for party and government positions. Like Chiang, they were eager that the party should not fail a second time.[78]

The Seventh Congress of the Kuomintang, held in October 1952, marked the conclusion of the reorganisation of the party. It did not emerge as a Leninist party, though the principle of democratic centralism was included in its reform programme.[79] Ideologically it opposed Marxism-Leninism vehemently. The Kuomintang ideology in principle committed the party to introduce democracy to China eventually. As for party discipline, the Kuomintang did not enforce this as strictly and effectively as a Leninist party usually did. In regard to party organisation, democratic centralism as practised in the Chinese Communist Party, which laid heavy emphasis on adhering to the party line, was not implemented.[80] What did emerge was a party which resembled a Leninist-type party in some ways — such as in its structure, its attempt to establish a party-state, its pervading of society, and its being an instrument of a kind of dictatorship — but it was one which had a different ethos.

As the decade progressed, the Kuomintang under Chiang penetrated virtually the entire social fabric in its attempt to create together a kind of party-state in Taiwan. It extended its control by building up an organisation to parallel the state administration. It dominated various functional groups in society, such as the military, trade unions, the media, farmers' associations, irrigation associations, the civil service and the educational establishment. It also established auxiliary organisations, the most important of which was the Chinese Youth Anti-Communist National Salvation Corps, under the control of Chiang Ching-kuo. The Corps was Chiang's instrument to indoctrinate young people at an impressionable age.[81] On the whole the Kuomintang was

---

77. Hermann to Eden, dispatch 41, 17 June 1954, FC1019/38, FO371/1102.
78. Lu, Ya-li, *op. cit.*, p. 113.
79. Shieh (ed.), *op. cit.*, p. 217.
80. Lu Ya-li, *op. cit.*, pp. 111–13.
81. Chiang Kai-shek: Tsung-chi, vol. 25, pp. 173–5.

relatively more successful in extending its control over the immigrant mainland community than over the native Taiwanese community.

Hand in hand with the reorganisation of the Kuomintang went Chiang's efforts to build up a new security and intelligence apparatus under the overall command of Chiang Ching-kuo. This began with the setting up of the "Materials Section", nominally under Chow Hung-tao but actually under Chiang Ching-kuo at the presidential office, in March 1950.[82] Step by step the younger Chiang gained domination over the remnants of the originally separate and competing intelligence-gatherers and secret police set up by the old "CC Clique" and Tai Li.[83] He also extended his control over the police and secured the support of successful commanders of Taiwan Garrison Command.[84] By 1958, Chiang Ching-kuo's control over the security and intelligence apparatus in Taiwan was complete.[85] His men were responsible both for intelligence activities overseas, including operations on the Chinese mainland, and for internal security including counter-intelligence duties. On the mainland, Ching-kuo admitted the loss of "several hundred" comrades in the 1950s. In Taiwan, the security apparatus successfully prevented Communist infiltration and kept watch on various political leaders to ensure none was plotting against Chiang Kai-shek.

The reorganisation of the party and the building up of an effective and efficient security and intelligence apparatus were clearly important if Chiang Kai-shek seriously wanted to reconquer the mainland. Throughout the 1950s Chiang preached that the recovery of the mainland would require 70 per cent political work and 30 per cent military efforts. Thus in a sense the political reforms of the 1950s were even more important as an indicator of Chiang's real intention. However, a review of the political reforms in this period does not suggest that they were introduced mainly to prepare for an offensive on the mainland, despite Chiang's rhetoric. The reorganisation of the Kuomintang, the extension of its power to include the community at large, even the massive strengthening of the security and intelligence

82. Reminiscences of Dr Kuo-cheng Wu, f.199; enclosure to Australian Embassy (Paris) to R.G. Casey, letter of 18 June 1954, FC1019/37, FO371/110202.

83. Li Shih-chieh, *Tiao-ch'a-chu yen-chiu* (Taipei: Li Ao ch'u-pan-she 1988), pp. 15–18.

84. Reminiscences of Dr Kuo-cheng Wu, ff.201–2.

85. K'o Lai-en (R.S. Cline), *Wo so chih-tao te Chiang Ching-kuo* (Taipei: Lien-ching ch'u-pan shih-yeh kung-ssy, 1990), p. 25.

services would have been needed in any case for the political set-up which Chiang wanted in Taiwan.

## Implications

Chiang Kai-shek's public commitment to a policy of recovering the mainland by force in the 1950s had important effects on political developments in Taiwan. On the one hand, it made the creation of a quasi-Leninist party-state more acceptable to the population, who found this preferable to Communist rule. On the other hand, the constant reminder of the existence of a powerful threat across the Straits kept Chiang, and the Kuomintang party-state, on their toes. They knew their government's legitimacy, based on its claim to be the government of the Republic of China, could be challenged relatively easily. They had to ensure their survival, not only by building up a potent defence force and a powerful party-state apparatus but also by performing as an efficient and effective government. Ideological commitment reinforced this requirement. Thus, despite the Taipei government's huge military expenditure throughout the decade, it insisted on spending its remaining limited resources on the steady improvement of the standard of living in Taiwan, even at the expense of rational long-term infrastructural development.[86] The vulnerability of Chiang's regime contributed to the emergence of what one political scientist called "the inhibited centre" in a powerful party-state.[87]

The existence of this paradox in Taiwan in this period was captured vividly by a neutral observer, A.A.E. Franklin, the British Consul at Tamsui, who wrote in late 1957:

If anything, it would be truer to say that the government is in complete and unquestioned control. Admittedly there is a somewhat unpleasant odour to it, since it has to lean heavily for its backing on the slightly totalitarian triumvirate of Army, Security Forces and Party. That the late Dr. Sun Yat Sen's rather threadbare Three People's Principles have conspicuously failed to invest the Kuomintang with much genuine, popular appeal, is beyond serious dispute. Nevertheless, difficulties notwithstanding, the government, by and large, manages quite comfortably—in fact surprisingly so. Moreover, the

86. "Review of US policy towards Formosa & the government of the ROC", n.d. (?1958), Annex B, f.1, NSC 5503—Policy towards Formosa & ROC, White House Files: Special Assistance to NSC Policy Papers Box 14, *Eisenhower Papers*.

87. Term used by Lu Ya-li.

margin of liberty within this semi Police [sic] State is much greater than is generally imagined in the world outside Formosa . . . The security authorities themselves, when searching for Communists, concentrate on Chinese mainland groups, not on the local population . . . [W]hat appears to be an idea widely accepted abroad, that everything which the Chinese Nationalist government touches is incompetent, incoherent and corrupt, is ridiculously exaggerated . . . [T]his government in fact has a good number of highly able, intelligent, hard working and honest men in it.[88]

While Franklin under-estimated the value of Sun's ideology as a means of enlisting support for Chiang's government and indoctrination, he was right in seeing the regime as a benevolent dictatorship.[89] It was a police state where the ordinary people had little to fear when going about their daily lives. The resultant political, economic and social stability in fact provided an environment conducive to economic development.

Whether Chiang's public commitment to reconquer the mainland slowed down development in Taiwan generally is a more difficult question to answer. In 1950 Chiang was already stressing the need to make a model province of Taiwan, which would require developing the province. Nevertheless his overriding concern then was to turn it into the base for his "revolutionary" struggle for the whole of China.[90] The land reform of the early 1950s was needed both for domestic reasons in Taiwan, and to give substance to Chiang's strategy of making Taiwan a model to appeal to the rest of China in his struggle against the Communists. By the late 1950s, however, even Chiang's private speeches indicated that he saw the two as entirely complementary to each other. But since he was not seriously planning a campaign on the mainland, it is reasonable to conclude that, for all practical purposes, his government was really devoting all non-military resources on the development of Taiwan itself.

There remains the question of whether Chiang inhibited development in Taiwan with the very heavy military expenditure involved in maintaining a standing defence force about 600,000 strong. In the 1950s, Chiang's military expenditure accounted for about 58 per cent of government expenditure, or 13 per cent of Gross National Product

88. Franklin to Lloyd, dispatch 84, 2 Dec. 1957, FCN1015/17, FO371/127452.
89. The land reform invested the KMT regime with considerable support, and it was presented as the implementation of Sun's ideology on improving the people's livelihood.
90. *Hsien Tsung-t'ung Chiang-kung yen-lun hsuan-chi*, p. 132.

(GNP). This is an enormous proportion by any standard. However, the review of the military development given above has demonstrated that in spite of all these expenses, between 1949 and 1958 Taiwan never had sufficient capabilities to defend itself against an all-out attack by its likely invader, the Chinese Communists. The apparently over-sized infantry army was, in fact, primarily a defensive rather than an offensive force. Even a shift in military priorities, from land to sea and air defence would have resulted in a very limited saving in costs, if any. The only realistic saving would have been to give up the offshore islands and cut their garrisons of about 100,000 soldiers, mainly infantrymen: a relatively low-cost item. But to compensate for this loss in capabilities, considerable, and expensive, air force and naval units would have had to be added. In any case this would not have been feasible in the early 1950s, because the ROC forces at that stage were not able to absorb the necessary, more sophisticated hardware for the air force and the navy. In the meantime, throughout the 1950s, the threat from the PRC was real. Taiwan survived because of American support. As long as Chiang's government and the people of Taiwan were not prepared to rely primarily on the United States for protection, the huge military expenditure could be justified by the need for defence.

## Conclusion

While Chiang Kai-shek believed that he had a mission to "re-conquer the mainland", he came to realise in the 1950s that this was not a prac-tical policy. However, for both emotional and political reasons he could not give up this aspect of his government's official policy, because it was the *raison d'être* for the maintenance of the ROC in Taiwan. Thus, when in 1958 Chiang and his government had publicly to give up the policy of retaking the mainland militarily, they insisted that this was merely a change of emphasis, a shift from stressing a military to a political solution. However, this claim was deceptive, as Chiang had since 1949–50 been talking privately of the task of recovering the mainland as a 70 per cent political, but only 30 per cent military — the same percentage publicly announced in 1958. The fact is that if Chiang and his government were to remove the reoccupation of the mainland from their political platform, questions as to the government's legitimacy and Taiwanese independence would have to be confronted. Seeing himself as a revolutionary, a nationalist and the successor to Sun Yat-sen, Chiang would not and could not contemplate this. Nor did the political environment in Taiwan in the 1950s encourage the Kuomintang government to face up to these questions.

The result was that politics in the ROC in Taiwan during the 1950s was conditioned by this official policy of recovering the mainland. This contributed to the establishment of a quasi-Leninist party-state with an inhibited centre, which willy-nilly eventually provided the political framework for Taiwan's move towards developing into a democracy in the late 1980s.

# 3

# IN SEARCH OF A NEW POLITICAL ORDER? POLITICAL REFORM IN TAIWAN

## Hermann Halbeisen

For several decades since their flight to Taiwan the Chinese Nationalists have committed considerable energies to maintaining a political order whose constitutive traits were established on the Chinese mainland. In spite of the fact that the institutions defined in the Constitution adopted in 1947 did not suit the conditions of the island in a number of ways, the preservation of this order and the extensive use of emergency laws enabled the Nationalist regime to maintain its rule over the island largely unaffected by the consequences of socio-economic change and intermittent popular demands for political reforms.

Having dismissed demands for political reforms for several decades by pointing to the still unresolved national crisis and the continuing struggle with the Chinese Communists, the ruling Kuomintang (KMT) reversed its position in the middle of the 1980s and initiated a process of political reform, aiming at a liberalisation of the domestic political scene and an adjustment of the Constitution to the conditions in Taiwan.

Translating the reform into political reality turned out to be difficult, however, as its scope and content became highly controversial. At the time of writing, nearly seven years after its start, only parts of the initial concept have been accomplished: the liberalisation of political life and a partial amendment of the Constitution. Considerable differences of opinion concerning the substance, scope and speed of constitutional reform still exist among and between the political parties represented in the National Assembly (NA), civic organisations and parts of the population.

The delay in conceptualising and implementing the reform stages has been the result of a number of different influences. From the start opinions within the KMT were divided concerning the scope and the potential risks of political reform. It was due to the unexpected death of one of the most influential promoters of reform within the party leadership, Chiang Ching-kuo, that political reform became enmeshed with the problem of succession. As the settlement of the succession became a priority for the various groups within the KMT, little capacity was left for the pursuit of political reform.

Taking advantage of the enlarged freedom of political action in the wake of the termination of martial law, a number of new political actors emerged and participated vigorously in the reform process. They introduced new topics and demands into the debate and began to propagate them emphatically both inside and outside political institutions. Some of the topics that became part of the reform debate challenged the premises upon which the KMT had initiated political reform, thereby further complicating the reform process.

Demands for changing or amending the political order in Taiwan were first put forward in the 1950s. The topics that constituted the demands of the political opposition during the 1970s and 1980s were to a considerable extent borrowed from the public pronouncements of the dissidents of previous decades. In order to accentuate continuities and discontinuities between the early demands for reforms and the concepts employed in the current debate, the following analysis of the reform process in Taiwan will begin with a short discussion of the features of the political system that developed there after 1949, and of the criticisms they brought about. It will then turn to the political reforms, providing a conspectus of the unfolding process and a short analysis of the diverging goals of the participants. Finally, the results of the reforms and their implications for future political developments in Taiwan will be discussed.

## The political system after 1949

Among the characteristics of the political order that developed in Taiwan after 1949, two are of special relevance for our inquiry: the ideas that define the origins and the end of the political order, and the application of these ideas in everyday politics.

Fleeing to Taiwan in 1949 the Chinese Nationalists carried with them their understanding of the identity and the aims of political order. The institutions of the Republic of China, as defined in the Constitution of 1947, were maintained, although they were conceived for the whole of China, for a population and territory exceeding those of the island of Taiwan many times over. The aim of the political order, Chinese nationalism as expounded in the work of Sun Yat-sen, also remained unchanged. Taiwan was considered part of China, the Nationalist government viewing itself as the sole legal government of China.

The Constitution of 1947 and the elected members of the three representative organs of the Republic, the National Assembly, the Control Yuan (CY) and the Legislative Yuan (LY), formed the core of a concept used by the Nationalists to assert the *fa-t'ung*, legitimacy of their rule, against growing criticisms. In the short and pointed definition of T'ao Pai-ch'uan, *fa-t'ung* meant "ruling the nation by means of the constitution",[1] a definition that seems to state something quite obvious. For the political situation in Taiwan, however, maintaining *fa-t'ung* implied serious limitations on the scope of legal political activities. On the one hand, governmental policies were oriented towards the needs of an ideal China. On the other hand, it led to the ossification of the membership of these representative organs, which continued to include those selected in the 1948 elections.[2]

The stress on the immutability of the Constitution and the political order it defined did not — in the perception of the Nationalist regime — contradict the fact that constitutive parts of this order were modified or temporarily annulled by emergency laws designed to cope with the exigencies of the Communist rebellion. Martial law and the "Temporary Provisions Effective during the Period of Communist Rebellion" limited or annulled personal liberties.[3] At the same time the Temporary Provisions modified the constitutionally defined balance of power among the institutions of central government by enlarging the powers of the president of the Republic at the expense of those of the Premier (the President of the Executive Yuan) on the one hand, and the power of the executive *vis-à-vis* the legislative branch on the other.[4]

1. Quoted in Cheng Mu-hsin, *T'ai-wan i-hui cheng-chih ssu-shih-nien* (Taipei: Tzu-li wan-pao, 1987), p. 110.

2. "The existing constitution had to be respected, no changes of its constituent aspects or its substitution were allowed. The object of constitutional practice to embrace all compatriots, i.e. the system of three representative institutions, elected in the early stage of constitutional rule, had to be maintained. Regarding an eventual passing away of its members, the nation had to find ways of replenishing the membership, in order to maintain a symbol of representing the whole of China." *Ibid.*

3. See Chapter 2 above, and Peng Ming-min, "Political Offences in Taiwan: Laws and Problems", in *China Quarterly* (*CQ*), no. 47 (1971), pp. 471–93.

4. "As a result, the declaration of martial law, the issuance of the emergency ordinance, and the adoption of other measures no longer had to be approved or confirmed by the LY. They became matters to be decided by the President and the EY. Although the LY could exercise its own initiative and adopt a resolution to request

Amendments to the Temporary Provisions increased the dominant position of the President even further through the establishment of a National Security Council as part of the presidential office. Its membership included the Presidents of the Republic and of the Executive and the Legislative Yuans, a number of ministers and members of the armed forces, thereby bridging the constitutionally envisaged division of powers. The President was also granted the power to take what steps were necessary to fill the vacant seats in the national representative organs. The legal basis for these "supplementary elections", which were held in Taiwan after 1969, consisted of presidential decrees until the LY adopted the Public Officials Election and Recall Law in 1980.[5]

The dominant position the President of the Republic occupied in the institutions of the state was further enhanced by the personalities of the incumbents. Both Chiang Kai-shek and his indirect successor Chiang Ching-kuo were "strongmen" and they held other important positions in the power structure of the regime, thereby making the office of the President the most important political office in the eyes of the population.[6]

The influence that the representative organs were able to exert was further reduced by the increasing age of its members after the Grand Justices suspended Article 47 of the Constitution, which called for regular elections. The election of additional members through supplementary elections was not sufficient to stop this decline. The continuing numerical superiority of the senior members (*tzu-shen tai-piao*), their growing distance from the values and requirements of a rapidly changing society and their often unconditional support of government policies allowed only rather limited improvements.

While the emergency laws altered the relationship between the national political institutions, they did not provide a legal framework for politics at the sub-national level. The laws needed to specify the

---

that the emergency measures be terminated, the EY could still send it back for reconsideration . . ." Jen Teh-hou, "The Constitutional Development of the Republic of China, 1949–1975: Law and Politics in Taiwan" (unpubl. Ph.D. thesis, New School of Social Research, New York, 1978), p. 70.

5. *Ibid.*, p. 282. The Public Officials Election and Recall Law was adopted in May 1980.

6. The interregnum of Yen Chia-kan was too short to qualify this assessment, the more so as the election of Chiang Ching-kuo made the office of the President once more into the most powerful position within the power structure.

constitutional provisions for local self-government were never passed;[7] local administration was instead carried out on the basis of a decree issued by the Executive Yuan (EY) in April 1950, the Regulation for the Enforcement of Local Government of Hsien and Municipality in Taiwan Province. This regulation did not provide for the popular election of governors, mayors of special municipalities or mayors/magistrates. In spite of continuing criticism concerning lacunae in the regulatory framework and constant demands for the direct election of governors and mayors, the decree continued to remain in force.[8]

The development of this political order with strong authoritarian and personality-oriented characteristics did not pass without numerous critical objections, or attempts to prevent its unfolding or to turn it in a different direction. The continuation of the martial law regime, even after the immediate threat from the Chinese Communists had eased, and the creation of the regime of personality centred on the person of Chiang Kai-shek became the main targets of criticisms.

In a series of articles dealing with topics of the day, published in the magazine *Free China Semi-Monthly* (*Tzu-you chung-kuo pan-yuek-k'an*) in the early 1950s, a group of intellectuals drew up a balance-sheet of the political conditions in Taiwan, of the chances for a reconquest of the mainland, and of the global situation. This was followed by a detailed critique of Nationalist policies in all important policy areas. One area that attracted special concern was the steady loss of influence suffered by the LY *vis-à-vis* the EY. The intellectuals saw the loss of challenges to the members of the LY, a result of the suspension of regular elections, and the lack of alternatives to the existing political parties as the main reasons for this development. Thus they advocated the foundation of a new opposition party as a way to remedy the debilitation of the legislative institutions and to reassert their control over the executive.[9]

7. The statutory bill, "General Principles of Provincial and Hsien Government", which was intended to clarify the relationship between the national government on the one hand and the regional and local governments on the other, had already passed its second reading in the LY in 1950 when the the EY decided to shelve the bill. Jen, *Constitutional Development*, pp. 172–3.

8. The content and results of the Second Amendment are discussed in this chapter, pp. 98–9.

9. Li Hsiao-feng, *T'ai-wan min-chu yün-tung ssu-shih-nien* (Taipei: Tzu-li wan-pao, 1987), p. 59.

A second development that raised the concern of the intellectuals was the attempt to change or to reinterpret the Constitution in order to enable Chiang Kai-shek to take up a third term of office as state president. The intellectuals vehemently opposed this plan and came out in favour of a strengthening of constitutional procedures. Instead of identifying the future of the nation with the continuing rule of one person they argued for a systematic grooming of political successors, a method they considered more in tune with the requirements of the nation and the necessities of the anti-Communist struggle.[10]

Although the coherent critique of political developments in Taiwan and the political ambitions of Chiang Kai-shek that the intellectuals put forward drew considerable attention among the public, it failed to achieve their aim. Assessing the experiences derived from the campaign against a third term of office for Chiang Kai-shek, the intellectuals came to the conclusion that political appeals alone were not sufficient to influence the interests of politically influential groups. They decided, therefore, to enter the field of practical politics and to realise one of their central demands, the establishment of an opposition party. The preparations for a new political party, the Chinese Democratic Party (*Chung-kuo min-chu-tang*), an effort that united intellectuals and politicians of mainland origins together with politicians of Taiwanese descent, were well advanced. After leading members of this initiative were arrested on charges of not reporting Communist agents in September 1960, the whole project was abandoned, however.[11]

The intellectuals critical of the authoritarian political system on Taiwan in the 1950s were mostly of mainland origin. Although they castigated the growing paralysis of political life as a consequence of maintaining the *fa-t'ung*, they did not question the Chinese identity of the political order. A more radical critique was formulated in political circles outside the island, however. Activists belonging to the groups of Taiwanese exiles that were organised in Japan and the US began to question the legitimacy of Nationalist rule over Taiwan and the proposition that the island was part of China. These groups, which were affiliated to the Taiwan Independence Movement (TIM),[12] were formed

10. *Ibid.*, p. 67.

11. Cheng, *T'ai-wan i-hui cheng-chih*, pp. 183–7; Li, *T'ai-wan min-chu*, pp. 74–82.

12. See Cynthia Yun Ping Weth, "Die Taiwanesische Unabhängigkeitsbewegung (Taidu) 1945–1978" (unpubl. Ph.D. thesis, University of Würzburg, 1981); A. James Gregor and Maria Hsia Chang, "Terrorism: The View from Taiwan", in *Terrorism*, vol. 5, no. 3 (1981), pp. 233–64.

in reaction to the events of 28 February 1947.[13] The suppression of the 1947 demonstrations proved to them the dictatorial nature of the Nationalist regime in Taiwan, a rule that was characterised by the oppression of one group of people, the Taiwanese, by another, the mainlanders. The political influence of the TIM in Taiwan itself was quite limited, but its ideas found some resonance among the Taiwanese students who went to study in the United States. Despite considerable efforts to spread their views in the island itself, it was only in the 1970s that the question of Taiwan's identity became a topic of political debate among opposition circles in Taiwan.[14]

The debate on the political order in Taiwan entered a new phase in the late 1960s. A new generation, whose political and social orientations were moulded by the conditions prevailing in post-war Taiwan, the experience of rapid economic and social development, entered the political scene. At the same time, the Republic of China was confronted with new challenges to its international position. The political situation in Taiwan itself, where symptoms of intellectual stagnation and political rigidity had become more pronounced, caused the young generation to raise demands for comprehensive political reforms with new vigour.[15]

Though a number of similarities existed between the social position and the political strategies of the young critics of the regime and the dissidents of the 1950s, the differences in their political aims were considerable. The key members of the 1960s were intellectuals, organised around a magazine, *The Intellectual (Ta-hsueh tsa-chih)*. The questions they discussed dealt only in part with domestic reforms; they were equally concerned about the implications of Taiwan's international relations. To protect the international position of Taiwan from the effects of the entry of the People's Republic of China into international organisations was one of their main motives. This was

13. See the studies by Günter Whittome, *Taiwan 1947: Der Aufstand gegen die Kuomintang* (Hamburg: Institut für Asienkunde, 1991); and Lai Tse-han, Ramon H. Myers and Wei Wou, *A Tragic Beginning* (Stanford University Press, 1991).

14. See Hermann Halbeisen, "Taiwanese Consciousness (T'ai-wan i-shih): Facets of a Continuing Debate", in E.K.Y. Chen, Jack F. Williams and Joseph Wong (eds), *Taiwan: Economy, Society and History* (Hong Kong: Centre for Asian Studies, Univ. of Hong Kong, 1991), pp. 235–50.

15. See Mab Huang, *Intellectual Ferment for Political Reform in Taiwan, 1971–1973* (Ann Arbor, MI: Center for Chinese Studies, Univ. of Michigan, 1976). A participant's view of these developments is provided by Ho Wen-chen, "Hsin-hai chüeh-hsing yün-tung", in Ho Wen-chen (ed.), *Ke Kuo-min-tang ti ching-yen* (Taipei: Ch'un-feung ch'u-pan-she, 1978), pp. 1–30.

reflected in their motto "Reform and protect Taiwan" (*Ke-hsin pao-T'ai*).
The political reforms these intellectuals advocated were that the island's
inhabitants should be adequately represented in the national parliamentary bodies (i.e. the National Assembly, the Legislative and the
Control Yuans), and that the position of these bodies in the institutional
framework should be strengthened. The first step should be the retirement of the present membership of the legislative organs, followed
by new elections in Taiwan.[16] In spite of a number of highly publicised
activities, the influence that these young intellectuals were able to
exert on the policies of the Nationalist government was quite limited.
The topics they introduced into the national political debate, however,
became part and parcel of the political programmes of the opposition
movement which developed during the 1970s.

The challenges to the political order in Taiwan reached an unprecedented level with the development of a new form of political opposition
in Taiwan, the Tang-wai. This movement incorporated nearly all the
main criticisms of the Nationalist political order that had been raised
in the decades before. It also managed to combine theoretical issues
with effective political action.[17] The political demands of the Tang-wai
were originally focused on the question of the population of Taiwan
being represented in the national parliamentary bodies. Since upholding
the *fa-t'ung* required strict limitations on any solution, the demands
spread that this concept should be abandoned and that all representatives
should stand for re-election. Publications by liberal intellectuals who
argued in favour of lifting martial law and implementing the provisions
of the Constitution added to the growing appeal of opposition demands
among the public.

Among some groups within the Tang-wai the conviction spread
that the problem of political order was intrinsically linked to the
question of identity, a position that found an increasing number of
adherents in the early 1980s. The statement by the Presbyterian Church
that "Taiwan was a new and independent nation",[18] was followed

16. Chang Ching-han *et al.*, "kuo-shih ching-yen", in *The Intellectual*, no. 46 (1971),
pp. 1–10. See also Huang, *Intellectual Ferment*, pp. 21–60.

17. For a brief discussion of the early development of the Tang-wai, see Hermann
Halbeisen, "Tangwai, Entwicklung und gegenwärtige Lage der Opposition in Taiwan",
*Zeitschrift für Politik*, vol. 29, no. 2 (1982), pp. 206–20.

18. Declaration of Human Rights by the Presbyterian Church in Taiwan, 16 August
1977. Marc J. Cohen, *Taiwan at the Crossroads: Human Rights, Political Development
and Social Change on the Beautiful Island* (Washington, DC: Asia Resource Centre, 1988),
p. 389.

several years later by a flood of publications trying to prove anthropological and cultural differences between Taiwan and mainland China. The debate on the existence of a separate "Taiwanese identity" (*T'ai-wan i-shih*) provided the arguments needed to challenge the concept that Taiwan was part of China. Corresponding with this idea on the political level were demands for self-determination, to let the inhabitants of Taiwan decide on the island's political status and its relation to China.[19]

At the beginning of the 1980s all constitutive elements of the established political order in Taiwan were exposed to growing criticism. In contrast to earlier periods, this was not just a sporadic phenomenon or limited to small circles of intellectuals and activists. Increased opportunities for political action, a growing number of politically active citizens and numerous political magazines that spread the political views of the Tang-wai to all parts of the island provided the basis for a greater awareness among the population of Taiwan of the deficiencies of the existing political order.

## The beginning of political reform

Although the legitimacy and exercise of its rule became the target of repeated criticisms, the Nationalist regime was able to fend off demands for a comprehensive change by pointing to the continuing national crisis. The Nationalist leadership was only prepared to allow improvements in the representation of the population of Taiwan in the national parliamentary bodies by introducing limited elections in 1968. In that year it conducted national elections to fill vacancies in the seats allotted to Taiwan. After 1972 these supplementary elections were held at regular intervals.[20] The number of additional seats created for these elections increased from 51 in the LY and 53 in the NA in the first elections, to 101 in the elections to the LY in 1989 and 84 in the elections for the NA in 1986. The number of seats in the CY was also increased.[21]

In the early 1980s the KMT could no longer ignore demands for

---

19. See note 13 above.
20. See John F. Copper and George P. Chen, *Taiwan's Elections: Political Development and Democratization in the Republic of China* (Baltimore, MD: University of Maryland School of Law, 1984), pp. 50–1.
21. The membership of the CY increased from fifteen in 1973 to thirty-two in 1987.

political reforms. Developments in Taiwan's society and within the party itself combined to increase the party leadership's sensitivity to growing criticisms.[22] The political opposition became more articulate in its demands, while the regime faced a loss of credibility among the politically active population as a result of the growing discrepancy between its self-characterisation as a democracy and the maintenance of a martial law regime. The growing senescence of the "senior representatives", whose numbers began to dwindle rapidly, endangered the human foundation of *fa-t'ung*. Meanwhile the "junior representatives" (*ts'eng-o tai-piao*), the basis of future legitimacy and continuing rule by the KMT, appeared less inclined to accept the continuing supremacy of their senior colleagues. Demands for reform originating from within the KMT became more widespread.[23] The continuing success the KMT enjoyed in the supplementary elections enabled the party's candidates to win comfortable majorities of seats regularly, assuaging fears among sections of the party leadership that complete re-election of the members of the national parliamentary bodies would be tantamount to a loss of power. Under these circumstances, the readiness of the party leadership to undertake political reform increased markedly.

This resolve was strengthened by several events. One was the number of political scandals that further tainted the image of the KMT in the eyes of the people.[24] Another was the growing popular speculation and apprehension as to the future development of the political situation in the island. These apprehensions focused on the political succession in the event of the premature death of President Chiang Ching-kuo, and the likelihood of a change of regime. President Chiang deemed it necessary to intervene personally and clarify the issues. He stressed that the eventual succession would take place according to constitutional procedures and that no member of his family would be a candidate for the office of President. He also dismissed the possibility of military rule after his death.[25]

22. See Chapter 4 below.
23. Interviews by the author in Taiwan during 1984–9.
24. Among the political scandals of this period, special mention has to be accorded to the Tenth-Credit Cooperative Bank in Taipei. The discovery of financial malpractices by the bank's management was followed by revelations of influence-peddling that implicated a number of KMT politicians in the LY and senior cadres of the party apparatus.
25. Interview with Chiang Ching-kuo, *Time Magazine*, 16 Aug. 1985, cited in Luo Hao, "Chiang Ching-kuo ta-k'ai cheng-chih chiang-chü", in *T'u-p'o cheng-chih chiang-chü* (Taipei: Feng-yün lun-t'an-she. 1986), pp. 23–4.

The process of political reform was formally set in motion by a decision of the Second Plenum of the Twelfth Central Committee of the KMT in March 1986. The plenum accepted a list containing the areas in need of reform and set up a commission charged with the drawing up of a precise plan of action. The list mentioned six areas where reform should be undertaken: (1) the strengthening of the national parliamentary bodies; (2) the legalisation of local self-administration; (3) the consolidation of laws on national security; (4) the establishment of a legal basis for civic organisations; (5) a rectification of public mores as well as a strengthening of social order; and (6) a clarification of the important tasks of the KMT.[26]

A reform commission consisting of twelve members (*shih-erh-jen hsiao-tzu*) was appointed, with the task of studying the problems and suggesting ways to resolve them. Members of the commission were selected from different opinion groups within the party, and comprised members of the conservative group of elder party leaders (*yuan-lao*) and younger technocrats in favour of reform, of both mainland and Taiwanese origins. Their selection underlined the fact that political reform was a matter of skill and expertise as well as a process of consensus-building, integrating divergent interests and calming the fears of several powerful groups within the party so as to focus in one direction.[27]

In spite of the fact that the list passed by the Second Plenum was limited to just a few topics and concentrated on reform within the existing political order, with the aim of strengthening its legitimacy through a limited adjustment to the conditions in Taiwan, the deliberations within the reform commission were tortuous and did not produce tangible results. Feeling against any kind of reform was strong among the conservative groups within the party. Their strong opposition was overcome on several occasions only by the personal intervention of the party Chairman.

The main efforts during the first phase of reform were concentrated on problems of liberalisation, political participation and democratisation. The lifting of martial law on 15 July 1987, after having been in force for thirty-eight years, put an end to one of the more notorious

26. Cited by Wu Wen-cheng and Chen I-hsin, "Entering the Age of Party Politics", *Free China Review*, vol. 39, no. 4 (1989), p. 53.

27. Short biographical information on the members of the commission is provided by Chiang Ai-fen, "Kuo-min-tang shih-erh-jen 'ke-hsin hsiao-tzu' ti chien-li", in *T'u-p'o cheng-chih chiang-chü, op. cit.*, pp. 52–61.

aspects of Nationalist rule in Taiwan. With the end of martial law limitations on civil liberties, such as freedom of speech or demonstration, the right to strike and a number of restrictions concerning the publishing of newspapers and magazines as well as their contents, were also abolished. However, in two areas these newly achieved freedoms were immediately curtailed by a new law on national security, which came into force soon after the end of martial law. This provided a basis for certain limitations to the freedom of speech and for a number of controls which the government deemed necessary as long as the conflict with the PRC was not resolved.[28]

The opportunities for political participation increased considerably, nevertheless. By amending the Law on Civic Organisation a legal basis for the establishment of new political parties was provided, albeit with several restrictions concerning their political programmes. They had to abstain from advocating Communism or secessionism, i.e. the establishment of an independent Taiwan. Notwithstanding these limitations the amendment kindled a wave of party formation. The number of parties hovered around seventy in 1992. Among the setting up of numerous tiny parties and several offshoots of the "friendly parties" (*you-tang*) of martial law days—the Young China Party (*Chung-kuo ching-nien-tang*) and the Democratic-Socialist Party (*Min-chu she-hui-tang*), both of which splintered into several new parties—came the foundation of the Democratic Progressive Party, or DPP (*Min-chu chin-pu-tang*). It exerted considerable influence on domestic political developments. Established in an act of defiance against the Nationalist regime in September 1986, i.e. before martial law was lifted, the new party united nearly all activists of the Tang-wai in one organisation. In spite of a pronounced factionalism and the departure of several popular politicians,[29] the DPP evolved into the most important political opponent of the KMT on the domestic political scene. The DPP was admittedly weakened by the loss of some leading members of the LY who went on to establish their own political parties. However, these breakaway groups, the Labour Party (*Kung-tang*) and the Social Democratic Party (*Min-chu she-hui-tang*), failed to make substantial inroads into the electoral basis of the DPP.

28. According to the text of the law it is illegal to use the right of assembly to advocate Communism or secessionism. The law also provides for the continuation of limited access to Taiwan for the inhabitants of the Chinese mainland.

29. Among the prominent politicians that have left the DPP for varying reasons are Wang Yi-hsiung, Chu Kao-cheng and Lin Cheng-chieh.

While the amendment of the Law on Civic Organisations and the establishment of new political parties marked a belated entrance into the period of party politics, the future shape of the new party system, at the time of writing, has not yet clearly emerged. Hopes for the development of a full-fledged two-party system were dashed in 1991, following the DPP's poor showing in the elections for the NA. Predictions of an eventual fragmentation of the party system, which were made after former DPP politicians established their own organisations, turned out to be premature as well. With the KMT recovering its predominant position and the DPP undergoing a series of intra-party struggles, the development of a "one and a half" party system of Japanese derivation seems most likely.[30]

The reform of the NA and the LY, it transpired, was more complicated. The KMT could not agree to demands for a complete re-election of members and the immediate pensioning off of the "senior representatives", because of strong opposition from conservative circles within the party and fears of endangering the party's claim to represent the whole of China. Its own approach took the form of a compromise containing strong financial incentives for the "senior representatives" to retire voluntarily within a fixed period of time but without any coercive measure.[31] This approach failed to have the desired effect, however, since few "senior representatives" were willing to comply. They chose instead to stay in office for as long as possible in order to maintain their influence on the direction of the reform process.

An advance towards the rejuvenation of the membership of the national parliamentary bodies came as a result of a decision by the Council of Grand Justices, which revised its earlier ruling on the duration of the mandate of the representatives elected in 1948. The Grand Justices declared in June 1990 that in the light of the changed national situation the assumptions of their earlier decision had to be reviewed, and they decided that the mandate of the "senior representatives" would end on 31 December 1991.

With the departure of the "senior representatives" within sight, a restructuring of the membership of the three parliamentary bodies (the NA, LY and CY) became a matter of urgency. The definition of the membership of the restructured representative organs constituted

30. For a discussion of the elections see Simon Long, "Taiwan's National Assembly Elections", *CQ*, no. 129 (1992), pp. 216–28.
31. The pensions could reach sums of up to NT$3.7 million, or around US$134,000.

the essence of the first step of constitutional amendments, which consisted of ten "Additional Articles" to the Constitution and came into force on 1 May 1990. The regulations were largely identical with an earlier decision by the National Security Council to reduce the number of seats in the NA, the LY and the CY. Since all these seats were to be contested in the "free areas" of the Republic of China, i.e. Taiwan and Penghu, with the exception of a few mandates for overseas Chinese, the number of representatives from Taiwan increased considerably. The restructuring of the representative bodies was to be accomplished in two steps. The first was that the number of representatives elected in Taiwan under the old structure in the LY was increased from eighty-nine to 120 in the elections of 1989, and to 150 in the elections to be held in December 1992. In a similar fashion the membership of the NA increased to 230 in the 1991 elections and was to rise to 375 in the elections of 1998, while the membership of the CY was to be increased to fifty-four persons to be elected indirectly in 1992.[32]

The procedures for electing the members of the three national parliamentary bodies contained one new element. In order to avoid the impression that the new representatives were only responsible to the electorate of their local constituencies, thereby putting the claim to represent the whole of China into doubt, an additional constituency was created at the national level. These parliamentarians, who were supposed to represent interests not taken into consideration in the local constituencies, were to be elected by proportional representation.[33]

With the promulgation of the Additional Articles the era of emergency laws finally came to an end, as the Temporary Provisions expired on the same date. The institutional arrangements that were founded on these provisions, the relationship between President and Premier in particular, remain unchanged, however. Article 8 contained transitional arrangements that allowed a number of laws based on the Temporary Provisions to stay in effect until July 1992.[34]

Domestic liberalisation exerted a strong stimulus on the island's political life. In addition to the establishment of new political parties

32. "Additional Articles of the ROC Constitution", *FCJ*, vol. 8, no. 32 (2 May 1991), p. 8.

33. Paragraph 4 of Articles 1–3 of the Additional Articles.

34. Articles 8 and 9 provide a legal basis for the retention of agencies that were created under the Temporary Provisions partly in violation of constitutional provisions, like the National Security Council and the Central Personnel Administration. *Ibid.*

and civic organisations, its effects became most obvious in livelier and multifarious newspapers and magazines. It also led to a significant rise in the importance accorded to the LY by the general public as well as by the executive branch of government.

Members of the LY have begun to reassert their constitutional rights. An increased number of members belonging to the opposition, and the significance the "junior representatives" had acquired for continuing Nationalist rule, were instrumental in strengthening the LY *vis-à-vis* the EY. Those members of DPP affiliation succeeded in gaining a reputation as a credible opposition, by aggressively using their powers to question government proposals or by exposing a number of questionable links between the government and the KMT. However, their readiness to seek publicity through confrontations and brawls, which was not matched by a similar enthusiasm to formulate practicable alternatives to government policies, has severely limited their claim to be a credible political alternative to the ruling KMT.[35] Efforts by the LY to increase its political clout further have been marred by a number of structural weaknesses that will limit its influence *vis-à-vis* the EY. Its activities continue to be hampered by strong factional tendencies that pervade both the KMT and the DPP parliamentary parties. Its capacity to scrutinize government proposals and to draft its own bills is severely limited. Differences of opinion between the parliamentary parties and party apparatus of both the DPP and the KMT, concerning their respective role in the policy-making process, continue to exist and create a constant source of conflict.

The stimulating effects of the termination of martial law were most visible in the print media. The *de facto* prohibition on the establishment of new newspapers and the application process for the publication of new magazines were both lifted. The strict limitations concerning the contents of publications became obsolete. The way was opened for the setting up of numerous new publications with widely divergent political and thematic orientations.[36] Having to compete with these new publications, the content of the two major newspapers, which used to be politically close to the KMT, has become more variegated and now includes topics that in martial law days were relegated to

35. See Gunter Schubert, "Constitutional Politics in the Republic of China: The Rise of the Legislative Yuan", *Issues and Studies*, vol. 28, no. 3 (1992), pp. 21–37.

36. In the meantime a number of magazines and newspapers ceased publication owing to economic problems. Among them were newly founded publications as well as several long-established ones.

the smaller papers like the *Independent Evening News*. Indicative of the degree of liberalisation that has taken place in the print media is the publication of a Taiwanese edition of *The Nineties*, the popular Hong Kong magazine of slightly leftist orientation that used to be banned under martial law.

The population has capitalised on the recently enlarged scope for political action through numerous demonstrations that have confronted the authorities concerned, be they the EY, the LY or the party headquarters of the KMT, presenting them directly with their demands and complaints. The causes motivating people to organise demonstrations have been multifarious, ranging from economic motives like the dissatisfaction with government policies that led to a crash of the highly speculative stock market, to social issues like the demand of ageing soldiers that the government redeem their land certificates, to demands concerning the content and speed of political reform. These demonstrations are evidence of a growing political commitment among the people of Taiwan. They also indicate that established procedures are suffering an increasing loss of credibility, which has motivated part of the population to try to realise their demands through their own actions, without relying on the good services of their representatives (*tzu-li ch'iu chi*).[37]

## The second phase of political reform

The political reforms conceived by the Second Plenum of the KMT represented a well-defined project initiated by the party leadership, which was undertaken with the strong personal involvement of the party Chairman. The nature of the reform, as well as the prerequisites for its realisation, underwent considerable changes as a result of the unexpected death of President Chiang and the pluralisation of the reform process in the wake of political liberalisation.

That political reform would encounter strong obstacles within the KMT itself became obvious at an early stage in the reform process, after the members of the "Committee of 12" had been appointed. Conservative circles within the KMT, among them members of the *yuan-lao* and the security services, articulated their misgivings about

37. An informative list on "Public Protest Activities, 1983–87" can be found in Jauhsieh Joseph Wu, "Toward Another Miracle? Impetuses and Obstacles in Taiwan's Democratization" (unpubl. Ph.D. thesis, Ohio State University, 1988), p. 142.

the termination of martial law in view of continuing menaces to national security.[38] Since these groups were well represented within the Committee of 12 they were able to influence its deliberations and delay its decision-making. Progress could only be achieved through the intervention of Chiang Ching-kuo, whose personal authority held the intra-party opposition in check.

After the death of Chiang Ching-kuo power relations within the party started to shift. Advocates of reform lost a decisive source of support, the party as a whole lost its dominating personality and its final arbiter in important decisions. Since the position that leading party members and politicians occupied within the hierarchy was to a certain extent determined by the sponsorship of the Chairman of the KMT, his passing naturally brought about a rearrangement of power relations within the party leadership. The speedy succession of Li Teng-hui to the positions of President of the Republic and temporary party Chairman only marked the beginning of a prolonged period in which problems of political reform were overshadowed by struggles for influence within the post-Chiang power structure.[39]

Chiang's death had a number of serious consequences for political reform which made changes in its conceptualisation and implementation imperative. It also strengthened the position of those groups that were opposed to reform. Without the authority of the party Chairman as a last resort to overcome opposition, the reform-oriented groups within the KMT had to make allowances for the numerous diverging interests within the party. To commit these interest groups to support specific solutions required lengthy negotiations; compromises were often achieved only by pushing complex problems to the side or by postponing their solution to a later date.[40]

The election of the President and Vice-President, scheduled for

38. For a detailed analysis of the participants and their arguments, see Sung K'e-han, "Chiang Ching-kuo kai-ke ti tzu-li", in *Chiang Ching-kuo pien-fa t'uei-hsin* (Taipei: Feng-yün lun-t'an-she 1985), pp. 30–7; and Wei Wu, "Ch'ung-man pien-chü ti T'ai-wan cheng-chü", in the same volume, pp. 38–46.

39. Conservative members of the Central Standing Committee expressed reservations about the immediate appointment of Li Teng-hui as temporary party Chairman, but were overruled in the ensuing vote. See Luo Hao, "Chiang Ching-kuo shih-shih hou ch'üan-li tou-chang ti nei-mu", in *T'ai-wan cheng-chüan chuan-yi nei-mu* (Taipei: Feng-yün l'un-t'an-she, 1988).

40. Cf. the position taken by the party leadership concerning constitutional reform and the reform of the party structure.

March 1990, put a group of conservative party members in a pivotal position to influence the speed and direction of the reform process. Dependent on the support of the "senior representatives" in the NA for his re-election, the incumbent, Li Teng-hui, was forced to assuage their apprehensions. Of particular concern to the "senior representatives" was an eventual relinquishing of the Chinese identity of the party and the state. Their fears arose from several factors, one being the fact that Li was of Taiwanese origin, which led some people to doubt his commitment to the goal of reunification. The other major cause of their misgivings was the demands for the complete re-election of the NA and the LY, with their negative effects for the representation of mainland China and demands for Taiwanese independence. These demands had been aired more outspokenly in the second half of the 1980s. In order to calm their fear and to counter the challenge by Lin Yang-kang, whose support derived from local Taiwanese politicians and conservative mainlanders,[41] Li Teng-hui and his supporters had to make several concessions to the senior members of the NA. They refrained from taking measures to expedite the retirement of the "senior representatives" from the national parliamentary bodies. In a related move, plans for the convocation of an assembly to discuss problems of national unification were made public. The National Unification Council (*Kuo-chia t'ung-i wei-yuan-hui*) was finally established in October 1990 to bring together participants of diverse persuasions. After extended deliberations the Council passed "Guidelines for National Reunification" (*Kuo-t'ung kang-ling*), which have since become the basis for the government's policy towards mainland China.[42]

The measures undertaken in this phase of political reform led to the pluralisation of the reform process. The numbers of participants increased, the KMT was no longer in a position to determine the speed and content of the reform process, but instead had to react to the

41. The candidates of the "minor current" (*fei chu-liu*) in the KMT were Lin Yang-kang, President of the Judicial Yuan, and Chiang Wei-kuo, younger brother of Chiang Ching-kuo and Secretary-General of the National Security Council. Although both controlled power bases of considerable size, for politicians of Taiwanese descent and Chiang loyalists among the NA representatives, they proved unable to overcome Li Teng-hui's popularity and the opposition of the top military leadership against Chiang Wei-kuo.

42. For the extended coverage of the establishment of Council, see *Hsin Hsin-wen* (*HHW*), no. 186–8 (1990); for the guidelines, see *HHW*, no. 208 (1991), pp. 34–42. For further details of this policy see Chapter 8 below.

initiatives of the DPP and a growing number of civil organisations. As the reform became bogged down because of internal problems in the KMT, the DPP was able to influence the domestic debate—and, to a certain extent, the discussions within the KMT as well—with its own proposals and demands.

The DPP was highly critical of what it considered to be an insufficient degree of liberalisation in domestic politics and a number of practices still employed by the authorities in the area of domestic security. Thus the DPP vehemently opposed the adoption of the National Security Law and the government's intention to treat a number of political activities as criminal acts by including them in Article 100 of the criminal law. Owing to the DPP's persistence, the government finally had to admit to the existence of a blacklist (*hei-ming-tan*) containing the names of political activists living abroad who were not permitted to return to Taiwan.[43] The DPP was also concerned with the still insufficient degree of democratisation of the political system. The party continued to demand a complete re-election of the national parliamentary bodies' members, and called for the direct popular election of the Governor of Taiwan Province and the mayors of Kao-hsiung and Taipei. Selection of the President of the Republic by direct popular vote became one of the main planks of the DPP's election platform for the NA elections of late 1991.

Constitutive elements of the political system in Taiwan and the identity of the political order were touched upon by the DPP's position on constitutional reform. In the debate over the desirability of amending the existing Constitution (*hsiu-hsien*) or writing a new one (*chih-hsien*), the DPP finally opted for the adoption of a new constitution. In fact one of the leading members of the DPP's headquarters published the draft of a new constitution in 1990, but his suggestions met strong criticisms within the party.[44] By formally declaring its support for the so-called "Taiwanese Constitution" (*T'ai-wan hsien-fa*), which became part of the DPP's election platform in 1991, the party had come out in favour of a complete reconstruction of the political system on the basis of a new identity. This decision carried one of the central demands

43. See Julian Baum, "Easing up, Somewhat", *Far Eastern Economic Review* (28 May 1992), pp. 18, 20.

44. This draft constitution was drawn up by Huang Huang-hsiung and was published under the name "Min-chu ta-hsien-ch'ang". It drew strong criticism from the New Wave faction, which considered the draft "too soft" on a number of points. Text of the draft in *Tzu-li chou-pao* (*TIWP*), no. 56 (29 June 1990), p. 7.

of the former Tang-wai to its logical conclusion. Advocating self-determination by the people of Taiwan, the Tang-wai had posed a challenge to the Nationalist understanding of Taiwan's identity as part of China and postulated that the future identity of Taiwan was still open.[45] By supporting the "Taiwanese Constitution" and amending its party platform the DPP has given a clear answer to the question of Taiwan's identity: the island has an identity different to that of China; Taiwan, defined as the island itself, Penghu, Quemoy, Matsu and some smaller islands, is considered to be a state with its own sovereignty.[46]

Motivated by concern over the slow progress of political reform, a number of groups and civic organisations tried to exert influence on the government and the KMT by organising public protests and demonstrations. Their proposals and demands added to the pluralisation of the reform process.

Notable among these efforts was that by a group of intellectuals and scientists, who as early as the days of martial law had engaged themselves in analysing social and political developments and suggesting ways to reach their solution. Reorganised as the Teng-she, they tried, through numerous commentaries and articles, to establish standards for further political development.[47]

In order to expedite constitutional reform and to unify the diverging views on this question, a considerable number of politicians without party affiliation, together with opposition politicians and scientists, organised a two-day meeting that debated and adopted a draft for a new constitution. At critical points when the conflicts within the KMT seemed to endanger the progress of reform or the resurgence of conservative influence seemed to be imminent, students and politically active members of the population began to organise demonstrations or hunger strikes and increased the pressure on KMT politicians to push ahead with political reform.

Substantial differences of opinion among the political élites of the KMT and the DPP on the priorities of political reform constituted an additional complication. Although a considerable number of politicians within the KMT and the DPP were in favour of political reform,

45. *FCJ*, vol. 8, no. 66 (30 August 1991), p. 2.
46. The draft of the "Taiwanese Constitution" was published in *TIWP*, no. 118 (6 September 1991), p. 13. For a short discussion of this draft see pp. 95–7, below. On the DPP party platform, see *FCJ*, vol. 8, no. 79 (15 October 1991), p. 2.
47. The commentaries of this group appear regularly in the newspapers published by the *Independence Post* group.

differing notions on the purpose and priorities of reform made cooperation between the two difficult. Concerning the relative importance
of reforming the political system and of solving the question of identity,
the chasm between the groups became impossible to bridge.[48] To the
reform-oriented groups within the KMT the gradual reform of the
political system and greater democratisation under conditions of domestic
stability enjoyed priority, while the question of identity was considered
to be of secondary importance. Maintaining the status quo seemed
to them the precondition for a successful transformation of the political
system.

A sizeable group among DPP politicians had a completely different
understanding of the priorities of political reform. To them a decision
on the identity of Taiwan with the aim of establishing a new state
enjoyed absolute priority. Political reform was a sensible undertaking,
but its full potential could only be realised in an independent Taiwan.
In other words, real democracy was only possible after Taiwan had
become an independent state. Taking a rather negative view of the role
the KMT had played and would continue to play in Taiwanese politics,
they saw little point in cooperating with the KMT, a political party
whose political orientation was China-centred, not Taiwan-centred.[49]
Belonging to the more militant wing of the DPP, these members of the
political élite put equal stress on mass demonstrations and parliamentary
action to realise their aims.[50]

The continuing differences of opinion within the KMT delayed
matters to the extent that the NA elections of December 1991 drew
near, which was bound to influence the domestic debate on political
reform and lead to a further politicisation of the reform process. The
two main contenders, the KMT and the DPP, both made their public

48. The following discussion is based on materials contained in Jauhsieh Wu,
"Toward Another Miracle?", p. 229.

49. This position was most clearly expressed by Yao Chia-wen, former party
Chairman of the DPP: "The reason why Taiwan has no democracy today is because
of the KMT government, that is a Chinese government, not a Taiwanese government.
In order to have democracy, we should recognize that we want a Taiwanese parliament.
That is to say, Taiwan should be independent so that democracy can be achieved."
*Ibid.*, p. 255.

50. Among the various factions of the DPP the New Wave Faction is most strongly
in favour of confrontational politics and preferring mass movements over parliamentary
action. See the statement by Hung Chi-chang, a leading member of the group, in
*ibid.*, p. 256.

comments on the future of reform in a way that would enhance their chances for success in the elections. While the DPP strove to include populist demands in their election platform, the KMT chose a completely different approach. It tried to avoid, as much as possible, any statement about tangible aspects of the reform. Both approaches were dictated by the peculiar problems the two parties were facing.. While the DPP had to resort to populist appeals in order to camouflage its organisational weaknesses, the KMT refrained from making statements on substantial issues and concentrated on matters of personalities instead, in order to maintain the precarious harmony within the party and postpone the conflict over concrete proposals till after the elections. Judging these strategies by the results of the elections, the KMT chose the more effective approach.[51]

## Differing approaches of the DPP and the KMT

In view of the fundamental differences concerning the identity and norms of political order that divided the KMT from the DPP and some of the civil organisations, it comes as no surprise that their ideas on the shape of the reformed political system also diverged widely. These differences are reflected in the DPP's draft for a new constitution and the KMT's suggestions for a limited reform of the existing Constitution. In spite of a considerable commitment among the adherents of both sides, their debates tended to concentrate on a few topics while at the same time neglecting a number of equally important considerations. These issues included the implications that a complete or partial reform of the political system would have for the stability of the entire system; the efficiency of the restructured institutions; and an appraisal of the political behaviour and political culture that had developed in Taiwan since 1949.

These deficiencies resulted from both the increasing polarisation of the objectives of political reform and the growing inclination by both parties to use the debates on reform as instruments to further their own goals. But they also pointed to a failure in the work of those institutions that were entrusted with the analysis and promotion of constitutional reform. The National Affairs Conference (*Kuo-shih hui-i*), charged

---

51. See Nieh Yu-hsi, "Ablehnung der Gründung eines neuen Staates in Taiwan", in *China Aktuell*, vol. 21 (1991), pp. 780–3, and Long, *Taiwan's National Assembly Elections*.

with the task of identifying areas of agreement among the proponents of differing reform proposals, succeeded only in compiling an inventory of the variety of opinions. The importance of this endeavour was further reduced by a number of political controversies and the resignation from it of several well-known scholars.[52]

The experiences of those NA members who were elected in December 1991 may also prove problematic. The majority of them had not previously been involved in political activities at the national level before, and were not renowned either for their special qualifications in the field of constitutional law or for wielding influence in the leading bodies of their respective political parties. Controversies over and decisions on constitutional issues will therefore not take place on the floor of the NA but in committees outside its jurisdiction. Taking into consideration the division of seats among the parties, these committees will most likely consist of the commissions and the Central Standing Committee of the KMT, whose decisions will have to be implemented by the party's members in the NA.

The fundamental differences between the advocates of constitutional reform and those demanding a new constitution were reflected in the substance and length of their outlines. The supporters of a new constitution drew up numerous voluminous drafts complete with equally substantial commentaries and explanations.[53] In contrast, the KMT limited itself to the publication of a number of principles guiding the debates on reform, and the outlines of the Additional Articles shortly before they were deliberated in the NA.[54]

Owing to limitation of space a detailed discussion of the drafts cannot

52. See Chiu Hungdah, "The National Affairs Conference and Constitutional Reform in the Republic of China", *Issues and Studies*, vol. 26, no. 12 (1990), pp. 12–22; and the extended coverage of the conference in *HHW* and *TIWP*.

53. The various drafts consist of the "T'ai-wan kung-ho-kuo chi-pen-fa ts'ao-an" drawn up by Lin Yi-hsiung, in *Independent Evening Post* (6 November 1989); a commentary by the same author entitled "T'ai-wan kung-ho-kuo chi-pen-fa ts'ao-an (Kuo-hui, ts'ung-t'ung, kuo-wu-yuan shuo-ming pu-fen)", in *Independence Morning Post* (7 November 1989), p. 5; the "Min-chu ta-hsien-ch'ang" by Huang Huang-hsiung, in *TIWP*, no. 56, (29 June 1990); and "T'ai-wan hsien-fa ts'ao-an" proposed by the DPP, in *TIWP*, no. 118 (6 September 1991), p. 13.

54. See "Chung-hua min-kuo hsien-fa ts'eng-hsiu t'iao-wen", in *TIWP*, no. 96 (5 April 1991), p. 2; " 'Hsien-fa ts'eng-hsiu t'iao-wen ts'eng-ting yao-tien' hsiu-cheng-an", in *TIWP*, no. 116 (20 March 1992); "Hsien-fa ts'eng-hsiu t'iao-wen ts'ao-an', in *TIWP*, no. 153 (8 May 1992), p. 4; "Additional Articles of the Constitution of the Republic of China", in *FCJ*, vol. 9, no. 44 (23 June 1992), p. 7; and note 33 above.

be undertaken here. What follows is a short discussion of the main features of the draft for a "Taiwanese Constitution", representing the position of the political opposition, and of the Additional Articles, outlining the position taken by the KMT. It will also in passing deal with the premises underlying the two documents and the characteristics of the political institutions they define.

The "Taiwanese Constitution" defines in eleven chapters and 108 articles the territory, political institutions, rights and duties of the citizens of a new state, the "Republic of Taiwan". Its territory consists of the island of Taiwan and the island groups of Penghu, Quemoy and Matsu, as well a number of smaller islands. The extensive catalogue of civil rights and duties contains a number of guarantees protecting the rights of the individual. Its citizens will enjoy the same participatory rights that are a part of the Nationalist Constitution, namely election, recall, initiative and referendum. The list containing the objectives of the state is expanded, mentioning, among others, stiff measures for environmental protection. Further economic growth will be tolerated only if it is not detrimental to the environment.[55] Several clauses are included to prevent an eventual reappearance of conditions that were prevalent under martial law, by making it illegal to prevent the return of a citizen to Taiwan or by prohibiting the armed forces from becoming involved in the mass media.[56]

The political institutions are organised according to a division of power that follows the liberal-democratic model and consists of three powers instead of the five advocated by Sun Yat-sen. The NA in its present form is discarded, since the state President will be elected directly by the people. The governmental system as outlined in the "Taiwanese Constitution" approximates the presidential system of the United States, with the President assuming the role of head of the executive branch, assisted by a state council. Legislative power is vested in an NA comprising 120 representatives, with powers similar to those enjoyed by the American Congress.

There are three fundamental differences that distinguish the draft from the Constitution now in force on Taiwan. The draft provides for the establishment of a special law court for constitutional affairs. This court will adjudicate on conflicting jurisdictions among government agencies, and between national and local governments, and

55. Article 19.
56. Articles 17, 13.

will rule on infringements of human rights by government agencies. Furthermore, the provincial level of government will be discarded, reducing the government structure to two tiers, the national and the local levels. It also gives special consideration to the rights of the various tribes of the aboriginal population.

The "Taiwanese Constitution" defines a political order that is deliberately conceived of as an alternative to the political order existing in Taiwan. The experiences of severe limitations imposed upon the individual under a system of emergency laws has resulted in special attention being devoted to the creation of safeguards for civil rights. Care has also been taken to proscribe the role which the mainstays of the present Nationalist regime can play in the new political system. It limits the latitude for the armed forces and for political parties as well. Although political parties' contribution to society is recognised by the inclusion of a special chapter and by the provision of certain benefits, the margins of their activities are defined rather narrowly.[57]

The Articles of the draft reflect not only experiences with the existing political order, a political order inspired by Chinese nationalism, but also expectations for the creation of a new political order in the island. Both of these, experiences and expectations, have been used very selectively by the authors, however. The upshot is a draft constitution which outlines a society with a pluralistic culture and a multilingual education and language policy, with comprehensive guarantees for individual liberties, with enlarged opportunities for political participation and with numerous checks that will prevent the state from extending beyond certain limits its influence into society. It provides the conditions for the realisation of an alternative model of society in Taiwan. Of the experiences gained under forty years of Nationalist rule the drafters only take into consideration those relating to domestic politics, i.e. experiences with an authoritarian government and a political party monopolising the sources of power. They are reflected in the special attention given to the provisions on the limitation of the exercise of power and the extension of political participation. What is missing is the provision of the conditions necessary to sustain the political stability needed to cope with the still precarious international position of Taiwan, and to counter certain domestic developments that may threaten the efficiency of the political system.[58]

57. Paragraph 4, Articles 42–6.
58. Suffice it to mention the growing tendencies towards factionalism and the decreasing integrative capacity of the political parties in Taiwan.

The KMT, in contrast, has constantly upheld its position that only a limited reform of the existing Constitution is required to provide the basis for further democratic development. This position is amply reflected in the party's principles for constitutional reform and the two sets of Additional Articles for amending parts of the existing Constitution. The party has failed, however, to present a consistent concept identifying the areas in need of reform and offering conclusive alternatives. In place of a comprehensive approach the KMT has offered only piecemeal solutions aimed at assuaging conflicts within the ranks of the party.

The first set of Additional Articles provided the basis for the restructuring of the three national parliamentary bodies, by defining their membership and by establishing the procedures for elections to them.[59] The second amendment, also taking the form of articles added to the Constitution, was adopted by the NA in May 1992. It provided for considerable changes in the institutional framework by modifying several decisions taken by the same body in 1990. Most strongly affected by the new regulations were the NA and the CY, whose status, powers and position within the representative institutions would have to undergo considerable changes. The duties and internal organisation of the Judicial and Examination Yuans were also brought into line with the requirements of the day. Other subjects affected by the second amendment included the objectives of the state, local self-government and the term of office of the President and Vice-President, which for both was reduced to four years.[60]

Although the final shape of local self-government has been left to future legislation, the NA has laid down guidelines to be observed by the LY in framing the new laws. They provide for the direct election of provincial governors and mayors/magistrates, and strengthen the position of the provincial and county assemblies.[61]

The changes in the organisation and the jurisdictions of the NA and the CY are in fact considerable. The status of the NA, whose term of office is shortened to four years and synchronised with that of the President and Vice-President, is enhanced. Henceforth, the NA will regularly receive a report from the President on the state of the nation, and will deliberate on national affairs and offer advice. The powers

59. *FCJ*, vol. 8, no. 32 (2 May 1991), p. 8.
60. *FCJ*, vol. 9, no. 44 (23 June 1992), p. 7.
61. Article 17, *ibid*.

of the NA in selecting the Presidents and Vice-Presidents of the CY, Judicial and Examination Yuans, as well as in choosing Grand Justices and members of the CY and the Examination Yuan, have been increased considerably. Although they are to be nominated by the President of the Republic they will have to obtain the confirmation of the NA.[62] The CY has not only lost these powers to the restructured NA but has also lost its status as one of the three parliamentary bodies of the ROC. With a membership reduced to twenty-nine persons, its powers are now limited to auditing government budgets and to censuring and impeaching public servants.[63]

This revised division of power does not provide a solution to the inconsistencies that characterise the "Five-Power Constitution". In some cases conflicts of jurisdiction are aggravated. By raising the status of the NA, the long-smouldering competition between the NA and the LY may have been rekindled. The revaluation of the NA and the retention of the CY do not indicate a desire to increase their efficiency. These developments are the inevitable consequences of an earlier decision by the KMT leadership to avoid any change in the existing institutional framework.

## *Future prospects for political reform*

Political reform has resulted in a perceptible liberalisation and democratisation of the political system. The retirement of the "senior representatives" and the future election of public functionaries in the "free territories" of the Republic of China mark the final step towards the Taiwanisation of the island's political institutions. The final date for the completion of the reform is, at the time of writing, still not within sight, however. More then seven years after reform was initiated, two central tasks—a decision on the system of voting for the presidency and the delimitation of the respective powers of the President of the Republic and the President of the EY—remain unaccomplished. The KMT is deeply divided on these issues, and any solution will have grave implications for the power relationships within the party. A possible solution acceptable to all the groups affected has not yet been raised.

The results of the NA elections in December 1991 have enabled the

62. Article 11, *ibid.*
63. Article 15, *ibid.*

KMT to shape the speed and content of constitutional reform according to its priorities. Controlling more than 75 per cent of the seats in the NA, the KMT is not obliged to accept the demands and proposals of opposition parties and independent representatives. The KMT's proposals for constitutional reform and its performance in the NA have been less than satisfactory, however. It has utilised its comfortable majority primarily to pre-empt a full-scale discussion on the objectives and scope of constitutional reform in the NA. But the KMT has been unable to overcome the continuing opposition to its plans by other members of the assembly. Unable to influence the deliberations, these members and the groups they represent do not feel obliged to relinquish their demands for a new constitution or to accept the majority decisions on amending the Constitution.

In conclusion, by concentrating on the two questions of identity and of reforming the existing or framing a new constitution the debate on constitutional reform has neglected a number of topics equally worthy of consideration. Intermingling questions of political reform with considerations of power politics, the parties concerned pre-empted the genesis of a discourse which might have overcome the conflicting positions or, at the very least, succeeded in reducing the antagonism between the groups involved. Under these circumstances constitutional reform will remain one of the main controversies concerning Taiwan in the foreseeable future.

# 4

# DYNAMICS OF TAIWAN'S DEMOCRATIC TRANSITION

*Hung-mao Tien*

When World War II ended in 1945, the Kuomintang (KMT) regime on mainland China took control of Taiwan from the Japanese, who had ruled the island for fifty years. Four years later, as China's civil war came to an end, the defeated KMT forces retreated to Taiwan.

President Chiang Kai-shek and his followers initially thought Taiwan would be a temporary sanctuary, a military and political base for the recovery of the mainland, which they had lost to the Chinese Communists. However, their defeat shattered the morale of Chiang's followers, who still had to face the uncertain fate of the widely expected Communist military onslaught.

In June 1950, the outbreak of the Korean War forced the Truman Administration suddenly to alter American policy regarding the security and future of the Taiwan Straits. On 27 June President Truman—previously uncommitted to Taiwan's defense—ordered the Seventh Fleet to patrol the island against any military action by the Chinese Communists. This change of US policy not only saved Taiwan's inhabitants from the terror and destruction of war, it also prevented the possible annihilation of the KMT forces by the Communists.

Beginning in late 1950, the US provided Taiwan with an aid programme that reached a total of US $1.5 billion by 1965, when it was finally terminated. American aid helped the KMT regime maintain its military strength and stabilise the shaky agrarian economy, which was experiencing terrible inflation.

From 1950 to 1952 the KMT also underwent a fundamental reorganisation to invigorate the party machine from the state of paralysis into which it had fallen while on the mainland. An authoritarian political system, based on a one-party dictatorship, was transplanted to Taiwan. Although the KMT regime frequently resorted to oppression, its iron-fisted rule evidently provided Taiwan with three decades of political stability that enabled the government to launch a steady course of economic development. In the 1950s, Taiwan's authorities successfully undertook a land reform programme that equalised land distribution and promoted agricultural production. Once the government had accomplished land reform, it switched to an industrial development plan that led to a prosperous export-intensive economy. By the end of 1991, Taiwan's two-way trade reached nearly US $139 billion, making the island nation's trade volume the thirteenth largest in the world. Its *per capita* GNP also surged to US $8,815, compared with a mere US $50 in 1952.

Taiwan's success in economic development has already received widespread attention; its evolution towards democracy, which process began in the 1970s, is only beginning to attract serious scholarly inquiry. Between 1987 and 1992, the KMT regime undertook major steps to liberalise society and implement democratic reform. Martial law, declared four decades earlier on the heels of China's civil war, was lifted, bringing to life a sense of psychological liberation across Taiwan's socio-political spectrum. Many restrictions on public rallies, group activity, travel to the mainland and mass media were removed. Opposition political parties were legalised following the creation of the Democratic Progressive Party (DPP) in 1986. The Temporary Provisions, which extended virtually unlimited presidential power and created extra-constitutional institutions to perform emergency functions, were suspended in May 1991. In December 1991, a popular election produced a completely new National Assembly that amended the constitution in April–May 1992. Institutional reforms of the national government accomplished at the time of writing have laid a better foundation for democratic rules and procedures.

The current transition from authoritarianism to democracy makes Taiwan one of the few nations in the Third World undergoing such a political experiment. It is one of only three such nations which had an entrenched one-party dictatorship prior to the formation of opposition parties. Compared with the other two regimes, Taiwan's ruling Kuomintang (KMT) is even stronger organisationally than the Republican People's Party in Turkey and the party of Revolutionary Institutions (PRI) in Mexico. Indeed, the KMT may be the only existing non-Communist party having all the organisational characters of a quasi-Leninist party.[1] Its relations with both state and society have

1. James A. Robinson, "The KMT as a Leninist Regime: Prolegomenon to Devolutionary Leadership through Institutions", paper presented at the annual meeting of Florida Political Science Association (Winter Park, FL, 20 April 1990), p. 2.

also demonstrated a strong functional resemblance to a Leninist corporatist state.

The KMT regime, however, differs from the Leninist states in three fundamental ways.[2] Its official ideology, based on Sun Yat-sen's "Three Principles of the People", commits the regime to an ultimate goal of representative democracy. In addition, the regime has adopted a capitalist economy that allows private enterprises and a certain social autonomy which in time can ferment political opposition. Finally, the KMT, unlike Leninist parties in socialist states, does not subscribe to the principle of proletarian dictatorship or the monopoly of political power.

Given the nature of the KMT regime and Taiwan's peculiar political environment, what is the explanation for the democratic changes that have transpired? There are at least three analytical perspectives that shed light on Taiwan's experience: first, the correlation theory that links socioeconomic preconditions to democratic transition; secondly, the genetic or causation theory that emphasizes the ruling élite's initiatives as principal imperatives for democratic reform, and thirdly, the interaction theory that views democratic evolution as a process of calculated struggles and interactions between the ruling élite and the opposition forces. Each of these theoretical perspectives explains certain aspects of Taiwan's democratic evolution; none of them alone fully explains the Taiwan experience, which has involved various phases of political development.

## *Requisite conditions for democratic development*

The correlation between certain socio-economic conditions and democracy was first systematically explored in the 1950s by Seymour Martin Lipset.[3] Since then, many scholars have followed this approach in explaining both political democratisation and the existence of a stable democracy. Briefly stated, the approach maintains that the presence of certain requisite conditions, such as a high literacy rate, rising

2. Yangsun Chou and Andrew J. Nathan, "Democratizing Transition in Taiwan" *Asian Survey*, no. 3 (March 1987), pp. 278–9; Tun-jen Cheng, "Democratizing the Quasi-Leninist Regime in Taiwan", *World Politics*, vol. XLI, no. 4 (July 1989), pp. 477–8.

3. Seymour Martin Lipset, "Some Social Requisites of Democracy: Economic Development and Political Legitimacy", *American Political Science Review*, March 1959, pp. 69–105.

*per capita* income, urbanisation, the emergence of a substantial middle class, and broad exposure to mass media, are conducive to the development of political democracy. Samuel P. Huntington classifies the relevant preconditions into four broad categories, namely a wealthy economy, a highly differentiated social structure with autonomy of social classes and groups, pressure from external sources, and a favourable political culture.[4] Writing on Southern European experiences of democratic transition, Philippe C. Schmitter emphasises the importance of a civil society in which "certain types of self-constituted units are capable of acting autonomously in defense of their own interest and ideals".[5] Taiwan's experience so far seems to confirm the validity of these arguments, perhaps with the minor exception of assessing the impact of political culture, which is harder to pinpoint one way or another.[6]

Four decades of success in economic development have created social and economic preconditions favourable to a democratic surge in Taiwan's politics. During 1953–90 Taiwan achieved an annual GNP growth rate of almost 9 per cent. Industrial output rose from 19.7 per cent of gross domestic product in 1952 to 42.3 per cent by 1990. Employment in industrial and service sectors has also grown to about 85 per cent of the total work force. The literacy rate has steadily risen to over 90 per cent.[7] Popular access to mass media and modern transportation is approaching the standards of many European nations. Income distribution in Taiwan is among the most even of all nations, despite recent signs of wider disparity caused by stock market and property speculations. The government's control of industrial production dropped from 56.6 per cent in 1952 to about 19 per cent in 1990, leaving a large private sector.[8] In the increasingly differentiated social structure, the middle-class now constitutes almost 40 per cent of the population. On the surface at least, there appears to be a positive

    4. Samuel P. Huntington, "Will More Countries Become Democratic?", *Political Science Quarterly*, Summer 1984, pp. 198–209.
    5. Philippe C. Schmitter, "An Introduction to Southern European Transitions from Authoritarian Rule: Italy, Greece, Portugal, Spain, Turkey", in Guillermo O'Donnell, Philippe C. Schmitter and Laurence Whitehead (eds), *Transitions from Authoritarian Rule, Prospects for Democracy* (Baltimore, MD: Johns Hopkins University Press, 1986), p. 6.
    6. Hung-mao Tien, *The Great Transition, Political and Social Change in the Republic of China* (Stanford, CA: Hoover Institution Press, 1989), pp. 24–35, 45–54, 196–204.
    7. *Taiwan Statistical Data Book* (Taipei: Council for Economic Planning and Development, 1991), p. 41.
    8. *Ibid.*, p. 89.

correlation between the existence of such social and economic preconditions and the evolution of democracy. These preconditions have
strengthened the formation of secondary associations. In recent years
many of these groups have been successful in social mobilisation; some
have achieved a considerable degree of autonomy from party-state
intervention. With social pluralism on the rise, this inevitably exerts
additional pressures for more democratic reform both within the
KMT and in the national political system as a whole.

*Democratic change as a consequence of the ruling élite's response
to challenges*

While correlation theory explains the positive impacts of socio-
economic preconditions for democratic development, they do not automatically lead to democracy. As Dankwart A. Rustow has observed,
the ruling élite's decision to pursue democracy can be as important
as the presence of certain prerequisites.[9] Samuel Huntington describes
Taiwan's transition to democracy as one of "transformation", which
involves decisions to change by the ruling élites rather than overthrow
of the regime by the popular-based opposition forces.[10] Related to this,
Taiwan's democratic reform so far has also met with the acquiescence
of the military; the absence of such agreement has negatively affected
the fate of many Third World nations in their transition to civilian-
dominated democratic rule.[11]

The KMT leaders' decisions to tolerate opposition parties and to
initiate overall democratic reform are factors that should not be ignored.
Historically speaking, the autocratic leadership of the late President
Chiang Ching-kuo (CCK) should be given credit for initiating significant political change. In 1972, when CCK became Premier, he significantly increased the appointment of native Taiwanese, previously

9. Dankwart A. Rustow, "Transition to Democracy: Toward a Dynamic Model",
*Comparative Politics*, no. 2 (April 1990), pp. 156–244.

10. Samuel Huntington, "The Context of Democratization in Taiwan", a keynote
address delivered at the Conference on Democratization in the Republic of China,
co-sponsored by the Institute of International Relations, National Chengchi University
and the Center for International Affairs, Harvard University (Taipei, Taiwan, 9–11
January 1989).

11. Myron Weiner, "Empirical Democratic Theory and the Transition from
Authoritarianism to Democracy", *American Political Science Association Newsletter*,
Fall 1987, pp. 861–6.

denied access to power, to the positions of provincial Governor and Vice-Premier. He also ordered the addition of popularly elected new members to the national representative bodies, thus starting the trend towards the KMT's pluralisation in the composition of its élite and its membership. During 1986–7 Chiang again played a leading role at critical junctures by insisting on reform initiatives. He appointed a twelve-man committee to study reform measures, and specified the suspension of martial law and the legalisation of the political opposition as priorities. Following the formation of the DPP in September 1986, some KMT inner circle élites advocated suppression, but were overruled by Chiang Ching-Kuo. When CCK died in January 1988, Li Teng-hui's succession proceeded smoothly because he had been hand-picked by Chiang, hence securing the pledge of loyalty from key party officials and the military leaders. With Chiang's mandate and the acquiescence of many military and party leaders, President Li has been able to continue liberalisation and democratic reforms despite periodic objections from the conservative élites.

In the light of this background, Chiang's and other KMT leaders' support for continuing democratic reforms are as important as the existence of socio-economic preconditions. Without the ruling élite's commitment to democratic transition, Taiwan's political situation could have oscillated in a vicious cycle of violent protest and political repression.

## *Theory of calculated interactions*

Authoritarian regimes seldom relinquish their monopolistic power voluntarily, making concessions not necessarily for the sake of normative commitment to democracy but for political expediency. This view attaches great importance to the growth of political opposition or civil society and its success in bargaining with the ruling élites that results in involuntary concessions to democratic demands. In their studies of certain Southern European nations, Adam Przeworski, José Maria Maravall and Julian Santamaria have stressed the importance of rationally calculated interactions between the ruling élite and the opposition forces in the transition towards democracy.[12] The Taiwan

12. José Maria Maravall and Julian Santamaria, "Political Change in Spain and the Prospects for Democracy", and Adam Przeworski, "Some Problems in the Transition of Democracy," in O'Donnell, Schmitter (eds), *Transitions from Authoritarian Rule* and Whitehead, pp. 72–3 and 50–8.

experience can also be attributed in part to the political entrepreneurship of opposition forces skilfully engaging the ruling KMT in game-like bargainings and interactions.[13]

In short, opposition movements in Taiwan are not instantaneous products that were brought into existence merely as a result of the KMT's reform initiatives. Rather, they have been steadily growing since the 1950s, albeit in a zig-zag course of dialectic evolution. In the 1950s and 1960s they were led by disenchanted mainlander intelligentsia and Taiwanese notables in frustrated efforts to form an opposition party and gain political footholds in the provincial assembly as well as in local government executive posts. Following the controversial 1977 election when a mass riot took place in reaction to the KMT's electoral irregularities, opposition movements intensified. The activists, drawn mainly from the newly emerging middle-class intellectuals and professionals, utilised street actions, squabbles on legislative floors, third party (liberal scholars) mediation and foreign pressures (US Congress), and worked through the overseas lobbying by anti-KMT elements, to enhance their bargaining position *vis-à-vis* the KMT.

In the face of opposition challenges, the authorities have progressively resorted to repression, mobilisation (controlled participation), limited admission to political participation in a quasi-party form, and eventually to full admission that legalises opposition parties. To be sure, there were confrontations and occasional crisis-ridden atmospheres. But the opposition's skilful tactics and restraints in mass protests, together with the KMT's step-by-step reform initiatives, have prevented the political situation from getting out of hand. So far, Taiwan has not encountered the severe political explosions that have characterised the democratic developments elsewhere, in South Korea, the Philippines and Latin America.

To be sure, there are hardliners and moderates both within the KMT and in the opposition. In the reform process, negotiation and struggle among protagonists for and entrenched opponents of democratic transition have frequently coalesced into a state of uncertainty. Within the KMT, many old guard and extremely conservative elements remain suspicious of the DPP; the latter is also saddled with an internal split in opposition strategy between radical advocates of Taiwan's independence and democratic reformers. Conflicts between protagonists and

---

13. Tun-jen Cheng, "Democratizing the Quasi-Leninist Regime in Taiwan", *World Politics*, vol. XLI, no. 4 (July 1989), pp. 486–95.

opponents could go on while political change is being consolidated. In order for democratic transition to progress smoothly, there is bound to be more interaction between the KMT and the opposition as well as between the hardliners and the moderates within both camps.

## Aspects of democratic change

*Emergence of civil society.* The structural configuration and functional relationship of the KMT, the state and organised groups in the Republic of China's (ROC) political system are essentially corporatist. Not only do the party and the state form closely interlocking ties, but the party-state also serves as the principal arbitrator that directs the organisation and activities of various civic groups. The KMT determines key personnel appointments in the government administration and the representative institutions. Major policies and laws are often initiated or approved prior to legislative action by the party centre. The party also penetrates the state structure by establishing disciplined intra-governmental party branches that follow the party directives.

Organised civic groups are regarded as the party-state's "transmission belts". Through legal restrictions and political controls, the party-state intervenes in the selection of leaders, the activities and even the budgetary appropriation of strategic groups such as those for farmers, workers, business-industrialists, youth and professionals. The interests of these groups are often articulated within the party-state by means of concertation and intra-institutional representation. Consequently, group autonomy is held suspect as the party-state seeks to utilise civil groups for political mobilisation and as auxiliary instruments for policy implementation. At times, organised groups have also become part of the party-state's social control mechanism.

In recent years, however, the KMT's ability to control interest groups and other secondary associations has been steadily declining. Despite the corporatist nature of the party-state, Taiwan's society has moved progressively towards a high degree of pluralism. Following four decades of continuing industrialisation and economic growth, Taiwan's social structure in the early 1990s has become highly differentiated. One result of this is the proliferation of secondary associations, rising from 2,560 in 1952 to 13,766 in 1990.[14] In the 1980s many of these associations made claims on the existing arrangement of the state-society

14. *Taiwan Statistical Data Book*, p. 299.

relations and demanded changes. The party-state has already lost control over some associations previously held under its tight corporatist grip — even in the strategically important sectors of farmers' groups and trade unions, alternative associations with clear autonomy. Several groups, such as the Taiwan Human Rights Association, the Association for Taiwan Farmers' Rights and the Autonomous Workers' Federation, for instance, are not only independent of KMT control but are also closely linked to the opposition parties.

An increase in the number of social movements is another indication of pluralism that challenges the corporatist structure. Since the early 1980s, various social movements have been rapidly on the rise. In 1987 alone there were about 1800 street demonstrations.[15] According to one writer, by the end of 1988 there had been a total of seventeen types of social movement in protest against existing public policies and the conduct of the party-state.[16] Other writers maintain that the proliferation of social movements has been politically inspired, with the intended purposes of challenging the authoritarian system and realigning the KMT structure of political subordination over civil society.[17] In short, social pluralism as manifested by the proliferation of associations, greater demands for group autonomy and politically charged social movements is rapidly changing the political landscape of the corporatist relationship between the party-state and the society.

This is particularly true with regard to the newly formed and issue-oriented public interest groups. Issues of concern to the general public as well as to numerous groups have been brought into the political arena. Concerned citizens are no longer content with the old approach of relying on existing institutions and procedures within the party-state to air their grievances. Popular consciousness over such matters as the deteriorating environment, consumer rights, equality of women, human rights and academic freedom has gradually assumed the form of social protest.[18] Their emergence has generally coincided with the

15. "A Survey of Taiwan: Transition on Trial", *The Economist*, 5 March 1988, p. 16.

16. Hsin-huang Michael Hsiao, "Emerging Social Movements and the Rise of a Demanding Civil Society in Taiwan", paper presented at the Conference on Democratization in the Republic of China (Taipei, Taiwan, 9–11 1989), pp. 7–21.

17. Chang Mao-Kuei, "Pa-shih nien-tai Tai-wan she-hui yun-tung feng-ch'ao yu cheng-chih chuan-fa" (Taiwan's Social Movements and Political Transition in the 1980s), *National Policy Quarterly*, no. 1, 15 March 1989, pp. 54–9.

18. *Ibid.*; also Sheldon R. Severinghaus, "The Emergence of an Environmental Consciousness in Taiwan", paper presented at the annual meeting of the Association for Asian Studies (Washington, DC, 18 March 1989).

growth of political opposition which has provided some social movements with mobilisation activists and helped create a liberalised environment for social action. Even groups traditionally under the party-state's strict corporatist control, such as the trade unions and farmers' associations, are subject to internal divisions that allow the political opposition to organise counter-groups for protest purposes. They are no longer singular, compulsory and non-competitive groups which are supposed to serve mainly as the party-state's "transmission belts."

*A competitive dominant party system.* Prior to the creation of the new Democratic Progressive Party (DPP) on 28 September 1986, Taiwan had maintained for almost four decades an hegemonic one-party system. The KMT monopolised political power and public resources. During local elections, the KMT allowed non-KMT candidates to run either as independents or under the labels of the Young China Party or the Democratic Socialist Party, two satellite parties founded on the mainland. The authorities made certain that any attempt to form a new party would be harshly crushed.

The opposition movement in Taiwan may be divided into three major phases of development. During the initial phase in the 1950s, political opposition, cast in the form of intellectual liberalism, was promoted mainly by a group of disenchanted mainlander intellectuals, many with KMT ties. Supported by a handful of local Taiwanese politicians, they made an unsuccessful effort to form the Chinese Democratic Party in 1960. Lei Chen, the principal organiser, together with some of his followers, was arrested on 4 September 1960 on a dubious charge of patronising Communist agents.[19] In subsequent years the opposition continued to exist, but never posed an organised challenge to the ruling KMT. Individual opposition leaders did score impressive victories in local elections, but coordination of a nationwide opposition movement was not seriously contemplated for fear of political reprisals. The opposition politicians tended to settle for localised activities and were generally reluctant to raise restricted issues such as the legitimacy of the regime or to challenge the validity of the government's fundamental policies.

The turning point came in 1977 when a mass protest in Chungli,

19. Lei Chen, *Lei Chen hui-i-lu* (Lei Chen's Memoirs) (Hong Kong: Ch'i-shih nien-tai she, 1978), pp. 28–9; Pan Chia-chieh, "Lei Chen an chung-yu ta-pai" (The Lei Chen Case is Finally Brought into the Open), *Shih-pao chou-k'an* (*China Times Weekly*), no. 212 (18 March 1989), pp. 52–5.

a small city in north Taiwan, against an irregularity in KMT vote-counting touched off a serious clash between angry voters and the police.[20] A district police station was burned and a number of casualties were reported. The incident signalled a growing popular disenchantment with the authorities' conduct in electoral politics. After that, the opposition forces, mainly consisting of indigenous elements, pursued more confrontational tactics and attracted an activist layer fundamentally different in age and political outlook to that of their predecessors. In the local elections that year, opposition candidates won one-quarter of the magistrates' and mayors' posts, as well as 30 per cent of seats in the provincial assembly. A new era of a nationwide opposition movement was dawning.

In the subsequent decade, the opposition movement showed two interrelated developmental tendencies. First of all, it made relentless efforts to become organised under a structural instrument. Operating under the common label of Tang-wai (literally, "non-KMT") it began to recommend candidates and to coordinate inter-constituency campaigns in the 1981 parliamentary elections. Three years later, a group of elected Tang-wai officials formed the Association of Tang-wai Public Officials for the Study of Public Policy, which was later renamed the Association of Public Policy Studies (APPS). The APPS, never fully accepted by the authorities as a legally constituted organisation, exercised quasi-party functions in electoral and other political activities.

The third phase of opposition development came in September 1986 when the Democratic Progressive Party (DPP) was created by the Tang-wai activists. In December 1986 it formally nominated party candidates for the parliamentary elections, ran a nationwide coordinated campaign and scored impressive gains in terms of both legislative seats and the popular vote.[21] It adopted a party constitution and a party platform, and established a nationwide organisational structure with headquarters in Taipei. But in the early 1990s the DPP remains at the early stage of party development. With a membership of only about 40,000 in 1992 and its activists factionalised, the DPP's future

20. Lin Cheng-chieh and Chang Fu-chung, *Hsuan-chu wan-sui* (Long Live Elections!) (Washington, DC: Taiwan Monitor Reprint, 1978), pp. 240–79.

21. Nicholas D. Kristof, "Opposition Party Strong in Taiwan Vote", *New York Times*, 7 December 1986, p. 3; and Patrick L. Smith, "Taiwan's New Opposition Party becomes Force to be Reckoned with", *Christian Science Monitor*, 8 December 1986, p. 15.

prospect as a major party remains cloudy. Its adoption of a party plank advocating a "Republic of Taiwan" as a new state has caused grave concerns in the KMT ruling circles and provoked harsh verbal reactions from the PRC authorities.[22] In addition, at least sixty-three other parties, all tiny, have registered with the government. Among them, the Labour Party, launched in December 1987 by a group of intellectuals and labour activists, has a potential social base among Taiwan's more than 5 million industrial workers.[23] However, a group of left-wing intellectuals and militant activists split from the party in 1988 to form a separate Worker's Party, thus severely undermining the Labour Party's political potential. Meanwhile, both the KMT and the DPP have made serious efforts to strengthen workers' allegiance to their respective causes.

Faced with this changing environment, the KMT's political system has moved from "hard authoritarian" to "soft authoritarian", while simultaneously pursuing its intra-party transformation.[24] More recently, the ruling party has been through two phases of internal change. During the 1970s and most of the 1980s the mainlander-dominated exclusionary and authoritarian party evolved into a pluralistic authoritarian party. Membership drives both intensified and diversified. By the late 1980s over 70 per cent of the more than 2 million members were reportedly Taiwanese, from broad social and economic backgrounds. Previously monopolised by the mainlanders, the KMT Central Standing Committee included only three Taiwanese in its roster as recently as 1973. Since then, Taiwanese members have steadily increased to nine in 1979 and to sixteen, or 52 per cent of the total of thirty-one, in 1991. At the Central Committee level, Taiwanese representation had only a token share throughout the 1960s, which gradually rose to 17 per cent of its 150-strong roster in 1984 and reached 40 per cent of the 180 committee members elected at the Thirteenth Party Congress in July 1988.[25] The average age of the members dropped considerably

22. Hung-mao Tien, *Brothers in Arms: Political Struggle and Party Competition in Taiwan's Evolving Democracy* (New York: Asia Society's Asian Update Series, December 1991), p. 6.

23. Shim Jae Hoon, "Taiwan, Clarion Call to Workers", *Far Eastern Economic Review*, 21 January 1988, pp. 18–19; *Chung-kuo shih-pao*, 18 January 1988, p. 3.

24. Edwin A. Winckler, "Institutionalization and Participation on Taiwan: From Hard to Soft Authoritarianism?", *CQ*, September 1984, pp. 482–99.

25. *Chung-kuo shih-pao (China Times)*, 13 July 1988, pp. 1–2.

from seventy to about fifty-nine years, reflecting the addition of almost 100 new members with diverse career patterns.

The second phase of party transformation, initiated in 1988, has manifested itself in the form of intra-party democratisation. Four events underscore such a change. The first is the death of Chiang Ching-kuo and the subsequent succession of Li Teng-hui as party Chairman. Chiang's departure means that the party is now without an autocratic leader; instead it increasingly operates with a form of collective leadership. This is clearly reflected in the decision-making Central Standing Committee meetings. In the past the committee gathered to listen to Chiang's instructions; by the early 1990s it was filled with lively discussion on policy issues. Second, two-thirds of the Thirteenth Party Congress' 380 delegates were competitively elected in 1988 by the party's rank-and-file members.[26] Moreover, thirty-three of the 180-member slate prepared by the party authorities for the Central Committee failed to win election at the party congress; instead, thirty-three write-in candidates were elected through their own efforts.[27] In the past, Central Committee members were designated by the party Chairman. Third, a significant number of Taiwan-elected KMT members in the National Assembly and the Legislative Yuan have openly defied the party's decision by calling for involuntary retirement of the 1947–8 cohorts in both chambers, demanding that parliamentary houses consist only of members elected in Taiwan. And finally, the party primary as part of the nominating process for the KMT candidates for public offices has been virtually institutionalised. In the 1989 parliamentary elections, more than 85 per cent of the candidates winning the primary vote were subsequently nominated by the party's Central Standing Committee.[28]

Intra-party democratisation has stirred up considerable debate as the diehards and many of the old guard continue to resist change and stress the party's revolutionary mission. Still, a clear majority of the party's power élite appear inclined towards transformation of the KMT into a democratic type of party. This issue was not expected to be settled until the outcome of the next KMT Party Congress in 1993. There has been public debate regarding the feasibility of restructuring the KMT according to the model of Japan's Liberal Democratic Party.

26. *Chung-yang Jih-pao* (*Central Daily News*), 16 May 1988, p. 1.
27. *Chung-kuo shih-pao*, 13 July 1988, pp. 1–2.
28. *Ibid.*, 17 August 1989, p. 3.

Given the profoundly authoritarian nature of the party structure and the existence of a powerful and conservative gerontocracy in its upper echelons, further transformation of the party will take time. But, as the KMT directs more attention to winning elections and its "revolutionary" mission is replaced with the commitment to constitutional democracy, one sees a distinct possibility for the party to continue its internal democratic change, now widely demanded by both its members and many reform-minded élites.

The KMT, still in control of state institutions and major social resources, will probably remain in power in the foreseeable future. The party has a massive membership and possesses extensive networks of institutional mechanism and local factions to mobilise voters. It also owns a large array of profitable enterprises. Moreover, popular election does not yet extend to the positions of ROC President, cabinet members or even provincial Governor. These posts will continue to be held by KMT members. On the other hand, opposition parties are likely to pose greater challenges to winning local executive posts as well as legislative seats at various levels of government, thus accumulating growing countervailing power to check the KMT's dominant position. In the elections held in 1989, the DPP candidates received 29.7 per cent and 38.3 per cent of the votes cast for parliamentarians and mayors respectively, as opposed to 59.7 per cent and 53 per cent for the KMT candidates.[29] Such figures indicate that the DPP-led opposition forces are no longer inconsequential.

*Institutional reform.* One of the central issues in Taiwan's democratic development concerns institutional change in the legislature and the ROC government. For almost four decades after 1949 the archaic national representative bodies were largely composed of individuals "elected" while on the mainland in 1947–8. Although natural attrition has taken its toll, by 1990 no less than 140 of the 216 Legislative Yuan (parliament) members and 630 of the 835 National Assembly members, who elect the ROC President and amend the Constitution, were still the 1947–8 cohorts, putting the Taiwan-elected members in a decisively minority position. As popular pressures for change mounted, the Council of Grand Justices, in an exercise of judicial review, finally ruled in 1990 that the entire group of mainland-elected representatives

29. Chu Yun-han, "Hsuen-chi yu cheng-tang" (Elections and Political Parties), in *Tai-wan ch'i-shih-pa nien ta-hsuen yen-t'ao-hui lun wen chi* (A Collection of Essays on the 1989 Elections in Taiwan) (Taipei: Shih-pao Wen-hsueh chi-chin-hui, 1980), vol. 1, p. 2.

must retire by the end of 1991. This appears to have resolved the most controversial issue regarding the national representative institutions.

Moreover, the demands for popular elections of the ROC President, Governor of Taiwan and mayors of Taipei and Kao-hsiung, the two largest cities, are now increasingly brought into political focus in public debate. Until now, all four ROC presidents have been preselected by the KMT ruling circle and then rubber-stamped by the National Assembly, as required by the Constitution. The President appointed the Premier and other cabinet members with the consent of the Legislative Yuan. Such a recruitment process has raised fundamental questions with regard to the democratic basis of the regime's legitimacy. These issues were not entirely resolved in the spring of 1992 when the new National Assembly, elected in December 1991, met to amend the Constitution. Methods and dates of election were not finalised due to strong disagreements among the Assembly members.

The idea that the Governor of Taiwan and mayors of Taipei and Kao-hsiung should be popularly elected appears to have strong support from both the opposition parties and a clear majority of the KMT members. The only unresolved question on such matters concerns the dates when these elections should take place. On the other hand, the popular election of the President remains a deeply divisive issue. The DPP and public opinion are strongly in support of such a direct election. However, powerful conservatives within the KMT are adamantly opposed to such a change, arguing in favour of an indirect election of the President either by the National Assembly or by some kind of electoral college system. To make the matter more complicated, a coalition of the DPP and other non-partisan reformers has recently adopted a political plank that proposes a new constitution of the "Republic of Taiwan" instead of merely revising the existing ROC Constitution, hence fundamentally changing the nature of Taiwan's national identity.[30] Such a proposal is likely to elevate the anxiety level of Peking's Communist regime and make the task of future institutional reform in Taiwan much more difficult. At the time of writing, a KMT–DPP compromise seems possible only if both sides agree to popular election of the President. Continuing KMT–DPP dialogues would determine whether the apparent "crisis" of constitutional reform is indeed manageable.

---

30. *Min-chung Jih-pao* (*Commons Daily*), 26 August 1991, pp. 1–4.

*Conclusion*

The democratic transition in the Republic of China in Taiwan is an enormously painful process. It involves transformation of a highly authoritarian and corporatist party-state system. It has to tackle simultaneously the issues of political democratisation and national identity which pits a large segment of the indigenous Taiwanese against the mainlanders who still adhere to the KMT-led "one-China" policy. There is also constant danger of potential military intervention from the Peking regime whose influence has already penetrated Taiwan's political arena. Worse yet, Taiwan's authorities are under pressure rapidly to engineer a stable democratic transition that has taken many industrialised democracies more than a century to accomplish.

Given the complexity of ethnic differences, partisan politics, factionalism and evolving Taiwan–mainland relations, democratic transformation in Taiwan still faces a bumpy road ahead. As the conservatives, reformers and radicals jockey for position, the crucial test for success in Taiwan's continuing political experiment probably lies in the skill and ability of leaders in both the KMT and the DPP to strike timely compromises regarding issues of national identity and political conciliation with the PRC. Such a prospect, if it is to be realised, requires establishing better ground rules for inter-party dialogue as well as re-arranging the KMT's relations with the state and society. Constitutional reforms made so far have altered the regime's authoritarian nature. A true democracy for Taiwan, nonetheless, would demand additional institutional changes.

# 5

# THE KUOMINTANG AND
# THE OPPOSITION

## Jürgen Domes

In the years since young officers overthrew an authoritarian dictatorship in Portugal on 25 April 1974, a worldwide wave of uprisings, revolutions and—in some cases—non-violent processes of transition swept away seventeen authoritarian dictatorships and three traditional autocracies, and converted the political systems of these twenty countries into representative democracies, of which eight or ten can be considered reasonably stable in the early 1990s. This worldwide wave, which my German colleague Martin Kriele has called "the democratic world revolution", has assumed many different features. In the Republic of China in Taiwan (the ROC), where the process of transition from a development-oriented authoritarian dictatorship to a representative system seems to be approaching its conclusion in the 1990s, the systemic transformation appears to have followed the pattern of a gradual, planned, controlled and long-term development. Here, a nationalist mass party, the Kuomintang (KMT), which dominated a single-party system, was formally organised according to Leninist structural principles. Its transformation into a leading force in a competitive party system is not only of great interest to a political scientist interested in the character of political parties, it must also be considered historically an almost singular case an of élite changing; as such, it is of considerable importance for the development of structural-functional analysis.

As some of the most able and competent international specialists have analysed the issues of political, constitutional and legal reform in Taiwan elsewhere in this volume I shall concentrate on the question of how the political forces which are active in the ROC today have developed since the late 1940s.

In this context, I would like to divide the political history of the ROC in Taiwan into three stages. First is the stage of consolidation of authoritarian rule, and its stable existence, which I date from 1949 to 1975 or 1976. Second comes the stage of pluralisation and incipient liberalisation, which I place from 1975 or 1976 to 1986. The final stage is that of full-fledged transition to competitive politics, which I date from 1986 to the present and beyond. In each of the first two stages, I shall give a brief, and therefore necessarily sketchy, overview of the development of the KMT and the opposition forces. For the third stage, I shall try to describe the interactions between the KMT and the now-organised forces of the opposition from the late 1980s up to the time of writing, and I shall, in the conclusion, outline some alternative possibilities for the future of party politics in Taiwan.

## Stage 1: authoritarian rule 1949–1975

After their defeat and their loss of the Chinese mainland to the Chinese Communist Party (the CCP) in late 1949, the Nationalist government, the organs of the KMT party machine and about 600,000 soldiers and 640,000 civilians, led by Chiang Kai-shek, fled to Taiwan. In 1950 these people from "outside the province" of Taiwan (*wai-sheng-jen*) comprised approximately 19 per cent of the island's population.

At this point, the KMT leadership was confronted with three major problems. First, the island was underdeveloped—there was even a severe shortage of food. Second, the KMT in general, and its ruling élite in particular, had lost all its prestige internationally as well as nationally. Third, the locally born Chinese in Taiwan, those who spoke the southern Fukien dialect (*min-nan-yu*) as well as the Hakkas, were mostly alienated from the party and quietly opposed the domination by the mainlanders.

In order to stabilise its hold on the island, the KMT ruling élite had to solve these problems. Therefore, Chiang and his close advisors enacted five major policies:

1. *Land reform*, which was implemented in three stages between 1949 and 1953. Together with the United States' support for the beginning of economic development this resulted in the elimination of food shortages in 1951. After that the food situation in Taiwan stabilised. Moreover, a series of four-year development plans was launched in 1953, beginning with the establishment of domestic light and consumer goods industries which minimised the need for imports.

2. Immediately after reassuming the leadership of the National government in early 1950, Chiang introduced a thoroughgoing *organisational reform* of the party which was concluded with the Seventh KMT Party Congress in 1952. In the course of this reform, those party members

who had cooperated with the Communists or had a definite record of corruption, plus many members who had fled abroad, were expelled from the KMT.

3. In the area which remained under KMT control, the party developed an intricate *network of party presence* at grassroots level and in all sectors of society. The party established social welfare stations in villages and city districts, and constructed a network of party cells which kept tight control over trade unions, farmers' associations, professional organisations and the whole educational system.

4. The KMT ruling élite which emerged from the party reform imposed strict discipline within the party. In order to prevent any serious challenge from opposition forces, the Nationalist government used *emergency orders* to impose a ban on the founding of new political parties and to outlaw strikes and demonstrations.

5. At the same time, the KMT increasingly *accepted locally born Taiwanese* as party members. Moreover, the ruling élite began to permit limited political participation through the gradual development of elections for local administration heads and, after 1951, representative assemblies on the local, county and provincial level. When the organisational reforms of the KMT were completed in 1952, the party had 380,000 members or 9.92 per cent of the island's adult population, 55 per cent of whom were in the military and 45 per cent civilians. At that time, only 14.47 per cent were of local Taiwanese origin. Hence the KMT at that time was chiefly still a party of the "mainlanders". Yet from the late 1950s gradual and quiet but fairly effective changes began to develop in the party's platform. Particularly in the area of economic policies, ideas of neo-liberalism replaced Sun Yat-senism. Under the influence of this programme of change, private ownership increased remarkably. While in 1952 just 44 per cent of the industrial production originated from private enterprise, this proportion had risen to 81 per cent in 1990. Economic planning was reduced to directives to establish frameworks for development, and a gradual de-regulation of prices began.

Under the impact of these policies, the party achieved quite convincing successes in economic development and was deeply entrenched in society by 1975. By then the KMT had approximately 1,450,000 members or 16.3 per cent of the adult population, with 58 per cent of its members being of local Taiwanese origin.

The party also established a tight authoritarian system. Opposition forces were confined to activities on the local level and were not allowed to develop national organisations. In order to demonstrate its monolithic character the KMT used the slogan: "there is no party outside the party, there is no faction inside the party" ("*tang-wai wu tang, tang-nei wup'ai*"). It was by allusion to this slogan that the name "*wutang wu-p'ai*" (no-party, no-faction) developed, under which the opposition forces challenged KMT candidates in local elections.

Besides these local forces, there were two minor parties: the Democratic Socialist Party and the Young China Party. Both had been established on the mainland before 1949 and had formed a coalition with the KMT. In Taiwan, they had deteriorated to mere satellite parties, mainly funded by the KMT and the government. Nevertheless, occasionally some local oppositionists used the names of these parties when competing against KMT candidates.

Between the mid-1950s and the early 1970s there were principally two opposition groups which prepared for competition with the KMT élite. These comprised a number of non-partisan intellectuals from the mainland on the one hand, and large parts of the locally-born urban upper class on the other. During the late 1950s, these groups attempted to organise around the monthly journal *Tze-you chung-kuo* (Free China) which was published by, among others, the eminent intellectual leader Hu Shih. The group that published this journal began in 1959 to prepare for the establishment of a new opposition party under the name "Chinese Democratic Party". This attempt, however, was thwarted by the ruling élite in 1960 when one of the prospective opposition party leaders, Lei Chen, was arrested and sentenced to a long prison term. From then on, in the 1960s and early 1970s, rigid party control and severe crackdowns on opposition groups characterised the authoritarian political climate in Taiwan. Nevertheless, opposition forces enjoyed limited opportunities to participate in local and provincial elections.

In elections of city mayors and county magistrates, for example, oppositionists gained one out of twenty-one seats in 1957 and four out of twenty-one in 1964. Only in 1972 did all twenty seats go to KMT candidates. In elections for the Taiwan Provincial Assembly, opposition representation reached its highest point with fifteen out of seventy seats in 1960, and its lowest with ten out of sixty-seven in 1968, the percentage of popular vote received by non-KMT candidates varying between 34.9 per cent in 1960 and 21.9 per cent in 1968. The average opposition share in Provincial Assembly elections stood at 29.5 per cent, with an average of 29.33 per cent in elections for mayors and county magistrates.

Notwithstanding such limited successes of the opposition forces, the ROC in Taiwan must on balance be considered an authoritarian dictatorship during the whole period from 1949 to the mid-1970s.

## Stage 2: pluralisation and incipient liberalisation, 1975–1986

In July 1972 Chiang Ching-kuo, the eldest son of Chiang Kai-shek, was appointed Premier of the Executive Yuan. After the death of his father in April 1975, Chiang Ching-kuo took over the leadership of the KMT as Chairman of the Central Committee (CC). He finally assumed the Presidency of the ROC in 1978.

From 1972 the character of the political system of the ROC started to change. In order to consolidate KMT rule and to increase popular support for the ruling élite in the face of economic difficulties which arose during the two energy crises in 1973–4 and 1978–9, as well as rising international isolation, Chiang Ching-kuo initiated two developments which began to dominate Taiwan politics in succeeding years. These two developments were: first, the Taiwanisation of the political decision-making bodies; second, an incipient pluralisation of the political system.

Membership of the KMT reached the figure of 1,886,000 in 1980, which was 17.98 per cent of all adults on the island. At that time, 67.23 per cent of the members were locally born Taiwanese, who also almost completely dominated positions in the local and provincial representative bodies, as well as headships of administrations at the local level that were held by the KMT.

When Chiang Ching-kuo assumed the premiership in 1972, for the first time a Taiwanese, the previous Speaker of the Provincial Assembly, Hsieh Tung-min, was appointed Governor of the island province. The positions of Mayor of Taipei, which had become a centrally administered city in 1967, and of Kao-hsiung, which became a centrally administered city in 1979, were from the beginning held by Taiwanese.

In the central leadership, too, the participation of locally born Taiwanese gradually started to increase. While there were only three Taiwanese out of nineteen members in the Executive Yuan Cabinet in 1972, their number had risen to seven out of nineteen by 1986. In the CC of the KMT 9.3 per cent of the members were Taiwanese after the Tenth Party Congress in 1969. The Eleventh in 1976 increased this share to 17.9 per cent, and the Twelfth in 1981 to 20.7 per cent.

In the central decision-making organ of the ruling élite, the Standing Committee of the KMT CC, the increase in locally born Taiwanese representation after the mid-1970s was even more striking. From 1952 to 1969 Taiwanese representation on that body had been limited to one out of seventeen members, or 5.88 per cent, and from 1969 to 1972 to two out of twenty-one or 9.52 per cent. In 1972, the proportion rose to three out of twenty-one (14.29 per cent), and in 1976 to five out of twenty-seven (18.52 per cent). In 1979 the figures were nine out of twenty-seven members, or exactly one-third; in 1984 it rose again to twelve out of thirty-one members or 38.7 per cent.

The process of pluralisation of the political system developed much more slowly than that of Taiwanisation. As early as 1969, fifteen new members of the National Assembly and eleven new members of the Legislative Yuan were elected in the first by-elections for the central parliamentary bodies to be held in the island since 1948. In 1972, the number of delegates newly elected in Taiwan to the National Assembly — this time for a definite six-year term — increased to fifty-three out of 1,411, or 3.76 per cent. In the same year, fifty-one new members were elected for a three-year term to the Legislative Yuan, a share of 12.56 per cent of that body at that time. Three years later, in the autumn of 1975, the share of newly elected members of the Legislative Yuan rose to fifty-two out of 396, or 13.13 per cent of that body. Yet these were only small and rather hesitant beginnings. More far-reaching decisions concerning pluralisation were being prepared for the second half of 1977. It appears that some time in the winter of 1976–7, Chiang Ching-kuo, in his capacity as Premier, asked the Research, Development and Evaluation Commission of the Executive Yuan to organise a report on issues of political reform from Western-educated social scientists in the ROC. By the spring of 1977 these social scientists seem to have proposed a set of internal recommendations which included the abolition of the emergency rule of 1949 and of press censorship; the passing of a law on political parties which would allow the establishment of new parties; and a gradual development towards the total renewal of the central parliamentary bodies, i.e. direct elections to the National Assembly and the Legislative Yuan and indirect elections to the control Yuan. For the implementation of this process the report suggested a period of fully fifteen years.

Yet the preparations of the ruling élite for pluralisation required a response. This developed as the opposition forces began to establish more closely knit unofficial networks by 1975. During this period, the old term "no-party, no-faction" was replaced by the phrase "personalities outside the party" (*"tang-wai jen-shih"*), which was increasingly abbreviated to "Tang-wai". The Tang-wai forces experienced a first breakthrough in the local and provincial elections of autumn 1977. The turnout of voters increased from 70.3 per cent in the previous local elections in 1972 to 80.4 per cent, and Tang-wai candidates, with one-third of the popular vote, won twenty-one out of seventy-seven seats in the Provincial Assembly. In the elections for Taipei City Council, Tang-wai candidates gathered 20.6 per cent of the popular vote and secured eight out of fifty-one seats. Moreover, with 29 per cent of the popular vote they won four of the twenty positions of mayors and county magistrates in the province of Taiwan.

By-elections for the National Assembly and the Legislative Yuan were originally scheduled for December 1978. At the outset the campaign for these by-elections promised to develop into a new push for the process of pluralisation. In October 1978, the government tolerated the officially illegal establishment of a "Tang-wai Campaign Corps" which organised joint advertisements and meetings staged by several candidates. On 15 December, however, American President Jimmy Carter announced the establishment of formal diplomatic relations with the People's Republic of China and the de-recognition of the ROC. This provoked a serious political crisis in the ROC. The KMT ruling élite reacted by immediately postponing the elections to an indefinite date. The process of pluralisation was in danger of being interrupted. The opposition, however, tried to keep this process alive by pressing for five demands at a "National Affairs Conference of Personalities outside the Party" (*"tang-wai jen-shih kuo-shih hui-i"*), held on 25 December. The five demands were:

—the release of all political prisoners;
—the freedom to establish new political parties;
—the abolition of press censorship;
—the total renewal of the central parliamentary bodies; and
—the popular election of the Governor of Taiwan and the Mayor of Taipei.

It should not go without notice that by the end of 1991 the first four of these five demands had been implemented and the last was in the process of being put into practice. Yet in 1978, the ruling élite was still not willing to grant the demands of the opposition immediately.

Nevertheless, in spite of the crisis which followed American de-recognition, the year 1979 became a period of further relaxation in domestic ROC politics. Within the KMT, intra-party group formation became characterised by the evolution of three coalitions. These were not factions in the sense of coherent circles based on alternative platforms and exclusive claims for political power, but rather latent, mainly issue-oriented groups. Younger social and natural scientists holding doctoral degrees from American and European universities, some developmental technocrats, and a large group of regional and local politicians from Taiwan, as well as a number of young members of the central parliamentary bodies who had emerged from by-elections, combined into a reformist coalition. This group argued that national security and social stability could best be guaranteed by an expansion of the parameters of participation and political competition in a controlled and managed process. On the other side of the political spectrum within the KMT, a traditionalist coalition developed, consisting mainly of representatives of the old factions which had dominated KMT politics before 1949, a majority of the active military leaders, a number of older bureaucrats, and some politicians who were at that time close to Chiang Ching-kuo. This group stressed national security as taking priority over the pluralisation of the political system and hence tended to emphasise the authoritarian features. Between these two groups, a centrist coalition, consisting mainly of the majority of developmental technocrats and a number of senior local and regional politicians, put its strongest emphasis on economic growth and attempted to strike a balance between reformist and traditionalist approaches.

During the first nine months of 1979 the reformist forces prevailed over the traditionalists and directed the government to tolerate a number of newly established opposition monthlies and bi-weeklies. The most important of these journals was the magazine *Mei-li-tao* (*Formosa*). Almost all opposition groups were represented on the editorial board of that publication. The more radical of them began in October to establish local offices of the journal, which could be considered the nucleus of the organisational network of a new opposition party. Then, on 10 December 1979 a large Tang-wai demonstration in Kao-hsiung turned violent and openly clashed with security forces.

The "Kao-hsiung Incident" strengthened the traditionalists within the KMT leadership at first. It was followed by an immediate new crackdown on the opposition, including the arrest of a number of opposition leaders and the banning of many of the opposition journals which had been established in 1979.

Such attempts by the traditionalists to stop the tendencies towards pluralisation, however, were short-lived. After June 1980, the moves towards pluralisation regained momentum. The KMT ruling élite decided to hold in early December 1980 the by-elections for the National Assembly and the Legislative Yuan which had been postponed in late 1978. In these elections, seventy-six or 7 per cent of the delegates to the National Assembly, and ninety-seven or 25.46 per cent of the members of the Legislative Yuan, were to be newly elected. The opposition forces, who had to run separately and without campaigning jointly as Tang-wai candidates, secured 27.09 per cent of the popular vote.

A further step in the pluralisation process was taken in the by-elections to the Legislative Yuan in December 1983, when ninety-eight (26.34 per cent) of the seats in that body were at stake. This time a number of Tang-wai circles were allowed to nominate candidates officially, and these won 18.96 per cent of the popular vote while other Tang-wai contenders gathered 11.3 per cent, so that altogether 30.59 per cent of the popular vote went to opposition candidates.

Soon after the 1983 elections, the Tang-wai forces attempted to improve their organisation, with the ultimate aim of establishing a new opposition political party. In May 1984, Tang-wai personalities who held elective offices decided to establish a "Tang-wai People's Representatives' Association for the Study of Public Policy" (hereafter: Tang-wai Public Policy Association). Immediately after the founding of this organization Chiang Ching-kuo ordered the government to tolerate its existence. Tolerance was also exercised when Tang-wai politicians formed a "Tang-wai Association for Campaign Assistance" in September 1985. This group nominated official Tang-wai candidates for the local and provincial elections in November 1985, and it ran a joint campaign for these elections. In the Taiwan Provincial Assembly, official Tang-wai candidates won eleven and other oppositional candidates (now mostly called *"wu-tang-chi"* or "non-partisan") seven out of seventy-three seats. In Taipei City Council there were now thirteen Tang-wai out of fifty-one members, in Kao-hsiung City Council ten out of forty-one members. Moreover, Tang-wai candidates secured four of the twenty-one positions of mayors and county magistrates. The share of the popular vote for officially nominated Tang-wai candidates for the provincial level assemblies stood at 15.97 per cent while other non-KMT candidates won 13.54 per cent so that altogether 29.51 per cent of the voters decided to support opposition politicians. Soon after the local and provincial elections of 1985, the development towards a pluralisation of the ROC political system accelerated once more.

In June 1986, the Tang-wai Public Policy Association decided to establish local branches in a number of cities in Taiwan. Traditional forces within the KMT élite correctly viewed this move as part of the preparation for the establishment of a new opposition party. Under the direct influence of Chiang Ching-kuo, the government nevertheless again decided to tolerate this move, thus indicating an increasing influence of the reformist coalition within the ruling élite.

There are indications that Chiang Ching-kuo informed the leaders of the opposition through private channels during September 1986 that no action would be taken against them if they went ahead with the founding of a new political party. Hence, on 28 September 1986, 138 Tang-wai personalities assembled in the partly government-owned Grand Hotel in Taipei and established the Democratic Progressive Party ("*Min-chu chin-pu tang*", or the DPP) and the government, although declaring this move "illegal", did not take any action.

With this event a new stage, characterised by the full-fledged development of competitive politics, began in Taiwan.

### Stage 3: transition to competitive politics, 1986 onwards

The first elections to be held in the ROC in Taiwan after the establishment of the DPP were the by-elections to the Legislative Yuan and the National Assembly on 6 December 1986. On the official ballots, the DPP candidates were still listed as "*wu tang-chi*". But the newly established opposition party used its name and emblem in its own campaign pamphlets and advertisements without interference from the authorities.

In the most important elections for 100 seats in the Legislative Yuan, DPP candidates received 24.55 per cent of the vote and independents 8.72 per cent, so that a total of 33.27 per cent of the vote was cast for candidates opposing the ruling party. In the Legislative Yuan the KMT won seventy-nine seats, the DPP twelve, independents six and the two satellite parties three. Of the eighty-four new seats in the National Assembly, sixty-eight went to the KMT, eleven to the DPP, four to independents and one to the Democratic-Socialist Party.

Strongly promoted by President Chiang Ching-kuo, the trends towards Taiwanisation and pluralisation gathered further momentum during 1987. Between late 1986 and the summer of 1988 the number of local-born Taiwanese members of the cabinet increased from seven to nine, out of a total of nineteen ministers. While 20.7 per cent of the members of the Twelfth KMT CC, elected in 1981, were local-born Taiwanese, in the Thirteenth CC, which was elected in 1988, this share increased to 38.7 per cent.

From 1986 to 1988 fourteen of the thirty-one members of the Standing Committee of the KMT CC were locally born Taiwanese. But in 1988 this share increased to sixteen, out of the same total, constituting a majority.

When President Chiang Chiang-kuo, whose health had been deteriorating since 1985, died aged seventy-seven on 13 January 1988, Vice-President Dr Li Teng-hui,[1] a locally born Taiwanese, succeeded him as both President of the ROC and Chairman of the KMT. Li was confirmed in the former capacity by being elected President by the National Assembly in March 1990; and in the latter, by the Thirteenth Party Congress of the KMT on 7 July 1988.

The three milestones in the process of pluralisation and the development of competitive politics are the abolition of the then thirty-year-old state of emergency on 15 July 1987, the lifting of most restrictions on newspapers and periodicals on 1 January 1988, and finally the formal legalisation of new political parties through the implementation of a Law on the Organisation of Civic Bodies in January 1989.

Also of great importance to the political development of Taiwan were the decisions of the Thirteenth KMT Party Congress, which was held from 7 to 13 July 1988. The congress confirmed and consolidated the policies of political reform, adding them to the party platform. These policies were concrete in some points but comparatively vague and general in others. By deciding to keep the characterization of the KMT in the party statute as "revolutionary", the congress refused to admit that the party was, in the summer of 1988, already but one political organisation competing against others on an equal footing in a representative democracy. Nevertheless, fully competitive politics was accepted by the congress in principle, as its platform now provided

---

1. Prof. Domes prefers to follow Dr Lee Teng-Hui's own spelling of his surname. However, for consistency this name is spelt "Li" throughout this volume.

for the promotion of a "healthy competition among political parties on a fair and rational basis".[2]

Competitive politics, in fact, developed further during the by-elections for the Legislative Yuan and the elections for the Taiwan Provincial Assembly, as well as those for Taipei and Kao-hsiung city councils and those for county magistrates and mayors, which were all held on 2 December 1989. For these elections, fourteen political parties altogether fielded candidates, but the real contest in the very lively campaign was between the KMT and the DPP. The results indicated significant losses for the KMT and a definite increase in voter support for the opposition.

In the by-elections for 101 seats of the Legislative Yuan the KMT won 59.27 per cent of the popular vote and seventy-two seats, the DPP 29.92 per cent of the popular vote and twenty-one seats, and independents and others 10.81 per cent of the popular vote and eight seats.

In the elections for the Taiwan Provincial Assembly and the two city councils, the KMT won a total of 65.03 per cent of the popular vote and 119 seats, the DPP 25.36 per cent of the popular vote and thirty-eight seats. The others gained 9.61 per cent, seating thirteen independents and one member of the Labour Party (*Kung-tang*).

The greatest advances were made by the opposition forces in the elections for the twenty-one county magistrates and city mayors in the province of Taiwan. Here, the KMT won 56.11 per cent of the popular vote, the DPP 30.13 per cent and independent candidates 13.76 per cent. In these elections, the voting strength of the non-KMT forces rose to 43.89 per cent altogether. In other words, the KMT secured only fourteen positions (three less than in 1985), the DPP six (four more than in 1985) and an independent one (one less than in 1985).

The process of full pluralisation of the political system received a further boost in June 1990. The Council of Grand Justices of the Judicial Yuan ruled that all members of the National Assembly, the Legislative Yuan and the Control Yuan who had been elected in 1947–8 and in Taiwan in 1969 would have to retire by 31 December 1991 at the latest. This decision provided for a total renewal of members of all central parliamentary bodies through elections. These elections were then set for the National Assembly on 22 December 1991 and for the Legislative Yuan on 19 December 1992.

The year 1991 saw the beginning of the last stage in the gradual

2. Platform of the KMT, passed by the XIIIth Party Congress, July 1988.

and controlled process of transition from a development-oriented authoritarian dictatorship to a pluralistic representative system. After a long period of bickering, the KMT leadership had decided to convene an extraordinary session of the National Assembly to pass constitutional amendments in order to provide the legal basis for a total renewal of the three central parliamentary bodies. With this decision the ruling party overrode protests from the major opposition party, the DPP, which wanted all constitutional revisions to be passed by a now renewed National Assembly. It also rebutted the arguments of its own traditionalist wing that there should be no change in the Constitution at all. In other words, the position of the centrist mainstream of the KMT led by President Dr Li Teng-hui prevailed. On 8 April, the 539 remaining delegates of the old National Assembly convened to debate the initial constitutional amendments. During the debates the DPP delegates walked out of the meeting, and the opposition party staged street protests of more than 10,000 demonstrators in Taipei on 16 and 17 April. This prompted Li Teng-hui to go on television with a dire address for the first time, stressing that "a responsible political party should follow legal procedures in voicing political views to solicit voters".[3] The President's speech calmed political emotions, and on 22 April the National Assembly approved a constitutional amendment providing for the total renewal of the National Assembly and the Legislative Yuan. The new National Assembly was to have 325 members, 225 of whom would be elected directly in multi-member constituencies in Taiwan according to the plurality rule, eighty "nationwide representatives" and twenty overseas Chinese representatives from party slates according to the proportional representation rule. In the Legislative Yuan, of the 161 members, 135 were to be directly elected in constituencies, twenty as "nationwide" legislators and six as overseas Chinese legislators from party slates. On 30 April, President Li enforced the constitutional amendment. At the same time, in a televised press conference, he formally declared that the so-called "Period of Mobilisation for the Suppression of Communist Rebellion" proclaimed in 1948 would be terminated on 1 May 1991, and the so-called "Temporary Provisions" for this period would also be abolished. He thus relinquished his extraordinary presidential powers. Full constitutional rule was restored. As a gesture of reconciliation, Vice-Premier Dr Shih Ch'i-yang announced on the same evening that

3. *Chung-kuo shih-pao/China Times* (hereafter CKSP), 18 April 1990.

the government would erect a monument to the memory of those Taiwanese and mainlanders who were killed during the uprisings of 28 February 1947.

During the following months both the ruling party and the opposition began to prepare for the elections to the new National Assembly, which were set for 21 December, and for the major revision of the Constitution which that assembly was to debate in the spring of 1992.

On 14 August, the central decision-making body of the KMT, the Standing Committee of the CC, decided to form a task force of fourteen members to discuss the constitutional amendments. This was to be chaired by Vice-President Dr Li Yuan-tsu.

The KMT opted to hold preferential primaries of a consultative character for the nomination of its candidates for direct elections on 18 August. Yet only 566,000 or 29.06 per cent of the 1,949,000 party members participated. This small turnout was mainly attributed to the fact that the primaries were not binding, and that the campaigning of the 397 candidates in the primaries was not very inspiring. Finally on 2 October the Standing Committee of the KMT formally nominated 192 candidates for the 225 direct National Assembly seats, of whom 173 had won in the primaries.

The central issue of the campaign for the National Assembly elections was set by the DPP that autumn. Countering Li Teng-hui's promulgation on 5 March of the "Guidelines for National Unification", which suggested a long-range process of rapprochement with the PRC in three stages, from August onwards large sections of the DPP started to call for the establishment of an independent "Republic of Taiwan". The DPP decided to organise an island-wide drive to promote a new application for the state's admission to the United Nations under this name. On 7 and 8 September, between 8,000 and 10,000 people took to the streets in Taipei in massive demonstrations in support of this move. There was also increasing activity by US-based members of Taiwan independence organisations, promoting the agitation for Taiwan independence, which resulted in a number of arrests and the expulsion of a number of Taiwanese-born American citizens.

Within the DPP, the radical *"Hsin Ch'ao-liu"* (New Wave) faction increased its pressure for the whole party to adopt the call for Taiwan's independence, fervently opposed by the ruling élite in Peking as well as by the KMT, in its platform. In order to counter this move, Li Teng-hui invited eleven leading locally born Taiwanese politicians and scholars, including two independents and four members of the DPP, to discuss the issue on 29 September. During the talks, he stressed that Taiwan "has remained as a sovereign nation for a long time",[4] and that "reunification between the two sides of the Taiwan Straits is something that cannot be achieved in the near future". He pointed out that there really was no necessity to declare Taiwan an independent state.

Li's appeal went unheeded. The Fifth Party Congress of the DPP, which met between 12 and 14 October, decided to add to its platform the call for a plebiscite on the establishment of a "Republic of Taiwan" independent from China. Hsu Hsin-liang, the candidate of the moderate "*Mei-li tao*" (Formosa) faction, who had opposed the call for independence, narrowly defeated his opponent Shih Ming-te (supported by the New Wave) in the election for party Chairman. However, the New Wave faction for the first time gained a majority on the DPP Standing Committee, winning six seats against four for the Formosa faction and one neutral member.

As a result political tension over the independence issue increased sharply, and politics in Taiwan seemed to be heading for a new and dangerous crisis. In late October and early November, however, emotions calmed down again.

Nevertheless, Taiwan's independence had been made the central issue for the 21 December elections. By making it so, the DPP decided to go for broke. It was a highly emotional campaign which endangered all attempts to build a basic political consensus in the island, a prerequisite for a successful completion of political reform.

The result of the elections to the National Assembly dealt a heavy blow to the DPP and the issue of Taiwan's independence. The KMT won an unexpectedly large landslide victory. Voter turnout was 68.32 per cent, almost seven percentage points lower than in the Legislative Yuan by-elections two years earlier. The KMT won 67.72 per cent of the vote and 254 seats in the National Assembly; the DPP 22.78 percent and sixty-six seats; the candidates of a hastily founded National Democratic Non-Partisan Alliance 2.16 per cent and three seats; the newly founded China Social Democratic Party (*Chung-hua she-hui min-chu tang* or the CSDP) 2.08 per cent and no seat; independents 3.09 per cent and two seats; and thirteen other political parties 2.17 per cent and no seat.

---

4. CKSP, 30 Sept. 1990.

In comparison with the Legislative Yuan elections of 1989, the KMT's share of the vote increased by 14.15 per cent, while that of the DPP dropped by 23.86 per cent. Hence the KMT is still by far the largest political force in the ROC in Taiwan. With its 1,949,000 members in August 1991, it organised 14.53 per cent of the adult population in the island. Although this share was lower than 17.98 per cent, the 1980 figure, it still means that every seventh adult citizen of the island state belongs to the ruling party, which has not ceased to be deeply entrenched in society and to hold a firm grip over a large share of the mass media. Locally born Taiwanese comprise 70.4 per cent of the party's membership, still less but much closer than in the 1960s and 1970s to the 83 per cent of the island's overall population that they account for.

Yet the ruling party is, at the time of writing, highly factionalised. In the Standing Committee of its CC there are, including Li Teng-hui, fifteen to sixteen reformists, eight traditionalists and eight or nine centrists. The reformists in the party leadership tend to be more moderate than some of the radical reformers among the KMT members in the Legislative Yuan and the National Assembly.

With approximately 40,000 members, the DPP is still an élite party. As we have seen, it is highly factionalised. But while the Standing Committee of the party's Central Executive Committee is currently dominated by a slight majority of the radical New Wave faction, the moderate Formosa faction succeeded in getting twenty of its thirty-eight candidates elected in the 1991 National Assembly elections. In contrast, only nine of the twenty-two candidates nominated by the New Wave faction and only six of the eighteen of the even more radical Taiwan Independence League faction were elected members of the Assembly. The DPP's major problem lies in the fact that it has not yet succeeded in developing a comprehensive and coherent policy platform.

In total there are (in late 1992) sixty-three political parties in the ROC in Taiwan. But the only one which may eventually gain some importance, apart from the KMT and the DPP, is the CSDP led by the German-educated former DPP Legislative Yuan member, Dr Chu Kao-cheng. This party has approximately 4,000 members and seems to be in control of reasonably large funds. With its consistent public policy platform of moderately social democratic persuasion, it seems to have made some impact in intellectual circles.

## Conclusion

What of the future of the KMT and the opposition in the ROC Taiwan?

With the exception of the National Assembly elections of 1991, electoral behaviour in Taiwan has actually been quite stable. In general, the KMT has steadily secured between 60 and 70 per cent and the opposition forces between 30 and 40 per cent of the overall votes.

One may well expect that in the elections for the re-constituted Legislative Yuan, which are scheduled for 19 December 1992, the KMT may fall back to a share of 60 to 65 per cent of the overall votes, while the DPP may again increase its share to 25 to 30 per cent or even more.

Although the issue of Taiwan's independence did not prove to be a strong vote-winner for the opposition, the DPP at present still supports the formal independence of the island from China. This insistence on the part of the DPP leaves three scenarios for political development on Taiwan after the elections. In the first place, if the DPP does not significantly increase its share of the votes, public support, and support within the DPP itself, for independence will further diminish. Thus the chances for developing a basic consensus on policies in the polity of Taiwan will improve. In the second place, if the DPP significantly increases its share of the votes, particularly if it should break through the 30 per cent mark, the agitation for Taiwan's independence will certainly intensify. This may well increase the danger to social stability on the island. Finally, if the results of the 1992 elections should be roughly the same as for the 1989 Legislative Yuan elections, they will increase confrontations in the political scene in the following years and will pose a danger to social stability. However, this will be less threatening than that raised in the second scenario.

# 6

## THE ELECTORAL MECHANISM AND POLITICAL CHANGE IN TAIWAN*

### Fu Hu

Despite the existence of a considerable number of works on political change, the role of the electoral mechanism in the transition of an authoritarian regime to a democracy is not adequately understood and is generally under-appreciated.[1] The existing literature on comparative democratic transition is mostly centred around social and economic factors as the independent variables, rather than around political ones such as electoral competition.[2] In my view, elections in Taiwan comprise the principal political mechanism behind changes of different kinds in this society. Such changes have, in turn, developed into a powerful

* The author wishes to acknowledge the valued contribution of Professors Yu-han Chu, Teh-yu Cheng and Shuang-lien Liang of the National Taiwan University, Dr Huo-yan Shyu of Academia Sinica and Professor Yin-lung Iou of Soochow University. He is also grateful to Dr Min-tong Cheng, Mr Chia-lung Lin, Mr Yu-tsung Chang and Mrs Wen-lang Chang for their excellent assistance and helpful comments. This chapter is based on the findings of a research project led by the author, with collaboration in some parts from Professor Yu-han Chu. The data base, including the results of three large-scale surveys on electoral participation, was collected under the research project and has proved highly valuable. Support for this research comes mainly from the National Science Council. Additional backing has also been received from the Central Elections Commission of the Executive Yuan. The views expressed here are those of the author alone.

1. Two notable exceptions are Paul Drake and Eduardo Silva (eds), *Elections and Democratization in Latin America, 1980–1985* (San Diego: Center for Iberian and Latin American Studies, University of California, 1986), and Bolivar Lamounier, "Authoritarian Brazil Revisited: The Impact of Elections on the Abertura", in Alfred Stepan (ed.), *Democratizing Brazil: Problems of Transition and Consolidation* (Oxford University Press, 1989).

2. There are many approaches. For the bureaucratic-authoritarian industrialisation model, see Bruce Cummings, "The Origin and Development of the Northeast Asian Political Economy: Industrial Sectors and Political Consequences", *International Organization*, 28 (2), 1984, pp. 253–64; and Guillermo A. O'Donnell, *Modernization and Bureaucratic-Authoritarianism: Studies in South American Politics* (Berkeley: Institute of International Studies, University of California, 1973). For the corporalist model, see Alfred Stepan, *State and Society: Peru in Comparative Perspective* (Princeton University Press, 1978). For the statist or historical-structural approach, see Thomas B. Gold, *State and Society in the Taiwan Miracle* (Armonk, NY: M.E. Sharpe, 1986). For world

political force for weakening the entrenched authoritarian rule and for pushing the democratisation process forward.

As in many other cases in the modern world, the authoritarian regime in Taiwan can essentially be described as an umbrella structure, with an hegemonic one-party system forming its backbone and with three main branches, "the ruling authority or élite", "political society" and "civil society", forming its supporting frames.[3] Through this structure authoritarian controls were dynamically transmitted through the one hegemonic party to the authority or élite, political and civil society. If the definition of democracy in a political society is that the people hold the freedom either to choose their ruling authority through competitive elections or to influence the policy-making process under different participatory modes, in a civil society it is that the people enjoy both individual and social freedom from the state, a state where the ruling authority is checked by the separation of power.[4] Then it can be said that the people of Taiwan, under the dominance of the said umbrella structure of authoritarian rule, were indeed lacking the full-scale freedom and rights of a liberal democratic society. This did not, however, rule out any practice of elections under the authoritarian regime. In fact, few modern authoritarian regimes in developing countries can exist without some form of a democratic façade.[5] However, the practice of

---

system theory, see Immanuel Wallerstein, *The Capitalist World-Economy* (New York: Cambridge University Press, 1979). A comprehensive discussion of modernisation theory on the relationships between levels of economic development and democracy in the 1950s and 1960s can be found in Charles F. Cnudde and Deane E. Neubauer (eds), *Empirical Democratic Theory* (Chicago: Markham Publishing Co., 1969). An intensive review of approaches on Taiwan studies can be found in Edwin A. Winckler and Susan Greenhalgh (eds), *Contending Approaches to the Political Economy of Taiwan* (Armonk, NY: M.E. Sharpe, 1988).

3. This theory was developed by Professor Fu Hu. For a detailed discussion, see Fu Hu, The Umbrella Structure of an Authoritarian Regime, *Twenty-First Century*, 5 (6), 1991, pp. 36–40.

4. This trinitarian definition of democracy can be found in Fu Hu, "The Myth and Practice of Political Democracy", paper presented at the Conference on the Democratic Future of China, Taipei, 1989. Hu believes that the transition to democracy involves more than a liberalisation of an authoritarian regime. Democratisation actually refers to the institutional establishment of political freedoms and rights in the state and in both political and civil societies.

5. For an insightful discussion, see Edward Epstein, Legitimacy, Institutionalization, and Opposition in Exclusionary Bureaucratic-Authoritarian Regimes, *Comparative Politics* (October 1984), pp. 37–54.

partial democracy with its limited underlying function is more instrumental than substantial in terms of securing a political monopoly by
one hegemonic party. In other words, a political system where there
are only partial and limited elections cannot be defined as a real democracy. Given such a distinction in our conceptions, we may regard partial
and limited elections as an independent variable when interpreting
the process of political change, whether it is de-authoritarianisation or
democratisation.

The elections held in Taiwan since 1949 have been partial and limited,
but they still produced a specific political mechanism which was conducive to the maintenance and transition of the authoritarian structure.
This political mechanism has been crucial and conspicuous in the following way: the effects of the elections are constantly changing, but their
impact has never diminished.

In this chapter I shall first give an historical account of how and why
elections were employed by the Nationalist Party or the Kuomintang
(KMT) as an instrumental mechanism to support its own authoritarian
regime. Second, I shall examine the impact of the elections, both as
a social catalyst and as a socialisation agent, on the structure of candidates and on voters' attitudes towards the regime. Third, I shall closely
examine the evolving process of the elections from authoritarian utili-
tarianism to the de-authoritarian mechanism and, most importantly, the
rise of the Democratic Progressive Party (DPP). A macro contour of the
emerging partisan competition between the KMT and the DPP will be
presented according to both the electoral turnout data and the survey
data for the 1983, 1986 and 1989 national legislative elections. In section
four, I shall deal with the nature and systemic significance of the recent
electoral competitions in terms of the social and political cleavages manifested in campaign issues and electoral choices at the level of candidates
and voters. Micro-level details will be further added to the profile of electoral competition. In the conclusion, I shall show how the empirical
findings shed light on the future of political change in Taiwan.

### *Elections and the consolidation of a one-party authoritarian regime*

After losing the civil war to the Chinese Communists in 1949, the KMT
regime moved to Taiwan with an authoritarian structure crippled and
in disarray. Even more serious was the challenge of winning legitimate
support from the Taiwanese people for its reconstruction and revival.
Only a little over a year had passed since Taiwan's restoration from

Japanese colonial rule when the tragic 28 February 1947 Incident took place.[6] The fifty-year-long historical separation and the trauma of the Incident made it easy for the Taiwanese people to harbour a "sense of being Taiwanese", thus creating a potential crisis over the question of their national identification with China. In addition, the fact that the political power of the KMT regime was dominated by mainlanders gave the Taiwanese people the impression of being under another type of colonial rule. These complex rifts between the mainlanders and the Taiwanese people had to be dispelled if the KMT regime wanted to secure the legitimate support of the Taiwanese people. Facing the double difficulty of dealing with a potential lack of domestic support from the Taiwanese people and an inner crisis of structural disintegration, the KMT's formula to re-establish its political authority over Taiwan was to create a theory of "revolutionary democracy". To secure the Nationalist revolution, the reform of the party structure towards one with more authoritarian control was favoured. In order to defuse any potential domestic unrest, a limited element of democracy was adopted to incorporate the Taiwanese people into the Nationalist political system. Allowing the domestic population to elect some public officials at a local level was, therefore, justified in order to achieve the necessary cultivation of domestic support for the ruling KMT. Certainly, "revolutionary democracy" gave the KMT a solid foundation in Taiwan. It satisfied the party's political élite who called for party reconstruction and, most importantly, won the support of the Taiwanese people for the legitimisation of authoritarian rule. The actual process and operation are outlined here.

First, based on an elaborate reform plan, the KMT restructured its organisation along Leninist lines with the leader at its core. The reframed system emphasised an anti-Communist revolution; the enforcement of martial law was justified under this banner. Under martial law the establishment of new political parties and newspapers was banned. The KMT regime also suspended some normal constitutional

6. On this date, there was a bitter and violent conflict between the mainlander-led Nationalist government and radical Taiwanese opponents, which ended in the bloody suppression of the radicals by the Nationalist army. This tragic incident has been widely mentioned and acknowledged ever since its occurrence, but it was not until the lifting of martial rule in 1987 that open discussion of it was no longer taboo. There are still serious controversies over its causes and effects among historians in Taiwan. We are not intending to look into this incident in detail in this chapter, except to refer to its traumatic character.

provisions in the name of "national mobilisation during the period of Communist rebellion".

After the conclusion of party reform, the function of the party apparatus was strengthened with the establishment of powerful functional units organised along both regional and sectoral lines.[7] At the grassroots level, the KMT utilised existing patron–client networks to establish a complex local political machine within the party structure throughout the island. Within each administrative district below the provincial level, the KMT nurtured and kept at least two competing local factions striving for public offices and other electoral offices in many quasi-state organisations such as farming associations and irrigation associations. More importantly, the KMT also allowed the local functions striving for a share of the region-based economic rents in the non-tradable goods sector to be distributed by the party-directed local spoils system.[8] Above the local level, the KMT controlled and demobilised all the modern social sectors through the pre-emptive incorporation of business and professional associations, labour unions, state employees, journalists, intellectuals, students and other targeted groups. The party apparatus filled all political space in society and party membership encompassed almost 20 per cent of the entire adult population.[9] Also, the KMT controlled the rents earned by natural monopolies and governmental procurement at national level and used the money to support the economic security of their loyalist followers. Finally, where indoctrination or cooptation failed, the security apparatus came into play. Under the rule of martial law, the security authority was prepared to suppress even a hint of political stirring. For the first three decades of its rule, the KMT faced a very disorganised and weak political opposition consisting primarily of defiant local factions which had no national political aims and posed little threat to the KMT's dominant position. Thus, for an extended period of time, the KMT successfully achieved a firm authoritarian rule in both political and civil societies through the use of factional clientalism and sectorial corporatism.

The second plan of the KMT's policy was its formal maintenance of a five-branch (Yuan) national government, with a functioning legisla-

7. See Edwin Winckler, "Institutionalization and Participation on Taiwan: From Hard to Soft Authoritarianism", *China Quarterly*, 99 (September 1984), pp. 481–99.

8. For an analysis of the mechanism for the cooptation of the local élite see Edwin Winckler, "National, Regional and Local Politics", in Emily Ahern and Hill Gates (eds), *The Anthropology of Taiwanese Society* (Stanford University Press, 1981).

9. The most recent figure of KMT party membership (1992) is reportedly around 2 million.

ture (Legislative Yuan) claiming to represent all the people of China, consisting of members elected in 1948 from the mainland. It also retained a four-tier administrative system designed for the whole of China, starting at national and then flowing down to provincial, county/city and town/borough level. This formal ruling hierarchy was indeed complicated enough, but the KMT never lost its control owing to the formation of the party-state-military triumvirate. Under this triumvirate, the relationship between party and government was hardly differentiated nor demarcated in terms of roles and interests.

Generally, key members of the cabinet were at the same time members of the Central Standing Committee of the party. In the legislative body, the representatives of party members were regarded as no more than loyal cadres. Party membership was always regarded as an asset and a necessary stepping-stone for anyone intending to follow a successful career in either the military or bureaucracy. In practice, the KMT dominated the decision-making process and monopolised the political resources of the state.

Thirdly, to bolster the legitimacy of the authoritarian regime, the KMT adopted limited home rule from 1950. The natives were allowed to elect their representatives up to provincial level and leading executives up to county/city level. Such elections were certainly partial and limited but, even so, still represented a step forward in the restructured authoritarian party system. The KMT utilised and manipulated the elections through its factional cliental. This enabled it to coopt the native élite and to incorporate local political and social forces into its superimposed party structure. Under such circumstances, local elections could only serve as an instrument for the KMT to consolidate its authoritarian regime. As a matter of fact, in the three decades before the mid-1970s the KMT was fully capable of controlling the elections and of successfully establishing support for itself in the very roots of society. As indicated in Table 6.1, the KMT faction candidates in the Provincial Assembly elections in 1950–85 always won by a large margin over the non-faction candidates, with an average of 83.32 per cent to 33.88 per cent. This clearly proves that the KMT authoritarian regime successfully gained electoral support through its practice of patron-clientalism.

## Impact of elections on cultural, socio-economic and political changes

As discussed above, the electoral system installed by the KMT regime at the local level was initially to have the effect of consolidating its legitimacy of one-party authoritarian rule. However, as local elections

Table 6.1.
LOCAL FACTION CANDIDATES IN PROVINCIAL ASSEMBLY ELECTIONS, 1950–85

| | 1950 | 1954 | 1957 | 1960 | 1963 | 1968 | 1972 | 1977 | 1981 | 1985 | Total |
|---|---|---|---|---|---|---|---|---|---|---|---|
| KMT Faction Cand. | 59.3% | 55.2% | 43.8% | 52.2% | 54.9% | 47.4% | 43.8% | 56.3% | 44 % | 42.6% | 49.95% |
| KMT Faction Cand. Elected | 75.4% | 78. % | 82.2% | 85.7% | 70.9% | 88.4% | 90.7% | 88.5% | 83.6% | 89.8% | 83.32% |
| Non-Faction Cand. Elected | 8% | 30 % | 39.7% | 40.3% | 47.2% | 38.4% | 43.6% | 42.5% | 18.8% | 30.3% | 33.88% |

*Sources:* Calculated from the Provincial Assembly Elections Data.

Table 6.2.
PSYCHOLOGICAL IMPACT ON VOTERS BY
ELECTIONS, 1986–9

|      | Most heavy % | Rather heavy % | Nothing special % | None % | Total % |
|------|--------------|----------------|-------------------|--------|---------|
| 1986 | 4.8(68)      | 18.6(264)      | 59.7(849)         | 16.9(240) | 100(1,421) |
| 1989 | 5.6(71)      | 18.2(232)      | 62.6(800)         | 13.6(174) | 100(1,277) |

*Sources:* See note 11.

continued, their recurring mechanism was gradually to transform both the nature and significance of the established authoritarian regime which the KMT was at pains to protect. Like a whirlpool, this recurring mechanism could both influence and absorb cultural, social and political changes in a "circumvolving function" with interactive dynamics which prompted the transformation process.[10] This delicate and dynamic process can be seen analytically in several areas.

Because of its competitive persuasion and all-pervading nature throughout society, across-the-board elections become the most effective agent of the political socialisation of the people, especially in a developing country. Lacking the empirical data on how local elections affected people from the 1950s to the 1970s, we can find this information from empirical research in the 1980s.[11] Table 6.2 shows that for citizen voters who responded, 23.4 per cent and 23.8 per cent, respectively,

10. For a detailed discussion on the concept of this function, see Fu Hu, The Circumvolving Function of Election and Political Development, keynote address at the Conference on Democratic Development of Modern China, jointly sponsored by the East Asian Institute, Columbia University, and the Association of Twentieth-Century Chinese History in North America, 23 September 1985.

11. My colleagues and I conducted three surveys for the 1983, 1986 and 1989 elections in February–June 1984, February–June 1987 and February–June 1990. The number of respondents from the island-wide population aged twenty years or more in each of the surveys was 1,629 (1983), 1,430 (1986) and 1,301 (1989). The surveys were based on multi-phased quota sampling at an individual level. City/county, district/town (or village) and precinct were selected by probability-proportional-to-size criteria; then quotas by electoral turnout were drawn, utilising both the official household registration data and the official elector registration record. For a detailed and more technical description of the sampling procedures, please refer to Fu Hu, Teh-yu Cheng, Min-tong Cheng and Yin-lung Iou, *Voting Behaviour of the Electorate* (in Chinese) (Taipei: Central Election Commission, Ministry of Internal Affairs, 1987), pp. 44–7; and Chia-lung Lin, "The Social Basis of the Democratic Progressive Party and the Kuomintang: A Comparative Study of Party Support among Taiwan's Electorate, 1983–1986" (in Chinese) (unpubl. MA thesis, National Taiwan University, 1988), pp. 67–79.

Table 6.3.
REFLECTIONS OF VOTERS ON ELECTIONS, 1986–9

|  |  | Positive % | No opinion % | Don't know % | Total % |
|---|---|---|---|---|---|
| Breaking through bounds of party politics and bringing new hope for democracy | 1986 | 40.0(128) | 6.6(21) | 51.5(171) | 100(321) |
|  | 1989 | 63.9(189) | 30.4(92) | 5.1(15) | 100(296) |
| Raising natives' position to take the lead in political development | 1986 | 9.1(29) | 9.4(30) | 81.5(260) | 100(319) |
|  | 1989 | 44.6(133) | 48.2(146) | 6.4(19) | 100(198) |
| Causing confusion over national identity and causing conflict between natives and mainlanders | 1986 | 10.5(33) | 10.2(32) | 79.4(250) | 100(315) |
|  | 1989 | 31.9(95) | 62.4(186) | 5.7(17) | 100(288) |

*Sources*: See note 11.

were most affected by the 1986 and 1989 elections of the members of the Legislative Yuan. A more significant finding was that among those who responded positively, there was an evident increase of 23.9 per cent (40 per cent in 1986, 63.9 per cent in 1989) in those who believed that elections were "breaking through the bounds of party politics and bringing new hope for democracy", as can be seen in Table 6.3. Also significant in Table 6.3 is the increase, by 53.5 per cent (9.1 per cent in 1986, 44.6 per cent in 1989), in the number of those who thought the elections were "raising natives' political position to take the lead in political development", while those reporting increasing worries about "causing confusion over national identity and causing conflict between natives and mainlanders" rose by 21.9 per cent (10.5 per cent in 1986, 31.9 per cent in 1989). Without doubt, the most striking effect of the elections was to provoke the people to greater political consciousness, as is reflected in their increased concern for political democratisation and Taiwanisation on the one hand and a conflict of identity on the other.

Our empirical research paid close attention to the basic political value-orientations or political culture of the voters in the elections of 1983 and 1989. To be comprehensively defined as outlined above, democracy was treated as a deconcentrated and responsible "ruling authority", a

Table 6.4.
## VALUE-ORIENTATIONS OF THE VOTERS, 1983–89

|  | 1983 | 1989 | 1983–9 change |
|---|---|---|---|
| Popular sovereignty | 68.3 | 76.2 | +7.9 |
| Individual freedom | 33.7 | 50.1 | +16.4 |
| Autonomous pluralism | 20.3 | 40.6 | +20.3 |
| Separation of powers | 46.8 | 64.4 | +17.6 |

*No. of cases*: 1,692 (1983), 1,301 (1989).
*Note*
Questionnaire included:
1. Two questions for "popular sovereignty": (1) No good for all people to claim to be owner of political power; (2) Should not disturb decision-making process of the government.
2. Three questions for "individual freedom": (1) Should not waste time in judicial process for punishing a cruel criminal; (2) Heterogeneous opinions would undermine social order; (3) Public opinion should be censored.
3. Two questions for "autonomous pluralism": (1) Too many social groups would break down the community harmony; (2) Too many parties would cause political disorder.
4. Two questions for "separation of power": (1) Checks and balances of power would make government ineffective; (2) Judges should accept the advice given by the executive branch.
*Sources*: See note 11.

sovereign and participant "political society" and a liberal and pluralist "civil society". Based on this trinitarian nature of democracy, we could further divide it into four principles for empirical observation of the electorate's value-orientations: (1) separation of powers, (2) popular sovereignty, (3) individual freedom, (4) societal freedom or autonomous pluralism.[12] The result of the voters' positive responses to these orientations can be found in Table 6.4.

If we follow Herbert McClosky's suggestion to set the level of 75 per cent of agreement as a "consensus" required by the characteristic of culture,[13] Taiwan's political value-orientations of culture as shown in

12. The orientation to democratic values was measured on a ten-item scale developed by Fu Hu and his colleagues. The items were designed to measure the respondent's value-orientation (approval or disapproval) towards five constitutive principles of a democratic political system, namely political equality, popular sovereignty and accountability, liberty, separation of power, and pluralism. For a thorough theoretical elaboration of the scale and an assessment of its measurement property, see Fu Hu and Min-tong Cheng, "Political Systems and Voting Behaviour: An Examination of the Construction of Theoretical Framework", *Proceedings of the Conference on Voting Behaviour and Electoral Culture* (in Chinese) (Taipei: Chinese Political Science Association, 1986), pp. 1–39. The original wording of all questions is available from the authors on request.
13. See Herbert McClosky, "Consensus and Ideology in American Politics", *American Political Science Review*, 58 (2), 1964, pp. 361–82.

*Fu Hu*

Table 6.5.
CULTURAL TYPES AND CHANGE, 1983-9

|  | 1983 | 1989 | 1983-9 Change |
|---|---|---|---|
| Traditional authoritarian | 23.5 | 11.1 | −12.4 |
| Modern authoritarian | 63.7 | 68.3 | +4.6 |
| Liberal democracy | 12.8 | 20.7 | +7.9 |

*No. of cases*: 1,692 (1983), 1,301 (1989).
*Sources*: See note 11.

Table 6.4 were hardly democratic. On a continuum from authoritarianism to democracy, the political culture of the voter respondents in 1983 fell into the category of authoritarianism. Popular sovereignty apart, this culture was also not free of the authoritarian shadow in 1989 because of the lack of consensus on individual freedom, autonomous pluralism and separation of powers. On the other hand, there was a shift of between 6.9 per cent and 20.3 per cent away from an authoritarian pole towards a democratic pole. Conceivably, as a momentum towards a political society, a consensus for popular sovereignty would in practice serve as a catalyst to push forward the changing process. Elections are beyond doubt crucial to contributing to the forming of this consensus.

For a more distinct and comparative observation, we can further distinguish three cultural types in the voters' responses to the four political value-orientations: (1) traditional authoritarian, indicating a negative response to all four; (2) modern authoritarian, indicating a positive response to at least one of the four; (3) liberal democracy, indicating a positive response to all four. A comparison of these types was made between 1983 and 1989; Table 6.5 shows that the majority of respondents fell into the modern authoritarian type with 63.7 per cent in 1983 and 68.3 per cent in 1989, an increase of only 4.6 per cent. A greater increase (7.9 per cent) was seen in the liberal democratic type, in contrast to a large decline in the traditional authoritarian type (12.4 per cent). By placing respondents in three categories of value-orientation types, the transitional nature of the political culture in Taiwan is fairly reflected in recurrent electoral participation.

In terms of the socio-economic structure, elections had influenced, and been influenced by, social changes in Taiwan. As they evolved, elections became the major instrument by which to assimilate the emerging economic and social forces into the political system. Facing recurring electoral challenges, the party-sanctioned local factional networks were more adaptable to socio-economic changes than the formal party apparatus. When traditional clientalist networks could no longer deliver votes as effectively as they had done previously, the faction-centred, or candidate-centred, clientalism was expanded to incorporate more secondary associations and regional business concerns, especially in the rapidly urbanised areas. Also, more and more new contenders were drawn into the electoral process competing for political access and economic privilege, since electoral success could be readily translated into instant social prestige and handsome economic gain. With an ever-expanding economy, both the cost and stakes of elections became ever greater for the established factions. Thus, as more social resources were mobilised into the electoral process, elections became more institutionalised. Elections became the institution in which the local political élite found their self-identity and upon which the entire local power structure rested. Increasingly, the national ruling élite found not only that they could not do without elections, but that they had to deal with rising pressure from both inside and outside the party for electoral openings at a higher level.

Coupled with the impact of both cultural and socio-economic changes, elections also incited political participation in terms of electoral activities in Taiwan. I have produced a Gutman-scaled framework to classify these activities into five types or levels according to their functional attributes in a political system:[14]

1. Sustaining (or supporting): serving to support the functioning of the electoral system. This included "reading candidates' campaign literature or reports about them" and "discussing the candidates' campaign with others".

2. Pleading (or petitioning): serving to appeal for or request more satisfactory outputs (or outcomes) from the electoral system. This included "urging relatives and friends to vote" and "making a date to go to campaign rallies with relatives and friends".

14. This five-level participation framework was elaborated by Fu Hu and his colleagues according to the basic concepts of the functional processes of a political system. The multidimensional participation ranked on the Gutman scale is also empirically proven. For a detailed discussion, see Fu Hu, "The Political Participation of Citizens on Taiwan", *The Proceedings of the Fourth Social Science Seminar* (Taipei: Sun Yat-sen Institute, Academia Sinica, 1985), pp. 363–97; and Min-tong Cheng and Fu Hu, "The Behavior of Electoral Participation of the People in Taiwan", *Bulletin of the Institute of Ethnology of the Academia Sinica*, B: 20, 1988, pp. 401–18.

3. Reforming: serving negatively to reject certain aspects of the electoral system and to demand their abolition or reform. This included "expressing doubts or criticism of the fairness of those managing the election" and "expressing dissatisfaction or criticisms of the electoral system and regulations".

4. Accelerating: serving positively to push forward the functioning of the electoral system by making various suggestions and exerting demands. This included "putting forward new ideas and suggestions for reforming the electoral system" and "suggesting that someone enter the election as a candidate".

5. Intervening: serving to intervene directly in the decision-making or

Table 6.6.
ELECTORAL PARTICIPATION AT FIVE LEVELS, 1983–9

|  | 1983 % | 1986 % | 1989 % |
|---|---|---|---|
| *Sustaining* | | | |
| Reading candidates' campaign literature or reports about them | 60.9 | 57.6 | 69.4 |
| Discussing the candidates' campaigns with others | 45.6 | 39.4 | n/a |
| *Pleading* | | | |
| Urging relatives and friends to vote | 33.9 | 51.3 | n/a |
| Making a date to go to campaign rallies with relatives and friends | 29.5 | 20.6 | 17.7 |
| *Reforming* | | | |
| Expressing doubts or criticism of the fairness of those managing the election | 7.6 | 14.1 | n/a |
| Expressing dissatisfaction or criticism of the election system and regulations | 6.1 | 11.6 | n/a |
| *Accelerating* | | | |
| Putting forward new ideas and suggestions for reforming the electoral system | 4.4 | 8.2 | n/a |
| Suggesting that someone enter the election as a candidate | 3.4 | 3.2 | n/a |
| *Intervening* | | | |
| Carrying out campaign activities | 7.3 | 5.3 | n/a |
| Personally serving as a candidate or campaign staff | 2.6 | 1.8 | 3.8 |

*No. of cases*: 1,692 (1983), 1,430 (1986), 1,301 (1989).

policy implementation process. This included "carrying out campaign activities" and "personally serving as a candidate or campaign staff".

The results of a comparative study of voter respondents in the 1983, 1986 and 1989 elections of supplementary members of the Legislative Yuan are shown in Table 6.6.

Owing to some revisions made in the questionnaire design, results of the 1989 election survey were not wholly comparable with earlier findings. However, we could still discern certain meaningful changes in the participatory structure, while the Gutman order of the five types or levels of participatory activities did not change much from 1983 to 1989. Most of the increases were witnessed at the higher levels of reforming, accelerating and intervening rather than in the lower ones of sustaining or pleading. For instance, in contrast to a decline in encouraging relatives and friends to go to campaign rallies, there were increases in expressing criticisms and putting forward suggestions for reform. In addition, the respondents who indicated that they had served as candidates or campaign staff increased from 2.6 per cent to 3.8 per cent between 1983 and 1989. These changes from lower-level participation to a higher level indicated that Taiwan's electorate were becoming more autonomous and sovereign-oriented towards democratisation.

As cultural and socio-economic structures brought about the changes as discussed above, the voices of Taiwan's political élites calling for broad and complete participation in politics grew so loud that they could no longer be contained by the "election plans" drafted by the KMT in the early years after it moved to Taiwan. If such voices were brutally suppressed, they could destroy the whole political environment. Therefore, the best strategy for the KMT was to tolerate them and to make concessions. It did this by loosening the revolutionary authoritarian system and accommodating calls for an enhanced democracy. The KMT had been able to maintain its authoritarian rule by relying on the theory of "revolutionary democracy", a means which is no longer effective. When reflected in the political structure, the following changes can be seen.

First, in the early elections, KMT nominees won with ease; in many constituencies, there was only one contender. However, as more and more of the party élite fought each other for nominations, disputes naturally increased. Then there were candidates who joined the elections by breaking party rules, as well as those who participated in the elections by withdrawing from the party. As they went unpunished the iron discipline of the authoritarian party lost its effectiveness. Under such circumstances, the KMT could not but relax the quota for candidates in some constituencies. For example, in the 1981 Provincial Assembly elections in which seventy-seven seats were at stake, the KMT nominated only thirty-eight candidates, leaving the remaining seats open for contention. The KMT adopted a primary system for the elections in 1989 but remained flexible in that party chapters could nominate non-winners in constituencies where the voting rate was less than 50 per cent. Though this flexibility was kept, the fact that the KMT started to adopt the primary system will doubtless greatly promote the democratisation of the party's authoritarian structure.

Second, as pointed out before, elections held in Taiwan were limited to local government and assembly seats. Elections for the governorship of Taiwan Province and parliamentary bodies were not open in the early years of the KMT's rule in Taiwan. As the pressure grew for wider political participation, the ruling authorities permitted elections for supplementary numbers of three chambers of parliament which was increased in 1980 and 1989. Elections had finally reached central government level after beginning at local government level. Indeed, all the senior members of the three representative bodies elected in 1948 on the mainland retired at the end of 1991. At the time of writing, more Taiwanese are expected to join the national ruling structure, which has been dominated by mainlander élites since 1949.

A third political consequence of cultural and socio-economic changes was the rise of a new breed of political opposition in the elections. With rapid urbanisation, diffusion of education and a general rise in material well-being, the opposition who dared to initiate an open challenge to the legitimacy of the KMT regime found more and more ready ears among an increasingly articulate, self-assured and economically secure electorate. This development culminated in the local elections of 1977, in which a loosely coordinated opposition group, bearing the label of Tang-wai (literally, "outside the party", i.e. the KMT), made considerable gains in contesting local and provincial electoral offices. From 1977, more and more activists dared to test the permissible limits of public defiance of political taboos.

On the eve of the aborted 1979 elections,[15] Tang-wai was firmly established with the forming of a formal island-wide campaign organisation—the Taiwan Tang-wai Campaign Corps. Afterwards, the

15. The 1979 elections were cancelled by the government at the end of 1978 immediately after the announcement of the normalisation of relations between the US and the PRC.

dissidents affiliated with Tang-wai moved cautiously towards forming a quasi-party despite the government's stern warnings of its resolve to enforce the legal ban on political parties. In the meantime, it became increasingly costly for the ruling élite to use repressive measures against popularly elected opposition leaders. To do this, the KMT regime had to pay a considerable price, at the cost of its own legitimacy as the ruling élite, as it soon discovered in the aftermath of the Kao-hsiung Incident, when a number of prominent dissident leaders were prosecuted and jailed for treason. After a short period of disarray, members of Tang-wai soon regrouped themselves and regained their electoral momentum in the 1980 elections. In the 1983 elections, the national leadership of Tang-wai was united under the Tang-wai Candidates' Campaign Support Committee, which established for the first time a formal procedure of endorsement. This *ad hoc* association was upgraded to a quasi-party organisation called the Public Policy Research Association in 1984. Finally, on the eve of the 1986 elections, a formal party, the Democratic Progressive Party (DPP), was formed.

This breakthrough had multiple effects on loosening the regime's authoritarian grip on society. It ignited a broadly based popular demand for political decompression and began the process of more rapid political liberalisation and democratisation. As a result, the KMT regime found itself reigning over a resurrected civil society expressing itself in the mushrooming of autonomous social groups breaking out of the out-dated corporatist strait-jacket in the upsurge of social protests and all kinds of contentious collective actions.[16] Thus cracks in the authoritarian order were widened even more and state power was substantially pushed back. Eventually the KMT regime was compelled to respond to these developments with an accelerated "Taiwanisation" within the party's power structure and a general political decompression culminating in the lifting of martial law and other long-time political bans on new parties and newspapers in the first half of 1987. As of 1992, more than sixty parties are registered with the government.

## The rise of the DPP in electoral competition

To understand the meaning of the rise of the Tang-wai/DPP in electoral competition, we need first to give an account of the popular support that came from the electorate.

16. See Yun-han Chu, "Social Protest and Political Democratization in Taiwan", *Political Science Review*, 1:1 (March 1990), pp. 65–88.

Table 6.7 presents a detailed tally of the percentage shares of the electoral votes received by the Kuomintang, Tang-wai/DPP and independent candidates[17] in the last four elections — those of 1980, 1983, 1986 and 1989. Owing to a system of dual representation,[18] the overall electoral return could be divided into two simple categories. In Table 6.7 the first section reports the percentage share of the total popular vote in the category of regional districts. The second section reports the percentage share in the category of occupational and aboriginal districts, and finally the third section reports the share of overall electoral returns.

As the data in Table 6.7 show, the Tang-wai/DPP candidates have gradually made inroads into the electoral competition since their meagre start in the 1980 elections. On that occasion, just one year after the Kaohsiung Incident, the opposition was in disarray. The hastily regrouped opposition camp had great difficulty enlisting enough candidates to run under the Tang-wai banner. Nevertheless, they still managed to place contenders in fourteen cities and counties (out of a total of twenty-one) and secure 9.5 per cent of the total return in the category of regional district votes and 8.28 per cent overall. Encouraged by the unexpected electoral gains, Tang-wai leaders stepped up their efforts to recruit more independent political figures. In the 1983 elections, under a new system

---

17. While it is very easy to tell the DPP candidates from the independents in the 1986 elections, it is not quite so straightforward to differentiate Tang-wai candidates from the independents for elections before the forming of the DPP. For the 1980 and 1983 elections credible sources can be readily found because in both elections Tang-wai candidates were formally united under some *ad hoc* national campaign organisations. Thus, for the 1980 elections, Tang-wai candidates are those identified by the Statement of Identification issued by the Association of Tang-wai Candidates for the Election of National Representative Bodies. See Lee, *The Forty-Year Democratic Movement in Taiwan* (Taipei: Independent Evening News, 1988), pp. 164–6. For the 1983 elections, Tang-wai candidates were those endorsed by the Tang-wai Candidates' Campaign Support Committee. See *ibid.*, pp. 189–91.

18. In Taiwan elections of national representative bodies are organised around a peculiar system of dual representation. While most representatives are elected from regional districts on the basis of more familiar geographical criteria, a disproportionately large number of seats are appropriated to six occupational districts on the basis of occupational criteria and two special districts have been set aside for the island's aborigines. This requires members of certain designated occupational associations and aboriginal voters to register on separate occupational or sub-ethnic rolls and vote on separate ballots. For example, in the 1986 elections, eighteen out of a total of seventy-two elected seats were appropriated to eight special districts which, however, only accounted for 13.3 per cent of total popular votes.

Table 6.7.

## ELECTORAL TURNOUT OF KUOMINTANG, TANG-WAI/DPP AND INDEPENDENT CANDIDATES, 1980–9

| | 1980 % | 1983 % | 1986 % | 1989 % |
|---|---|---|---|---|
| *Regional Districts*: | | | | |
| Kuomintang | 72.1 | 70.5 | 66.7 | 59.7 |
| Tang-wai/DPP | 9.5 | 18.9 | 24.6 | 29.7 |
| Independent | 18.4 | 10.6 | 8.8 | 10.5 |
| *Occupational and Aboriginal Districts*: | | | | |
| Kuomintang | 82.4 | 87.5 | 84.7 | 65.5 |
| Tang-wai/DPP | 1.3 | 3.1 | 6.9 | 19.9 |
| Independent | 16.3 | 9.4 | 8.4 | 14.6 |
| *Overall*: | | | | |
| Kuomintang | 73.64 | 72.86 | 69.06 | 60.6 |
| Tang-wai/DPP | 8.28 | 16.68 | 22.22 | 28.2 |
| Independent | 18.09 | 10.46 | 8.72 | 11.2 |

*Sources*: The electoral turnout data of individual candidates were provided by the Central Election Commission of the Executive Yuan, and the data of candidates' party affiliation were based on Lee, *The Forty-Year Democratic Movement in Taiwan* (Taipei: Independent Evening News, 1988).

of formal endorsement, Tang-wai-endorsed candidates contested all twenty-three cities and counties. Together they won 18.9 per cent of the popular vote in the category of regional districts and 16.7 per cent overall.

In contrast, the total popular vote received by the KMT candidates steadily declined from 73.6 per cent in 1980 to 60.6 per cent in 1989, and in the critical category of regional districts from 72.1 per cent to 59.7 per cent. The Tang-wai/DPP's total electoral gain rose from a mere 8.3 per cent in 1980 to 28.2 per cent in 1989. The most obvious changes took place in the total electoral returns for the independent candidates. These dropped from 18.1 per cent in 1980 to 8.7 per cent in 1986. It is clear that the rise of the DPP in electoral terms cost the independents as well as the KMT candidates. This also means that the rise of the DPP signified a transformation of the electoral opposition from an unorganised amalgamation of independent candidates into a formal island-wide political alliance.

Another important development accompanying the rise of the DPP is that more voters developed partisan attitudes towards one of the two parties. Apparently, owing to intensified electoral competition, the growing national significance that the elections acquired, and the increased symbolic meaning accorded to a party label, have accelerated the growth of partisanship among the electorate.[19] There also emerged a strong tie between a voter's party preference and his or her vote decision. To some degree, the DPP has successfully turned this limited electoral process into a political contest between the two parties at national level. The DPP exists not only as a party in name but is increasingly being viewed by the electorate as a party in practice.

In my post-election survey of the 1983 elections, more than half of the partisan voters indicated that they did not have a clear preference for either party (see Table 6.8).[20] Three years later, more than 70 per cent of partisan voters had acquired a party preference in one direction or another.[21] The chi-square statistics indicate that the positive association between party preference and electoral choice is extremely strong for the 1983 data and even stronger for 1986.[22] This partisan structure of the electorate has become an important and predictable source of electoral support. Both parties drew more than half of their popular vote in 1986 from the respective groups of party well-wishers.

In summary, the rise of the DPP in recent electoral competitions has been quite significant. While the DPP candidates have so far carried less than a quarter of the popular vote, the systemic meaning of its electoral

19. Of course, we do not rule out the possibility that this is also because more people have become more willing than before to express their party preference, owing to the general relaxation of the political atmosphere. However, this hardly explains why we witness a corresponding growth in party preference towards the ruling party.

20. In this and the following analyses, respondents who voted for independent candidates are excluded and only those who voted either for a KMT-endorsed candidate or a DPP-endorsed candidate are included, in order to make a clear-cut comparison.

21. Our items measure party preference, not party identification, which requires not just an attitudinal orientation towards a party but the development of a psychological attachment to a party. For a thorough discussion of different measures of partisanship, see Herbert Asher, "Voting Behavior Research in the 1980s: An Examination of Some Old and New Problem Areas", in Ada Finifter (ed.), *Political Science: The State of the Discipline* (Washington, DC: American Political Science Association, 1983), pp. 354–60.

22. I do not mean by this that many voters choose a particular candidate solely because of his or her party preference. I recognise that the importance of party preference in vote decisions needs to be compared with other factors. A comprehensive analysis of modes of voting decisions at an individual level is not of concern here; rather, I am interested mainly in assessing the significance of the rise in partisanship at the system level. For a comprehensive analysis of modes of voting behaviour, see Hu, Chen and Iou, *Voting Behaviour of the Electorate*.

Table 6.8.

GROWTH OF PARTY PREFERENCE AMONG ELECTORATE
AND ITS RELATION TO ELECTORAL CHOICE, 1983–6

*Year 1983*

|  | | Party preference | | |
|---|---|---|---|---|
|  | Pro-KMT | None | Pro-DPP | Total |
| Vote for | 427 | 443 | 44 | 914 |
| KMT candidates | 95.96% | 78.27% | 49.44% | |
| Vote for | 18 | 123 | 45 | 186 |
| DPP candidates | 4.04% | 21.73% | 50.56% | |
| Total | 445 | 566 | 89 | 1100 |
| *Chi-Square Statistic* + 133.5 | | *P* = .000 | *D.F.* = 2 | |

*Year 1986*

|  | | Party preference | | |
|---|---|---|---|---|
|  | Pro-KMT | None | Pro-DPP | Total |
| Vote for | 474 | 204 | 22 | 700 |
| KMT candidates | 94.80% | 78.16% | 19.47% | |
| Vote for | 26 | 57 | 91 | 174 |
| DPP candidates | 5.20% | 21.84% | 80.53% | |
| Total | 500 | 261 | 113 | 874 |
| *Chi-Square Statistic* = 328.9 | | *P* = .000 | *D.F.* = 2 | |

*Sources:* See note 11.

challenge is qualitatively different from its previous electoral opposition.
First, the DPP is a formal party organisation rather than just a statistical
sum of non-KMT candidates. With its leadership and organisation, the
DPP can integrate its popular support from various constituent bases
into a coherent national political programme. The DPP, as a party, has
already won its identity among a substantial portion of the electorate.
Its rise has actually bolstered the growth of partisanship among the electorate. More importantly, the DPP has built its electoral support largely
on the demand for a comprehensive political reform to realise majority
rule. To a degree, the rise of the DPP has elevated elections increasingly
to a test of the legitimacy of the KMT regime. Of course, much of the
above observation still needs to be substantiated empirically at the micro
level, to which we now turn.

## The social and political cleavages manifested in recent electoral competitions

My micro observations on the nature of electoral competition are at two levels — at the level of the candidate and correspondingly at the level of the individual voter. First, I examine the campaign manifestos employed by the candidates of the two camps to attract voters, especially those voting for an issue. This will help to verify the kinds of socio-economic or ideological interests that the KMT and DPP candidates respectively represented, or the kinds of social or political cleavages they intended to exploit. Next, I compare the social and political composition of KMT supporters with that of DPP supporters. This will reveal the kinds of social and political cleavages and the degree of their intensity empirically manifested in the electoral competition.

I apply content analysis to the platforms that the candidates prepared for dissemination in the official campaign bulletins of the 1986 elections. For a systematic comparison of the candidates' positions on issues, I have compiled a list of thirty-four often-cited issue statements extracted from the candidates' platforms as expressed in their campaign pamphlets, posters and official campaign bulletins in the elections of 1983 and 1986. Table 6.9 presents a complete list of those issue statements. Furthermore, to evaluate the systemic significance of these issue statements, I have grouped these thirty-four issue statements into three categories — national identity, political regime and public policy — depending on the level of political objects under concern. Within each category, items were broken up into their respective sub-categories. In Table 6.9, the four items belonging to the level of national identity were divided into two sub-categories: items underscoring the Chinese complex and items underscoring the Taiwanese complex.[23] The twelve items belonging to the level of the political regime were also divided into two sub-categories: items underscoring regime maintenance and items underscoring democratic reform. The eighteen items belonging to the level of public policy were classified into five sub-categories: items underscoring the concern for national development, social

23. The Chinese complex refers to a value-orientation which favours the ultimate unification of Taiwan with mainland China and insists on the inseparability of Taiwan and China both politically and culturally. The Taiwanese complex, on the contrary, favours a separate identity for Taiwan both politically and culturally.

Table 6.9.
CANDIDATES' CAMPAIGN PLATFORMS:
CONTENT ANALYSIS, 1986

|  | KMT candidates (N = 51) | DPP candidates (N = 17) |
|---|---|---|

### I. ISSUE POSITIONS WITH REGARD TO NATIONAL IDENTITY

*Chinese complex*

|  | KMT | DPP |
|---|---|---|
| 1. To adhere to the unification of Taiwan with mainland China on the basis of Three Principles of People, and oppose separatism and localism | 25 | 0 |
| 2. To love the national flag and protect the name of the country with a view to glorifying patriotism | 1 | 0 |

*Taiwanese complex*

|  | KMT | DPP |
|---|---|---|
| 3. Taiwan's political future should be determined by all the residents on the island of Taiwan | 0 | 17 |
| 4. To recognise the history, language and culture of Taiwan, with a view to deepening the identification with the land of Taiwan | 0 | 13 |

### II. ISSUE POSITIONS ON POLITICAL REGIMES

*Regime maintenance*

|  | KMT | DPP |
|---|---|---|
| 5. To strengthen the leadership apex and oppose defamation of the leader | 2 | 0 |
| 6. To have sympathy for the country's present unusual situation and give firm support to government policies | 0 | 0 |
| 7. To oppose mass protest and street demonstrations in order to maintain the order of society | 2 | 0 |
| 8. To maintain the harmony of society and ban the expression of radical political ideas | 0 | 0 |
| 9. Oppose too many political parties coming into being, and so enhance the nation's political stability | 0 | 0 |
| 10. To centralise political power and curtail external constraints to establish a government of high calibre | 0 | 0 |

[continued on next page

Table 6.9. *(cont.)*

|  | KMT *candidates* (N = 51) | | DPP *candidates* (N = 17) | |
|---|---|---|---|---|
| *Democratic reform* | | | | |
| 11. In favour of the general re-election of national representative bodies with a view to expanding political participation | 0 | | 17 | |
| 12. To oppose both the abuse of and the monopoly of political privileges | 0 | | 17 | |
| 13. To realise the independence of justice and completely eradicate the interference of politics | 1 | | 17 | |
| 14. To uphold the freedom of forming new parties, with all parties having equal opportunities to compete and to form a government | 0 | | 17 | |
| 15. To immediately lift the ban on martial law with a view to protecting basic human rights | 0 | | 17 | |
| 16. To lift the ban on establishing new newspapers and other mass media such as television stations, with a view to promoting freedom of speech | 0 | | 17 | |

III. ISSUE POSITIONS ON FIVE TYPES OF PUBLIC POLICIES NATIONAL DEVELOPMENT

|  | | % | | % |
|---|---|---|---|---|
| 17. To make good use of foreign reserves to promote national development | 8 | 16 | 13 | 76 |
| 18. To advance economic development and improve the environment for foreign trade | 24 | 47 | 15 | 88 |
| 19. To upgrade the transportation system and improve traffic conditions | 28 | 55 | 2 | 12 |
| 20. To promote research on leading-edge technology and enhance national defence | 15 | 29 | 0 | — |
| *Social security* | | | | |
| 21. To protect the right to making a livelihood for farmers, workers and fisherman | 29 | 57 | 15 | 88 |

Table 6.9. *(cont.)*

| | KMT candidates (N = 51) | | DPP candidates (N = 17) | |
|---|---|---|---|---|
| | % | | % | |
| 22. To take good care of veterans, reserve military personnel and the families of military personnel | 16 | 31 | 0 | — |
| 23. To increase the income of military personnel, civil servants and teachers | 31 | 61 | 0 | — |
| 24. To improve the income of the lower classes and narrow the gap between the poor and the rich | 5 | 10 | 4 | 24 |
| 25. To instal unemployment and health insurance for the entire population and increase welfare benefits | 42 | 82 | 17 | 100 |
| *Post-materialist values* | | | | |
| 26. To legislate a consumer protection law in order to protect consumers' rights | 16 | 31 | 10 | 59 |
| 27. To protect women's rights and eliminate discrimination against women | 18 | 35 | 15 | 88 |
| 28. To protect the ecological environment and eliminate environmental pollution | 42 | 82 | 17 | 100 |
| 29. To streamline the armed forces and shorten the duration of military service | 1 | 2 | 14 | 82 |
| *Improvement in foreign relations* | | | | |
| 30. To break through the diplomatic predicament and return to the international community | 16 | 31 | 16 | 94 |
| 31. To promote athletics as a national movement and take part in international competition in order to win honour for our country | 5 | 10 | 1 | 6 |
| *Administrative reform* | | | | |
| 32. To reform the tax system in order to ease the burden of the people | 30 | 59 | 6 | 35 |
| 33. To increase the police force and maintain law and order | 21 | 41 | 0 | — |
| 34. To keep government officials free of corruption and sweep away bribery | 26 | 51 | 15 | 88 |

security, post-materialist values,[24] improvement in foreign relations and administrative reform.

For content analysis, I went through the official bulletin to see which of the thirty-four statements or their equivalents were adopted by which party-endorsed candidates,[25] and then aggregated the findings to yield a sum at party level for each of the thirty-four items by counting how many candidates of the same party adopted a particular issue statement or its equivalent. The results are reported in the right-hand columns of Table 6.9. My analysis of the official campaign bulletin of the 1986 elections shows that the KMT and DPP candidates clearly diverged on issues in the categories of national identity and political regime, but converged on most issues in the public policy category. A common feature of the platforms of the DPP candidates is that they all highlighted issues concerning alternative views about the national identity. Statements underscoring self-determination and local identity were cited by all DPP candidates. DPP candidates also unanimously endorsed issue statements concerning democratic reform, such as "general re-election of the national representative bodies", "the freedom of forming new parties" and "protecting basic human rights". This is in direct contrast with the concentration of KMT candidates on public policy issues. As many as half of the KMT candidates took a clear stand on the issue of national identity. Nearly all, however, avoided taking a clear stand on the issues concerning the political regime. Unlike the 1983 elections, almost none of the KMT candidates during the 1986 elections stood up to defend the necessity or legality of the existing authoritarian arrangements.[26] This points to the possibility that many were to some extent tacitly in favour of issues concerning democratic reform.

On the issue items concerning economic growth, social security, post-materialist values, improvement in foreign relations, and administrative

24. For the concept of post-materialist values, see Ronald Inglehart, *The Silent Revolution: Changing Values and Political Styles among Western Publics* (Princeton University Press, 1976).

25. Only candidates who ran in the regional districts and who were officially endorsed by either the KMT or the DPP parties are included in the analysis. This includes fifty-one KMT-endorsed candidates and seventeen DPP-endorsed candidates. In the KMT camp, party endorsement means that candidates had received either party nomination or party approval. There was no such distinction within the DPP camp. See Lee, *The Forty-Year Democratic Movement in Taiwan*, pp. 189–91.

26. Because we only based our content analysis on the official campaign bulletin of the 1986 elections, it does not cover many issue statements concerning systems maintenance that were adopted widely by KMT candidates in 1983 and dropped by most KMT candidates in 1986. This contrast is in itself a significant indicator of the change in the island's political climate during those three years.

reform, the two party candidates converged most of the time. However, there was a major qualification in that the DPP candidates avoided all issue statements with the implication of enhancing state power. In contrast, many KMT-endorsed candidates adopted the issue position for a strong defence, for improving the welfare of civil servants, the military and veterans, and for expanding the police force.[27]

Our content analysis confirms the anti-system as well as the anti-state nature of the campaign waged by the DPP candidates. The DPP candidates and the KMT candidates were clearly differentiated on the issue of national identity. The DPP candidates had tried to set the tone of the elections in terms of regime legitimacy, while the KMT candidates tried to direct the focus of the elections on public policy issues. Also clear from our content analysis is that neither the KMT candidates nor the DPP candidates tried to project images in class or group terms: candidates of both parties made appeals to (or avoided offending) voters of all social stripes, from the business élite to the lower classes, from consumers to environmentalists, and from tax-payers to crime victims. The only exception is that only KMT candidates claimed to present the interests of state employees.

Much of what I have just said about the nature of the electoral competition based on an analysis of the candidates' platforms was echoed by what I found at the level of the individual voter. To examine the social base and value base of party support, I included four independent variables — value-orientation towards democracy, the attitude towards national identity,[28] sub-ethnic origin and socio-economic class[29] — in a

27. Specifically, they are items 20, 22, 23 and 33.

28. For the attitude towards national identity, two questions were introduced: "Do you agree or disagree with the following statement that, for the larger goal of the unification of the whole of China, we should readily renounce localism?" and "Do you agree or disagree with the following statement that to build a better Taiwan is more important than the unification of China?" Before combining the two to yield composite measure of the sentiment of national identity, a respondent's score on a Likert scale for the second question was inverted to align it with the first question.

29. According to occupation, each respondent was classified into one of the following six social class categories: farmer, labourer, state employee, middle-class, capitalist and other. The farmer category included rice farmer, dairy farmer and fisherman. The labourer category included manual workers and non-managerial white-collar workers in the private sector. The state employee category included civil servants, military personnel and policemen, employees of state enterprises, the KMT party and Youth Corps officials and public school teachers. The middle-class category included the professional, technician, engineer and manager. The capitalist category included shop owners and business people, large and small. Finally, the "other" category included housewives, students, the unemployed and the retired.

multivariate analysis. Only in a multivariate framework can the relative influence of each of these variables on a voter's party choice be evaluated when the effect of other variables and the complex interactive relation-shipships among them are taken into account.[30] Because most of the variables are categorical in nature, I conducted the analysis within the framework of the log-linear analysis,[31] as seen in Table 6.10.

Based on the log-linear analysis, we can gauge the nature of electoral competition in terms of the socio-political compositions of the two voter groups. First, as expected, mainlander voters are the most dedi-cated supporters of KMT candidates while Hakka voters are the least supportive of the three major sub-ethnic groups. Second, it is clear that KMT candidates drew relatively more votes from state employees, farmers, and housewives and retirees, the two largest groups in the category "Others", while DPP candidates gained relatively more sup-port from the middle class, capitalists and working class, all three classes in the modern private sector. This is a very significant result. It suggests that in Taiwan, a state-dominated society, the more salient aspects of socio-economic cleavage are not defined by capitalist production rela-tions but by state power. Economically speaking, the middle class, capitalists and working class are all relatively less dependent on the state and, socially speaking, it is more difficult to incorporate members of the three groups in the modern (and mostly urban) sector into the factional clientalist networks.

Equally significant is the finding that voters with positive scores on the democratic value scale are relatively less likely to vote for a KMT candidate than a DPP candidate by odds of 0.87. Also, voters with a positive score on national identity, i.e. in the direction of upholding Chinese identity, are relatively more likely to vote for a KMT candidate than for a DPP candidate by odds of 1.71. This shows that a value-orientation to democracy and a national identity attitude are signifi-cantly correlated with party choice even when the effect of a voter's sub-ethnic origin and socio-economic class, and the complex interactive relationships among them, are taken into account. Furthermore the direction of association is fully consistent with the findings of our content analysis.

30. Again, in this analysis, only the KMT voters and the DPP voters are included in order to make a clear-cut comparison.

31. For an introduction to the log-linear model, see Stephen E. Fienberg, *The Analysis of Cross-Classified Categorical Data*, 2nd edn (Cambridge, MA: MIT Press, 1981).

Table 6.10.
SOCIAL AND IDEOLOGICAL CORRELATES OF ELECTORAL
CHOICE, 1986: MULTIDIMENSIONAL LOG-LINEAR
ANALYSIS

| Effects | KMT | DPP | KMT/DPP |
|---|---|---|---|
| *Main Effect on Party Choice* | 1.752 | 0.571 | 3.07 |
| *The Effect of Origin* | | | |
| 1.  Min-nan* | 1.146 | 0.873 | 1.31 |
| 2.  Hakka* | 0.672 | 1.489 | 0.45 |
| 3.  Mainlander | 1.300 | 0.770 | 1.69 |
| *The Effect of Class* | | | |
| 1.  Farmer | 1.207 | 0.829 | 1.46 |
| 2.  Labourer | 0.917 | 1.091 | 0.84 |
| 3.  State employee | 1.174 | 0.852 | 1.38 |
| 4.  Middle class | 0.766 | 1.305 | 0.59 |
| 5.  Capitalist | 0.882 | 1.134 | 0.78 |
| 6.  Others | 1.140 | 0.877 | 1.30 |
| *The Effect of Identity* | | | |
| 1.  Positive | 1.309 | 0.764 | 1.71 |
| 2.  Negative | 0.764 | 1.309 | 0.58 |
| *The Effect of Democratic Legitimacy* | | | |
| 1.  Positive | 0.933 | 1.071 | 0.87 |
| 2.  Negative | 1.071 | 0.933 | 1.15 |
| *The Interactive Effect of Origin and Democratic Legitimacy* | | | |
| 1.  Min-nan | | | |
| (*a*)  Positive | 0.745 | 1.343 | 0.55 |
| (*b*)  Negative | 1.343 | 0.745 | 1.80 |
| 2.  Hakka | | | |
| (*a*)  Positive | 1.141 | 0.876 | 1.30 |
| (*b*)  Negative | 0.876 | 1.141 | 0.77 |
| 3.  Mainlander | | | |
| (*a*)  Positive | 1.177 | 0.850 | 1.39 |
| (*b*)  Negative | 0.850 | 1.177 | 0.72 |

*The Min-nan and Hakka are local people speaking different Chinese dialects. The former were
    originally immigrants from the Fukien province of China, and the latter from Canton province.
N = 953
D.F. = 105.    Likelihood-Ratio Chi-Square = 72.5    Prob. = 993
*Sources*: See note 11.

The relations between sub-ethnic background and party choice and between democratic value and party choice, however, are more complex than at first appears. Our model points to a complicated interactive effect of sub-ethnic origins and democratic values. Essentially, this means the relation between one's belief in democratic values and electoral choice is conditioned on one's sub-ethnic background. For Min-nan voters, a positive orientation to democratic values is negatively associated with voting for KMT candidates. For Hakka and, in particular, mainlander voters, the picture is entirely different. Mainlander voters who score positively on the democratic value scale are actually relatively less likely to support a DPP candidate. It is possible that mainlander and Hakka voters did not perceive the KMT regime as being as undemocratic as the DPP alleged it to be. Also, the two groups might regard the anti-system strategy of the DPP candidates as a little too disruptive for a stable transition to democracy, while Min-nan voters found the demand for democratic reform quite congenial with the emphasis on Taiwanese identity, given their dominant position in the island's sub-ethnic make-up.

Our log-linear analysis results allow us to ascertain that in Taiwan a substantial portion of voters are quite perceptive on the clear differences in political platforms between KMT and DPP candidates. There exists a high degree of cognitive congruence between voters' own political attitudes and their electoral choice. This suggests that the political strategy of the DPP candidates was, to a degree, effective, especially among the Min-nan voters. But only to a degree. In the final analysis the cumulative odds between voting for a KMT candidate and voting for a DPP candidate, considering every possible combination of social and political atttributes, are still far greater than 1.0 in most cases.[32]

32. The cumulative effect of two or more social and attitudinal attributes can be calculated by taking the multiplicative product of relevant odds. For example, a voter of mainlander sub-ethnic origin who is a state employee and takes a positive stand on national identity items is relatively more likely to vote for a KMT candidate than a DPP candidate by odds of 3.99. This figure is the product of 1.69 (the effect of sub-ethnic origin), 1.38 (the effect of socio-economic class) and 1.71 (the effect of national identity). By taking into account the base-line KMT/DPP odds ratio (3.07), we can infer that a voter with the above socio-political attributes is on the whole more likely to vote for a KMT candidate than a DPP candidate by a 12:25 ratio. Taking a more typical combination, a voter with Min-nan sub-ethnic origin who is a member of the middle class and takes a negative stand on national identity items is on the whole more likely to vote for a KMT candidate than a DPP candidate by odds of only 1.38, where $1.38 = 3.07 \times 1.31 \times 0.59 \times 0.58$.

Table 6.11.
ISSUE VOTERS AMONG KMT AND DPP SUPPORTERS, 1986 (%)

| | Issue voting | Non-issue voting | Total |
|---|---|---|---|
| KMT Voters | 195 | 558 | 753 |
| | 25.9% | 74.1% | 194 |
| DPP Voters | 65 | 129 | 194 |
| | 33.5% | 66.5% | |
| Total | 260 | 687 | 947 |

*Chi-Square Statistic* = 4.1     *D.F.* = 1     *P-level* = 0.043

*Sources*: See note 11.

The above analysis also suggests that the underlying political cleavages over democratic legitimacy and national identity issues are just as significant as social cleavages along sub-ethnic and socio-economic class lines. Socio-economic cleavage in Taiwan was less salient in past elections than in other developed counties because political and sub-ethnic cleavages cut across the socio-economic divide. Data also reveal a potential tension between issues of democratic legitimacy and Taiwanese identity, in particular in the eyes of mainlander and Hakka voters. It is possible that Hakka and mainlander voters worried about the entanglement of the demand for democratic reform with an emphasis on Taiwanese identity.

However, it is important to point out that the above multivariate model does not constitute a fully fledged model of voting decisions at an individual level. As the data of the 1986 elections' survey indicate,[33] only about one-third of the DPP supporters indicated that their chosen candidate's campaign issues had significantly affected their voting decision (see Table 6.11). The proportion of issue voters is even lower among the KMT supporters. Almost three-quarters (74.1 per cent) of KMT supporters indicated that other non-issue factors, such as a candidate's own calibre or character, party affiliation, and social connections in the form of lineage, communal affinity and group association, were influential.[34]

33. Just as in the log-linear analysis, in the following statistical analyses only KMT and DPP voters are included for a clear-cut comparison.
34. For a comprehensive analysis of modes of voting decisions among the electorate, see Hu *et al.*, *Voting Behaviour of the Electorate*.

For a further examination of the above issues, we can directly explore the issues which actually activated the issue voters and the KMT and DPP. In the survey, each respondent who indicated that his or her chosen candidate's campaign issues had significantly affected his/her voting decision was provided with the same list of thirty-four often-cited issue statements, and was asked to pick one or more items that he or she regarded as most appealing during the campaign. As in the earlier content analysis, the thirty-four items were grouped into three categories — national identity, political regime and public policy — and within each category items were further broken up into their respective sub-categories (see Table 6.9 for a complete list and classification scheme).

Table 6.12 shows the differences in issue preference between KMT issue voters and DPP issue voters. The figures indicate that ninety-three KMT issue voters (or as many as 47.9 per cent of all KMT issue voters in our sample) and only two DPP issue voters picked at least one of the issue statements underscoring the Chinese complex. Sixty-four DPP issue voters (or as many as 97 per cent of all DPP issue voters) did not pick any of the issue statements underscoring the Chinese complex. Also we see that 43.9 per cent of DPP issue voters found items underscoring the Taiwanese complex appealing, while only 5.6 per cent of KMT issue voters did the same.

The figures in Table 6.12 show that more than half (51.8 per cent) of the KMT issue voters found items underscoring the system maintenance appealing. Or to put it somewhat differently, of the 105 issue voters who picked at least one item in the system maintenance sub-category, 101 were KMT supporters. In contrast, 83.3 per cent of DPP issue voters picked at least one item in the democratic reform sub-category. Overall, all four sub-categories — the Chinese complex sub-category and the Taiwanese complex sub-category at the level of political community, the system maintenance sub-category and democratic reform sub-category at the level of political regime — are highly discriminant. Taken together, they can help us tell a KMT issue voter from a DPP issue voter with greater predictive power.

In contrast, public policy issues are not discerning at all. Table 6.13 displays the differences in issue preference between the two groups of issue voters over five sub-categories of public policy issues. Only issues emphasising improvement in international status can help us tell a KMT issue voter from a DPP issue voter. As the very high probability levels of chi-square statistics suggest, issues in the other four sub-categories

## Table 6.12. KMT AND DPP ISSUE VOTERS: NATIONAL IDENTITY ISSUES AND POLITICAL REGIME ISSUES, 1986

| | National identity | | | | Political regime | | | |
| | Chinese complex | | Taiwanese complex | | Regime stability | | Democratic reform | |
| | Yes | No | Yes | No | Yes | No | Yes | No |
|---|---|---|---|---|---|---|---|---|
| KMT voters | 93 | 101 | 11 | 184 | 101 | 94 | 62 | 133 |
| | 47.9% | 52.1% | 5.6% | 94.4% | 51.8% | 48.2% | 31.8% | 68.2% |
| DPP voters | 2 | 64 | 29 | 37 | 4 | 61 | 55 | 11 |
| | 3.% | 97.0% | 43.9% | 56.1% | 6.2% | 93.8% | 83.3% | 16.7% |
| Total | 95 | 165 | 40 | 221 | 105 | 155 | 117 | 144 |
| N = 260 | p < .000 | | p < .000 | | p < .000 | | p < .000 | |

*Sources:* See note 11.
*Note:* Refer to Table 6.4 for item composition of each type of national identity and political regime issues.

Table 6.13.

## KMT AND DPP ISSUE VOTERS: FIVE TYPES OF PUBLIC ISSUE, 1986

| | National development | | Social security | | Post-materialism | | International status | | Administrative reform | |
|---|---|---|---|---|---|---|---|---|---|---|
| | *Yes* | *No* | *Yes* | *No* | *Yes* | *No* | *Yes* | *No* | *Yes* | *No* |
| KMT voters | 67 75.3% | 125 74.0% | 108 73.5% | 86 76.1% | 58 74.4% | 136 74.7% | 26 60.5% | 168 77.4% | 94 73.4% | 99 75.6 |
| DPP voters | 22 33.3% | 44 66.7% | 39 59.1% | 27 40.9% | 20 30.3% | 46 69.7% | 17 25.8% | 49 74.2% | 34 51.5% | 22 48.5% |
| *Total* | 89 | 169 | 147 | 113 | 78 | 182 | 43 | 217 | 128 | 131 |
| N = 260 | p = .94 | | p = .73 | | p = 1.0 | | p = .03 | | p = .80 | |

*Sources:* See note 11.

attracted as many KMT issue voters as DPP issue voters. Clearly, in the eyes of the issue voters, the distance between the two parties was measured on a scale of system legitimacy rather than on a scale of policy performance. By now, it becomes quite clear that the electoral contest was centred more around alternative views about the political system itself than around the conflict of interest among clashing socio-economic classes, a result perfectly consistent with the result of our content analysis, and this is especially true for the issue voters. What is remarkable is that the conclusions are much the same for the electorate at large as revealed by our multivariate log-linear analysis.

## Conclusion: the prospect for democracy in Taiwan

My analysis has now come full circle. I have explored and illustrated the whirlpool functions of the electoral mechanism in Taiwan in terms of cultural, socio-economic and political changes. Indeed, the KMT's authoritarian rule has been considerably frustrated under this mechanism and some positive developments for the transition to democracy have already occurred. I should also point out that although the KMT has outgrown the stage of the hegemonic one-party system, a fully competitive party system has not been well established at the time of writing. Moreover, although competition between political parties has promoted and aroused an upsurge in social movements, the KMT still controls to a certain extent most social organisations, schools and the mass media. It appears that as the KMT's authoritarian rule wanes, the picture of a new civil society and political society is becoming clearer. Nevertheless, that picture is not yet very distinct because the society as a whole is not fully autonomous.

What is more worrying is that, while elections have pushed democratic reforms ahead, movements calling for Taiwanese identity and independence have entailed the entanglement of democratic reform with identity issues which would not only tend to push reform into oblivion, but also hinder the path of "transition through transaction"[35]; a polarised conflict might follow. By nature, the DPP's appeal for "a new

35. For an elaboration on transition through transaction, see Donald Share and Scott Mainwaring, "Transitions through Transaction: Democratization in Brazil and Spain", in Wayne A. Selcher (ed.), *Political Liberalization in Brazil: Dynamics, Dilemmas, and Future Prospects* (Boulder, CO.: Westview Press, 1986) and Donald Share, "Transitions to Democracy and Transition Through Transaction", *Comparative Political Studies*, 19:4 (January 1987), pp. 525–48.

country with a new constitution" is no longer political reform within the system but a political revolution of the system itself. With such an appeal on hand, elections can only work to win the people's support for revolution and enhance the legitimacy of oppositionists. Ironically, just like the KMT which developed the theory of "revolutionary democracy" upon moving to Taiwan, those oppositionists are in reality also using elections as an instrument to realise their revolution. If the opposition continues to appeal for a "new country with a new nation", what will be the impact on the KMT's authoritarian rule? In the past, the KMT has had to make political concessions and shrink revolutionary privileges in order to cope with the pressure of expanding political participation. If the expanding participation is transformed into pressure for revolution and independence, it will give the KMT every reason not to disentangle its authoritarian control further and to slow down the process of democratisation. From another angle, if the appeal of independence cannot win the people's support in elections, will oppositionists shelve this issue and turn to pursuing democratic reforms within the existing constitutional system?

From the above explorations it is clear that the electoral process precipitates political change which, in turn, tests the mechanism of the electoral process. What is revealed in this process of interaction is that elections are still at a crossroads in Taiwan and have not yet structurally stabilized under the framework of democracy. The future of Taiwan's electoral democracy remains uncertain.

# 7

# TAIWAN'S QUEST FOR IDENTITY IN THE SHADOW OF CHINA

## Thomas B. Gold

Objectively and subjectively, Taiwan's relationship with the Chinese mainland has never been consistent. Neither have the two ever been well integrated. Beginning in the 1970s, fundamental internal changes in Taiwan's social structure occurred simultaneously with a dramatic realignment in its ties with the global community, including mainland China. This has brought to the fore a questioning of Taiwan's identity.

This chapter explores the question of Taiwan's identity under the Chinese shadow as a political issue and then examines efforts to craft and define such an identity, primarily through works of culture.

### The triple Chinese shadow

Taiwan's economy, polity, society and culture all evolved under what I see as a triple Chinese shadow.

First is the geographic shadow. Located only 100 or so miles across the choppy waters of the Taiwan Straits from mainland China, events in Taiwan cannot help but be influenced more or less by the continent. Taiwan has performed various functions for the mainland by virtue of its geographical proximity. From its origins as a frontier settled primarily by peoples from the Malay and Polynesian regions, the island became one of the major recipients of emigrants from the mainland. These came in large part from southern Fukien Province (the Min-nan region), whose people also ventured to Hainan (China's second largest island) and throughout Southeast Asia. Taiwan was the base from which Cheng Ch'eng-kung marshalled forces in the hope of recovering the mainland from the Manchus in the seventeenth century. It was a spot where pirates and other renegades could hide and rest.

As a recipient of settlers from the mainland, the sparsely populated island fell under the shadow of Han Chinese culture, in particular that of Min-nan. The local dialect (Hokkien or Minnan) is the same as that spoken across the Straits. Popular religious beliefs are also similar, and

Taiwan's patron goddess, Ma-tsu, was a native of Fukien where she is worshipped as well. Confucian ethics were also brought over and Taiwan's emerging gentry élite duplicated the practices of its counterpart on the mainland, including studying the classics, taking the civil service examinations and performing a number of quasi-official tasks in their communities. The Confucian family system became dominant. Even though settlers may have changed the identification of their "native place" (*lao-chia* or *chi-kuan*) from the mainland to Taiwan, there was no escaping the fact that they constructed a Han Chinese social, political, economic and cultural system on the island. Some travelled back and forth regularly, maintaining close contacts with relatives on the mainland, even to the extent of keeping property there.[1]

The second type of Chinese shadow is the government of the Republic of China (ROC) which re-established itself in Taiwan after it was driven off the mainland by the Chinese Communists in 1949. Taiwan had been liberated from fifty years of Japanese occupation in 1945, regaining its status as a Chinese province, when it suddenly found itself the temporary seat of the ROC state apparatus under the leadership of the Kuomintang (KMT), or Nationalist Party. The KMT moved quickly and ruthlessly to establish its hegemony over the island and to lead the interrelated spheres of economic, political and cultural life in civil society. Having been reorganised in the early 1920s by agents of the Comintern as a Leninist-style organisation, although without a Marxist ideology, the KMT imposed a corporatist political structure on the island, ensuring that there was only one officially recognised organisation to represent particular social interests, and that the party monopolised appointments to public offices as well as government activities and political life more generally. The educational system, media and cultural affairs were under the direct and pervasive control of party leadership and censorship (sometimes self-imposed). Mandarin was taught as the official national language and the use of Taiwanese dialect in the media was drastically curtailed. The calendar adopted the system of counting years based on the founding of the ROC in 1911. Thus, 1970 became "Year 59 of the Republic".

All of this was nominally in the interests of the larger goal of recovering the mainland from the Communists. All other parochial interests

---

1. An excellent study of the evolution of a migrant family to gentry status is Johanna Menzel Meskill, *A Chinese Pioneer Family* (Princeton, NJ: Princeton University Press, 1979).

had to be sacrificed in order that all forces be mobilised for this over-riding sacred mission. In the terms of Antonio Gramsci, the KMT constructed a "collective national-popular will", articulating what it determined was the dominant ideology.[2] It did not tolerate heterodox challenges to this orthodoxy. This attitude grew out of the party's Leninist heritage but found conducive soil in China's traditional intoler-ance of heterodox ideas or organisations.

Taiwan thus became, in the KMT's view, the location of the legiti-mate government of all of China. The United States and most of the rest of the world acceded in this. The island thus had to bear an extremely heavy political burden. This became weightier. The Communists declared war on traditional Chinese culture and religion, attacking Con-fucian values, destroying temples, torturing practitioners and scholars of tradition, banning traditional operas and other literary works and trying to create fundamentally new types of individuals and personal relation-ships. The Nationalists, in response, promoted a revival of Chinese tradi-tion, teaching Confucianism in the schools, promoting traditional art forms, sponsoring some traditional practices and permitting others. This is ironic, as the KMT, like the Communist Party, grew out of the iconoclastic May Fourth Movement of the 1910s, which spearheaded an attack on Chinese tradition as the major obstacle to the country's moder-nisation and ability to withstand imperialist aggression.[3]

Although the regime acknowledged that Taiwan had regional partic-ularities, like any other locality in China, the KMT assiduously pro-moted the idea that the island was the repository and guarantor of Chinese tradition as well as the mainland's rich diversity.[4] The national political bodies, such as the Legislative Yuan and National Assembly, kept in place delegates representing mainland districts even though they were divorced from their constituents. Regional cuisines and operas flourished and native place associations were established. Popular culture stressed mainland roots, addressing history and life on the mainland, not the island. Politically and to some extent culturally, then, Taiwan

2. Chantal Mouffe, "Hegemony and Ideology", in Chantal Mouffe (ed.), *Gramsci and Marxist Theory* (London: Routledge and Kegan Paul, 1979), pp. 168–204.

3. Myron L. Cohen, "Being Chinese: The Peripheralization of Traditional Identity", *Daedalus*, 120 (?), Spring 1991, pp. 113–34, 129.

4. This is one way in which Taiwan differs from such other peripheral Chinese societies as Hong Kong and Singapore. Neither of them makes political claims over the mainland or conceives of itself as having any particular mission *vis-à-vis* Chinese history, culture or politics.

became a microcosm of pre-1949 mainland China as interpreted by the KMT.

Ironically, while telling its people that Taiwan was an integral part of China, the KMT forbad contacts with the mainland, establishing in effect a great wall across the Straits. The works of significant but left-wing modern Chinese writers such as Lu Hsun, Pa Chin, Mao Tun, Ting Ling, Ts'ao Yu and others were banned in the island, meaning that the people of Taiwan had extremely limited knowledge of events on the mainland after the Northern Expedition of 1926–28.[5]

The third Chinese shadow cast over Taiwan is that of the Communist-led People's Republic of China (PRC). It has occupied the mainland since 1949 and has oscillated in its threats to Taiwan. In the 1950s it employed military means to attack the offshore islands occupied by Nationalist troops. In the 1960s and 1970s it promised to "liberate Taiwan". Since the 1980s, it has advocated reunification under the promise of "one country, two systems". The Chinese Communist Party (CCP) has urged the KMT to engage in party-to-party talks. It has encouraged it to abandon its "three-no policy" (no negotiation, no compromise, no contact) and open the "three exchanges" of mail, trade, and air and shipping. Beginning in the late 1980s, the PRC actively solicited Taiwanese capital investment, trade and tourism. However, it has refused to renounce the use of force should Taiwan declare independence or go nuclear. (This formerly included an alliance with the Soviet Union, but since the USSR's dissolution in 1991, the status of this condition is unclear.) So the Chinese mainland under the CCP remains, in many ways, the final arbiter of events in the island of Taiwan.

The Communists have also tried to keep Taiwan, as the ROC, out of international organisations where it might be considered some sort of legitimate political entity separate from China. The ROC has maintained its seat in the Asian Development Bank, which it joined after the PRC was established, but it has lost its seat in virtually every other international organisation to Peking. In recent years it has rejoined some of them in the guise of a local authority – Chinese-Taipei, for instance. At the time of writing, Taiwan is coming very close to rejoining the GATT, an organisation which Peking also dearly wishes to join. Taipei has come up with the clever moniker, "Customs Territory of Taiwan,

---

5. Despite the ban, the works of some of these authors, Lu Hsun in particular, circulated underground in Taiwan.

Penghu, Kinmen and Matsu" for this purpose. Peking maintains that even this entity cannot join until the PRC is admitted.

In sum, Taiwan cannot escape its geographical, cultural or political situation under the shadow of China. Late in their occupation, the Japanese tried to eradicate Chinese culture and remake the Taiwanese as Japanese.[6] It is unclear how deeply or widely this campaign penetrated; in any event, that the Japanese committed energy and resources to this conversion is a testimony to the strength of Chinese tradition in the island. The Han who emigrated brought their Chinese traditions with them. Since 1945 the KMT and the CCP have identified Taiwan as a province of China, whatever the country's official name might be.

## The identity question

Political regimes may determine an official "identity" for a people but, subjectively, the identified may contest this designation. The last decade of the twentieth century has witnessed a tragic, almost inconceivable explosion of ethnic conflict. This has occurred with particular ferocity in some parts of the world where it had been assumed that tight political control, enforced assimilation and time had soothed away age-old hatreds. I have Yugoslavia and the former Soviet Union in mind. As sociologists see it, "ethnicity refers to cultural practices and outlooks of a given community that set them apart from others".[7] This differs from "race", which refers primarily to physical characteristics and which is to a large extent a concept imposed by other groups. Of course, the two often overlap, but the important thing is that ethnicity relates to *self-identification* as a distinct group.

Theories of ethnicity abound, but one factor worth noting is the way this "self-identification" grows out of one group's interrelations with other groups, which may include the state.[8] Dru Gladney argues

6. Ch'en Hsiao-ch'ung, "1937–1945 Nien T'ai-wan Huang-min-hua Yun-tung Shu-lun" (An Account of the 1937–1945 Taiwan *kominka* Movement), in Ch'en K'ung-li (ed.), *T'ai-wan Yen-chiu Shih-nien* (Ten Years of Research on Taiwan) (Hsia-men University Press, 1990), pp. 362–79.

7. Anthony Giddens, *Introduction to Sociology* (New York: W. W. Norton, 1991), p. 298.

8. See the very interesting discussion in Hill Gates, "Ethnicity and Social Class", in Emily Martin Ahern and Hill Gates (eds), *The Anthropology of Taiwanese Society* (Stanford University Press, 1981), pp. 241–81, especially pp. 243–9.

that "the notion of *Han zu* or *Han min* (Han nationality) is an entirely modern phenomenon".[9] It grew out of Dr Sun Yat-sen's efforts to mobilise all Chinese against the Manchu's Ch'ing dynasty. Sun contended that there were five Chinese peoples: Han, Manchu, Mongol, Tibetan and Muslim. The Communists assert that among the Chinese (*Chung-kuo jen*) there are now fifty-six groups—they use the term "nationalities" (*min-tsu*; there is no separate word for "ethnicity" in Chinese)—the Han and fifty-five minorities (*shao-shu min-tsu*). Some of these are amalgams of groups which the Communists put together.

China is a geographically enormous country and history and topography have combined to create significant differences within the Han. No one denies the distinct regional disparities of dialect, cuisine, popular beliefs and to some extent dress and physique. A major source of Chinese humour derives from mocking the dialects and peculiarities of people from different regions of the country. The Han resist using the term *min-tsu* to label such differences. However, I agree with Harry Lamley that it is perfectly proper to use the term "sub-ethnic" to refer to subcultural distinctions within the Han.[10] Members of such groups do not deny they are Han but also strongly identify with their native place. This continues in many cases even if they have moved elsewhere. I have met Shanghainese who migrated to places as different as Hsi-an and Kui-yang (and Taiwan, of course) who still speak Shanghai dialect, eat Shanghai food and maintain a strong sense of being Shanghainese, all hallmarks of "ethnicity".

In the Taiwan case, this sub-ethnic self-identification can have at least two dimensions. It can mean the "native" Taiwanese (those whose ancestors came to the island prior to 1945) as opposed to people from other provinces, and also differences among the Taiwanese. The latter refers on the one hand to immigrants whose native places were Ch'uan-chou or Chang-chou in Fukien, and the Hakka, most of whom came from Kwangtung Province and speak a very different dialect from Min-nan, Cantonese or Mandarin. These groups engaged in often violent conflicts in Taiwan during the Ch'ing dynasty.[11] In fact,

9. Dru C. Gladney, *Muslim Chinese: Ethnic Nationalism in the People's Republic* (Cambridge, MA: Harvard University Press, 1991), p. 82.

10. Harry J. Lamley, "Subethnic Rivalry in the Ch'ing Period", in Ahern and Gates (eds), *The Anthropology of Taiwanese Soviety* pp. 282–318.

11. In addition to Lamley, *ibid.*, see Hsu Wen-hsiung, "Frontier Social Organization and Social Disorder in Ch'ing Taiwan", in Ronald G. Knapp (ed.), *China's Island Frontier* (Honolulu: University of Hawaii Press and Research Corporation of the University of Hawaii, 1980), pp. 87–105; and Meskill, *A Chinese Pioneer Family*.

Taiwan had a terrible reputation for social unrest and violence. Fifty years of Japanese rule and then KMT governance erased many of these mainland-based differences among the Taiwanese. However, there remain self-conscious distinctions, albeit much slighter, among Taiwanese in Taiwan today, such as those from Taipei and those from T'ai-chung or Kao-hsiung, for instance. These distinctions are primarily dialect-based.

The issues of a "Taiwan identity" and who can share in it are fraught with sensitive and dangerous political implications. If the term is used to refer only to "Taiwanese", namely those whose "native place" (*chi-kuan*) is listed as "Taiwan" (*pen-sheng-jen*, i.e. people of this province) in government records, then it excludes people from other provinces (*wai-sheng-jen*, usually translated "mainlanders"). At the extreme, this could open the gates to an expulsion, potentially violent, of non-Taiwanese from positions in the government and even from the island itself. All citizens of the ROC have an official "native place" in their identity papers. This is passed through the father, so the grandchildren of a man born on the mainland share his native place, even if they have never set foot there. Should an expulsion of mainlanders occur, where do these descendants fit?

If "Taiwan identity" means "who does this island belong to?" it raises issues of the very legitimacy of the KMT's rule. The KMT has based its monopoly over Taiwan's political system on its claim to be the legitimate government of all of China, temporarily squeezed into one province. In this view, it has to maintain representatives from the entire nation in key positions to keep alive the idea of a continent-wide Republic of China, and to remain prepared for eventual recovery of the entire territory. If the people of Taiwan determine that they do not want to carry this burden but prefer to identify themselves as only the citizens of this island, whatever it is called as a country, then the KMT's legitimacy as the dominant force in the island, as well as the arbiter of the "collective national-popular will" is at stake. Admittedly, the KMT underwent a very dramatic "Taiwanisation" in the 1980s and early 1990s and is no longer identifiable as a "mainlander" party. But it officially keeps alive the idea that Taiwan has a special and sacred role to play in Chinese national politics. So questioning this and raising the idea of a unique "Taiwan identity" as well as "self-determination" by the people of the island as to its future, are political dynamite.

Naturally, the Communists see this too. So the issues of a Taiwan or Taiwanese identity and that of self-determination raise tensions in Peking and fortify the PRC's resolve not to renounce the use of force should this trend culminate in a declaration of independence. The Communists can bear with the increased presence of Taiwanese in the regime, if that is the basic essence of the demand for "self-determination" raised by many opposition politicians. But they sense that it really means independence, which they cannot tolerate.[12]

The issue of a separate Taiwan identity has broader international implications as well. Should there be a move to translate this idea of a distinct identity beyond self-determination to independence, then other countries would be compelled to consider recognising this new country and thereby incurring the wrath of the PRC. When the ROC tries to join or rejoin international organisations, or when there is a massive popular demonstration for Taiwan's admission to the United Nations, other countries need to consider not only their own interests but what the PRC might do to retaliate (primarily in relation to trade), should they opt to recognise Taiwan as a separate political entity from the PRC.

## The evolution of identity as an issue

In this section, I will review the conjunctural changes in Taiwan's internal social structure, political system and relation with the rest of the world, as well as changes on the mainland and the global political system, which have given rise to the current effort to define a Taiwan identity.

Although the issue of Taiwan's international status has been raised from time to time,[13] the decade of the 1970s significantly heightened the problem. It began in 1971 with the ROC's failure to recover a group of potentially oil-rich islands (Tiao-yu-t'ai) occupied since the end of World War II by the United States. The Americans turned them over to Japan and the KMT could only protest weakly. This brought an

12. Lin Chin, " 'T'ai-wan tzu-chueh' Li-lun Chi-pen T'e-cheng Fenhsi" (Analysis of the Basic Features of the Theory of "Taiwan self-determination"), in Chu T'ien-shun (ed.), *Tang-tai T'ai-wan Cheng-chih Yen-chiu* (Research on Contemporary Taiwan Politics) (Hsia-men: Hsia-men University Press, 1990), pp. 220–33. Lin suggests that the KMT secretly supports this movement as a way of maintaining anti-Communism and its ultimate control. Also, Chu T'ien-shun, "Hsi-p'ing 'Chung-kuo I-shih' yu 'T'ai-wan I-shih' ti Chiu-ke" (Analysis of the Dispute over "Chinese Consciousness" and "Taiwan Consciousness"), pp. 234–47 in the same volume.

13. For a review of the issues, see Ralph N. Clough, *Island China* (Cambridge, MA: Harvard University Press, 1978).

uncharacteristic outburst by patriotic and frustrated university students and ROC citizens abroad.

Possibly the seminal event was the assumption in 1971, after many years of failure, of the China seat in the United Nations by Peking. The ROC delegates left in humiliation. Just prior to the UN vote permitting this, American National Security Adviser Henry Kissinger, acting on behalf of President Richard Nixon, made a secret visit to Peking to begin negotiations on normalisation of relations. Nixon, as staunch a foreign supporter of the KMT as anyone, visited the mainland the following February and signed the Shanghai Communiqué with Premier Chou En-lai. In the Communiqué, the United States "acknowledged" that Chinese on both sides of the Straits "maintain" that there is only one China, including Taiwan. The US did not "challenge that position". During the first years of the decade there was a general sense of panic in the island, and a high rate of emigration, of mainlanders in particular.

Over the course of the 1970s, virtually every country in the world which had recognised the ROC as the legitimate Chinese government shifted its diplomatic ties to the PRC. In the middle of the decade, Indochina became Communist and the Americans stepped up their withdrawal from the region. In January 1979, the United States recognised the PRC. Although it had been in the works for some time, this move set off another round of panic in Taiwan. By losing its international status as the ROC, including the support of its closest ally, the mainlander-dominated regime thereby lost the fundamental pillar legitimising its monopoly over Taiwan's politics. It tried to take the high ground, arguing that although Communist-inspired international perfidy had compromised the morals of other countries, which had then abandoned the ROC, the KMT itself would not surrender. Rather, it would redouble its efforts to maintain the dream of mainland recovery. But such bravado could not convince most citizens, who felt increasingly humiliated by their international isolation and new status as a pariah state up there with Israel and South Africa.

The 1980s saw the convergence of several domestic and international trends which had further impact on the question of Taiwan's identity. In particular, they raised, increasingly publicly, questions about the KMT's right to monopolise the definition of the collective national-popular will and to dominate what Marxists refer to as the "superstructure", namely the system of laws, values, education, media, popular culture and political activities.

Taiwan's economic growth had brought in its wake a number of fundamental social structural changes which affected the KMT's ability to maintain the sort of close or uninhibited control over society that it had established in the 1950s as a result of its autonomy from local society.[14] First, along with industrialisation, labour shifted increasingly from the primary sector to the secondary. In 1952, 56.1 per cent of the labour force was in the primary sector; by 1990 this figure was down to 12.9 per cent. Manufacturing saw a rise from 12.4 per cent to 32 per cent over the same period.[15] Although Taiwan's industries are widely dispersed, nonetheless there was a significant migration from the countryside to the cities.

The government invested heavily in education, so that by 1991 the illiteracy rate was below 7 per cent (down from 42.1 per cent in 1952), and by 1990 no less than 57 per cent of the population aged sixteen years or more had completed secondary school.[16] Official *per capita* income passed US$8,800 in 1991.

From the 1960s on, Taiwan's economy became increasingly internationalised. Exports drove the phenomenal growth and foreign investors poured in. Taiwan's business community had to become conversant with international ways of conducting business. They needed to travel extensively. Seeing the world and opening to the world, through investment, tourism and foreign — mostly American — popular culture, society became more cosmopolitan. So, both structurally and in terms of consciousness, Taiwan's society grew quite complex, much too complex and tied to global affairs to be administered in an authoritarian fashion by a small tightly knit cohort. The KMT's legitimacy came to be based increasingly on continued economic growth as the opportunity to recover the mainland faded. As a result, it concentrated its efforts on improving the investment climate for domestic and foreign capital, requiring continued opening up.

Of course, the KMT itself had changed over the course of these decades.[17] It recruited increasing numbers of Taiwanese and, under

14. On the relative autonomy of the KMT state from Taiwanese society, see Thomas B. Gold, *State and Society in the Taiwan Miracle* (Armonk, NY: M.E. Sharpe, 1986), especially Chapter 5.

15. Council for Economic Planning and Development, *Taiwan Statistical Data Book, 1991* (Taipei: Executive Yuan), p. 16.

16. *Ibid.*, p. 7.

17. I discuss much of this in more detail in Thomas B. Gold, "Taiwan in 1988: The Transition to a Post-Chiang World", in Anthony J. Kane (ed.), *China Briefing, 1989* (Boulder, CO: Westview Press, 1989), pp. 87–108.

President Chiang Ching-kuo, promoted many of them into responsible leading positions in the party and state. These Taiwanese included Chiang's successor, Li Teng-hui. These new recruits, Taiwanese and mainlanders, were younger, better educated and more cosmopolitan than their elders, which influenced internal party affairs as well as the party's relations with society. Because the KMT held elections for both local and (some) national bodies, the citizens of Taiwan gained experience of electoral politics. Social change and change within the party inhibited Taiwan's political centre.[18] This increasingly emboldened dissidents who began publicly to raise previously taboo sensitive issues.

In the middle of the decade there were also some scandals which had serious impact on the KMT's domestic prestige, resulting in what some saw as a profound crisis of confidence.[19] One such scandal was the involvement of top security officials in the assassination, in Daly City, California, of the writer Henry Liu (Chiang Nan) who had been preparing an unflattering biography of Chiang Ching-kuo. There was also a major financial scandal involving top cabinet members and the Tenth Credit Cooperative, an organ of the Cathay Business Group. These occurred against the background of a serious economic downturn, lack of effective or imaginative leadership by the state, and concerns over Chiang Ching-kuo's health and choice of successor.

In addition to objective structural change, Taiwan's citizens began to take more initiative in social and political affairs. Although these figures are not further disaggregated, there has been an explosion in the number of civic organisations in Taiwan. These numbered 2,560, with a membership of 1.3 million people, in 1952 and increased to 13,766 in 1990, with a membership of 10.9 million individuals and 241,964 groups.[20] Of course, many of these are established and run by the party, but increasingly, especially with the passage of the Civic Organisations Law in 1989, they are autonomous. This indicates the dramatic expansion of civil society in this once party-dominated authoritarian corporatist society.

Besides these formal organisations, there have been numerous social

18. Lu Ya-li, "Political Modernization in the ROC: The Kuomintang and the Inhibited Political Center", in Ramon H. Myers (ed.), *Two Societies in Opposition: The Republic of China and the People's Republic of China after Forty Years* (Stanford, CA: Hoover Institution Press, 1991), pp. 111–26.

19. Hu Fu and Liang Shuang-lien (eds), *Hsin-hsin Wei-chi* (Crisis of Confidence) (Taipei: Tun-li Publishing Co., 1986).

20. *Taiwan Statistical Data Book, 1991*, p. 299.

movements addressing a range of issues.[21] These include consumers, environmental protection, anti-nuclear, women, indigenous peoples' ("aborigines") rights, labour, farmers, Hakka rights. They enjoy more or less formal organisation.

Throughout the 1980s, the major political story was the effort by dissidents, many of them disillusioned former KMT rising stars, to establish a new political party.[22] The KMT had been adamant in its refusal to permit this development, although it tolerated non-party affiliated candidates in elections. Beginning in 1986, with Chiang Ching-kuo's blessing, the KMT initiated a dialogue with members of the Tang-wai, or non (KMT)-party activists, an unofficial coalition active since the late 1970s. In September, the opposition established the Democratic Progressive Party (DPP). Not only was it not suppressed, at the end of the year it ran candidates in elections for national and local slots, winning many key ones.

Trends outside Taiwan also affected domestic politics. One was the demonstration effect of "people power", most notably in the nearby Philippines. Although the social, economic and political situations of the ROC and the Philippines differ drastically, nonetheless dissidents in Taiwan drew inspiration from the success of a popular movement in overthrowing a long-sitting dictator.[23] And Taiwan's rulers likewise took note of the inglorious collapse of a formerly unassailable political leader. Massive demonstrations in South Korea also provided lessons for the rulers and opposition of Taiwan. Soviet leader Gorbachev's *perestroika* and *glasnost* reforms also attracted attention.

Returning to the theme of the shadow of China, there is no question but that the dramatic reforms undertaken by the Chinese Communists after the Third Plenum of the Eleventh Central Committee in December 1978 had repercussions in Taiwan. The reformers, led by Teng Hsiao-p'ing, Chao Tse-yang and Hu Yao-pang, all but abandoned the previous development strategy and adopted a bold yet vague platform called

21. See Hsin-huang Michael Hsiao, "The Changing State-Society Relation in the ROC: Economic Change, the Transformation of the Class Structure, and the Rise of Social Movements", in Ramon H. Myers (ed.), *Two Societies in Opposition*, pp. 127–40. Also, Chang Mao-kuei, *She-hui Yun-tung yu Cheng-chih Chuan-hua* (Social Movements and Political Transformation) (Taipei: Kuo-chia Cheng-ts'e Yen-chiu Tzu-liao Chung-hsin, 1989).

22. See, among other sources, Tien Hung-mao, *The Great Transition: Political and Social Change in the Republic of China* (Stanford, CA: Hoover Institution Press, 1989).

23. This was made clear to me in interviews with DPP activists in autumn 1986.

"socialism with Chinese characteristics". In effect, they concentrated their energies on economic development rather than political or social revolution. Through a reworking of Marx, they claimed that China was in "the primary stage of socialism", requiring a great degree of flexibility in economic life in order to build just the sort of advanced industrial economy which Marx predicted would give birth to socialism. They introduced a number of policies and laws to create an investment climate suitable for foreign investors as well as a new domestic private entre-preneurial class. Rather than continuing to promote world revolution, the CCP advocated cooperation, with each country following its own developmental path in line with its capabilities. Astonishingly, given its very recent antipathy to this, the CCP spoke approvingly of the idea of an international division of labour and discussed the appropriate niches China could occupy. It established Special Economic Zones, based on Taiwan's Export Processing Zones, to achieve this.

These reforms began in the rural areas and then moved into the cities. From a focus on economics, some leaders tentatively raised the matter of political reforms, including the notions of introducing a professional civil service and separating the party from the government. These political reforms gained momentum until the winter of 1986–7, when conservative figures opposed to the reform programme in general launched an attack that brought down Hu Yao-pang, a staunch advocate of political reforms. Little progress was made after that time, with the T'ien-an-men Massacre of 1989 and fall of Chao Tse-yang figuring as a nadir of democratisation on the mainland.

From the perspective of Taiwan, the mainland reforms posed a very fundamental question. If the Communists had, in effect, given up doctrinaire Communism and were to a large degree, although without saying so explicitly, actually adopting the KMT's development strategy (derived from the writings of Sun Yat-sen), then why should the KMT maintain its staunch anti-Communist stand and the tight political control it claimed was required to prevent a Communist takeover?

The Communists also promoted new ideas for reunification with Taiwan, especially after signing a treaty with Great Britain for the return of Hong Kong in 1997 under a formula called "one country, two systems". Many former foreign supporters of the KMT, watching the Communists press forward with reforms, also began to question the stubbornness of the KMT in refusing to engage in some sort of official liaisons with their increasingly reasonable foes.

By the late 1980s there was also popular pressure within Taiwan to remove many of the obstacles blocking contacts across the Straits. In particular, many ageing former soldiers desired to visit their native places and re-establish contacts with their families. This grew into a protest movement, and in November 1987 President Chiang implemented a new policy permitting home visits for these men. That opened a flood-gate to people from all sectors of society, Taiwanese as well as main-landers, to visit the continent as journalists, tourists and business prospectors. Trade volume, carried on indirectly, neared US$6 billion in 1991, which is probably very under-estimated. Approximately 3,000 Taiwanese companies admitted to having investments on the mainland — again, indirectly — with a value around US$3 billion.[24] Ironically, it was after the 4 June 1989 killings in T'ien-an-men and the withdrawal of many foreign companies from the mainland that Taiwanese capital arrived with a bang.

Since the accession of Li Teng-hui, a Taiwanese technocrat, as President of the ROC and Chairman of the KMT in January 1988, the issue of Taiwan's relations with the mainland and the rest of the world has become a publicly debated issue in the island. On the one hand, there is an increased material relation across the Straits, but on the other, voices calling explicitly for Taiwan's independence, and not just self-determination, have been loud and strong. In the 1989 elections, some members of the DPP formed a "New Country Alliance" and published a constitution for a new country. In the 1991 elections, the party's plat-form called outright for independence. Although the DPP suffered a loss at the polls, in large part because the electorate saw this stance as irresponsible and reckless, this once taboo issue is now front and centre in the public's mind.

In this section, I have tried to indicate some of the central factors which have recently created a climate conducive to the discussion of Taiwan's identity. Domestically, social and political changes have called into question the KMT's definition of Taiwan's identity as the tempo-rary seat of China's legitimate government and repository of its tradi-tions, and even its legitimate right to determine it. Internationally, the PRC's reforms have altered opinion outside and inside Taiwan as to the necessity of maintaining a separate political existence from the mainland, with some people advocating closer ties and others promoting independence.

24. Qingguo Jia, "Changing Relations across the Taiwan Strait", *Asian Survey*, 32 (3), March 1992, pp. 277–89; p. 279.

In the next section, I examine some efforts in the cultural realm to fashion a distinct Taiwanese identity.

## Crafting a Taiwan identity

In this section, I will discuss some examples of central elements of a "Taiwan identity". These include a legacy of being overrun by outsiders and resistance; rural origins; and the experience of undergoing rapid modernisation.

The process of distinguishing and crafting a Taiwan identity can be seen in many ways. Owing to the long years of KMT-mainlander hegemony over the collective national-popular will (one of the shadows of China discussed earlier), this process could not be explicit; it may not have even been a conscious undertaking as such. Certainly, until the late 1980s it could not take place openly in the political sphere. A useful place to look for this process is in the cultural realm. Here again, it is hard to prove that the producers originally or consciously intended their works to serve the function of crafting a Taiwanese identity; with the *hsiang-t'u* (nativist) fiction of the early to mid 1970s, the project was more to explore the lives of the common people of the island, and many writers and critics sought to link this output with the larger post-May Fourth stream of modern Chinese literature rather than to emphasise its unique "Taiwaneseness". But it needs to be stressed that for writers to take the common people of the island of Taiwan as the subject of serious literary production was a significant breakthrough in itself.

Writing in the 1959 edition of his brother C.T.'s *A History of Modern Chinese Fiction*, T.A. Hsia accused writers in Taiwan of being merely escapists. Even stories with a real setting were populated by unbelievable characters:

> The Taiwan writers today, especially writers of fiction, are content with being mere daydreamers. I do not know of a single novel published in Taiwan in the last ten years that deals seriously or humorously with the life of the peasants, workers or the petty bourgeois class of teachers and government clerks to which the writers themselves belong.[25]

Lucy Ch'en (Ch'en Jo-hsi) saw some change and vigour in the writing by the early 1960s, mainly as a result of T.A. Hsia's efforts in his short-lived journal, the *Literary Review*, but was still dissatisfied:

25. C.T. Hsia, *A History of Modern Chinese Fiction, 1917–57* (New Haven, CT: Yale University Press, 1961). Appendix on Taiwan by T.A. Hsia, pp. 509–29, 511.

Most established literary men are afraid or too lazy to expose and analyze
either their own inner selves or the changing society around them. Why do
they not write about the changes in the cities with their new factories and
the thousands of young men and women who come in from the farms to
work in them . . . or about the farmers who must still stoop to push into
the mud every individual shoot of rice, but who now wear blue plastic
raincoats from Japan instead of the old straw cloaks . . . Formosa has a great
many things to write about. And sooner or later Formosan writers will
have to take up the challenge.[26]

C.T. Hsia omitted his brother's essay from the 1971 edition of the
book, claiming that Taiwan was now experiencing something of a
literary renascence. Part of that was what critic Yeh Shih-t'ao had referred to as "*hsiang-t'u*", or nativist, literature in a seminal 1965 essay.[27]

As Jing Wang notes, *hsiang-t'u* fiction brings together political, socio-
economic and literary elements.[28] Although emerging in the 1960s,[29]
its expansion during the early 1970s was clearly related to Taiwan's
international setbacks, a public call by some liberal intellectuals for
reforms[30] and attention to some of the costs of rapid industrialisation.[31]

Its evolution into a self-conscious movement can probably be dated
from August 1977. At a KMT-sponsored Symposium of Literary
Workers, several participants lambasted *hsiang-t'u* literature as, among
other things, "worker, peasant, soldier literature" comparable to that
produced under Communist direction on the mainland. This only added
to its attractiveness to disaffected and alienated young intellectuals who

26. Lucy J. Chen, "Literary Formosa", in Mark Mancall (ed.), *Formosa Today* (New
York: Praeger, 1964), pp. 140–1.

27. "T'ai-wan ti Hsiang-t'u Wen-hsueh" (Taiwan's Nativist Literature), in *Yeh Shih-
t'ao Tso-chia Lun-chi* (Collected Essays on Writers by Yeh Shih-t'ao) (Kaohsiung: San-
hsin Publishing Co., 1973), pp. 1–12. Jing Wang points out that the term can be traced
back to the Japanese period before the outbreak of the war with China. This is on
pp. 48–9 in the essay cited in the next note.

28. Jing Wang, "Taiwan *Hsiang-t'u* Literature: Perspectives in the Evolution of a
Literary Movement", in Jeannette L. Faurot (ed.), *Chinese Fiction from Taiwan: Critical
Perspectives* (Bloomington, IN: Indiana University Press, 1980), pp. 43–70.

29. *Yeh Shih-t'ao* especially pp. 143ff.

30. Mab Huang, *Intellectual Ferment for Political Reforms in Taiwan, 1971–73* (Ann
Arbor, MI: Center for Chinese Studies, University of Michigan, 1976).

31. The major collection of critical essays from the late 1970s reveals themes and con-
tradictions in the literature, including its relation to nationalism and critique of "wor-
shipping foreign things" (*ch'ung-yang mei-wai*) so prevalent among intellectuals. See Yu
T'ien-ts'ung (ed.), *Hsiang-t'u Wen-hsueh T'ao-lun Chi* (Collected Discussion on Nativist
Literature) (Taipei: Yuan-liu Publishing Co., 1978).

began to engage in political activity in support of the newly emerging Tang-wai. From this time, some writers, such as Yang Ch'ing-ch'u and Wang T'o, joined the opposition, while others, such as Hwang Chun-ming, studiously avoided it.[32]

As part of the trend to examine their own roots[33] and cast their efforts in a larger stream of Taiwan-oriented literature, *hsiang-t'u* activists also translated from Japanese and reprinted works by Taiwanese writers from the Japanese period. The works of these forebears had a strong anti-imperialist strain in addition to detailed depictions of rural life.[34] As examples I would cite Wu Cho-liu and Yang K'uei, two writers who lived well into the Nationalist period and served as models for later *hsiang-t'u* writers-cum-activists. Wu's novel *The Orphan of Asia* examined Taiwanese life in all sectors of society under the Japanese.[35] His bleak novella, *Potsdam Section Chief*, written just after retrocession, addressed a different form of occupation—the government and civilian carpetbaggers from the mainland who swarmed into Taiwan just after Japan's surrender. (The Allies' Potsdam Proclamation of July 1945 confirmed the intention to return Taiwan to China upon Japan's defeat.) It is a harbinger of Hou Hsiao-hsien's 1989 film, *A City of Sadness*, which also explored the clash between mainlanders and Taiwanese in the early days after retrocession, culminating in the violent 28 February Incident.

Yang K'uei became involved in social activism while studying and working at menial jobs in Japan. His stories, such as "The Newspaper Boy" and "Mother Goose Gets Married", combined anti-imperialism with a concern for the common people. He was repeatedly jailed by the Japanese and again by the KMT, spending his later years tending a flower garden opposite the main gate of Tunghai University in T'ai-chung.[36]

Celebrating the anti-imperialist strain of these early works could be seen as an unsubtle reference to what some would call Taiwan's neo-

32. Yang and Wang were arrested after the Kaohsiung Incident of 1979.

33. The American television drama, *Roots*, was shown on Taiwan television at this time and had a wide social impact.

34. A collection of translated works which emphasises these links is Joseph S.M. Lau (ed.), *The Unbroken Chain: An Anthology of Taiwan Fiction since 1926* (Bloomington, IN: Indiana University Press, 1983).

35. A song of the same name by Lo Ta-yu (discussed below) from the mid-1980s took Indochinese refugees as its subject.

36. See the essays on Yang K'uei in the special issue of *T'ai-wan Wen-I* (Taiwan Literature), 94 (15 May 1985).

colonialist subjection to both the mainlanders and their American
backers, as well as American and Japanese capital.

Although its author claims to be avowedly unpolitical, Hwang Chun-
ming's exuberant *Sayonara Tsai-chien* is as vicious an attack on Taiwan's
multifaceted resubjection to Japanese imperialism as can be imagined.[37]
An employee of a trading company has to entertain Japanese clients,
which involves taking them whoring in his hometown. These men comprise the "Thousand Beheadings Club", a name derived from the life-
time goal of a samurai but now referring to sleeping with a thousand
different women. The story is replete with references to both Japanese
popular culture's enduring influence in Taiwan and to the revived
economic presence. In a twist, the protagonist-interpreter sets the
Japanese up to be mocked and cheated by the women. Then, during a
train ride, he intentionally misinterprets a conversation between a
university student and the visitors to humiliate the Japanese over their
repeated atrocities against the Chinese and to raise some nationalist
(Chinese) pride in the youth.

Hwang's best-known works are microscopic presentations of daily life
in Taiwan among a variety of lower-class people — farmers, prostitutes,
gong-beating public announcers, signpainters, advertising sandwich-
men.[38] They richly convey a sense of place, rhythms of daily life and
transition, mostly due to the necessity to adjust to externally derived
influences. They lend themselves to the cinema screen very well and
many have been successfully transformed into films. In addition to these
screen adaptations, the internationally acclaimed films of mainlander
Hou Hsiao-hsien, scripted with mainlander Chu T'ien-wen and Wu
Nien-chen, have also preserved a slice of unhurried Taiwanese small-
town life in much simpler times.

One of Hwang Chun-ming's most moving stories is "Sea-Gazing
Days",[39] about a young prostitute who was sold first by her birth
parents and then by her foster parents to a brothel. She deliberately

37. An English version is available in Hwang Chun-ming, *The Drowning of an Old
Cat and Other Stories*, translated by Howard Goldblatt (Bloomington, IN: Indiana
University Press, 1980), pp. 217–70.

38. For an excellent discussion of Hwang as a regional writer, see Howard Goldblatt,
"The Rural Stories of Hwang Chun-ming", in Jeannette L. Faurot (ed.), *Chinese Fiction
from Taiwan*, pp. 111–33.

39. Translated as "A Flower in the Rainy Night", Joseph S.M. Lau and Timothy
A. Ross (eds), *Chinese Stories from Taiwan: 1960–1970* (New York: Columbia University
Press, 1976), pp. 195–241.

becomes pregnant by a fisherman without his knowledge. At the end, with her baby and a sense of self-dignity and social status, she visits his village. This touching story was made into an equally moving dance by the noted Taiwanese choreographer, Martha Graham-trained Lin Hwai-min, and performed by his Cloud Gate Dance Ensemble.[40]

Although not in Hwang's league artistically, Yang Ch'ing-ch'u is another writer unquestionably rooted in the nitty-gritty daily struggle of Taiwan's common people. Some of his more interesting stories focus on the social consequences of Taiwan's rapid industrialisation. In this category I would cite "Born of the Same Roots".[41] The setting is in a fancy hotel, at the wedding of the youngest of three daughters. Each daughter represents a different stage in the business career of the father, a parvenu who symbolises Taiwan's explosive accumulation of wealth. The eldest is illiterate, has never even seen an automatic door before and is all at sea at the garish wedding festivities. Her husband drives a pedicab, a vehicle soon to be prohibited in the cities. But he cannot pass the written test for a driver's licence and is doomed to failure. The ugly, haughty bride is the youngest, graduate of a home-economics finishing school, marrying a university graduate who will whisk her off to the United States. The middle daughter is in college but does not look down on her big sister. The plotless story is primarily an interior monologue of the eldest sister's humiliation and bleak prospects.

The themes of rootedness in the countryside and small towns, and the effects of modernisation also recur in the songs of the doctor-turned-songwriter, Lo Ta-yu. I would first call attention to his song, "Lu-kang, Small Town". The singer, now in Taipei, inquires about details of life in Lu-kang, a city in central Taiwan regarded by many as the heartland of Taiwanese culture, the site of one of the island's most impressive Ma-tsu temples. The chorus rails against Taipei, Taiwan's main metropolis:

> *Taipei is not my home,*
> *My home doesn't have neon lights.*
> *Lu-kang's streets, Lu-kang's fishing villages,*
> *People lighting incense in the Ma-tsu temple.*

40. Lin recently presented a dance drama about aborigines. In addition to his very "Taiwanese" works, he has also created modern interpretations of traditional Chinese myths. See Bruce Einhorn, "Dance Troupe Stresses Taiwanese Identity", *Asian Wall Street Journal Weekly* (18 May 1992), p. 11.

41. Translated in Vivian Ling Hsu (ed.), *Born of the Same Roots* (Bloomington, IN: Indiana University Press, 1981), pp. 228–36.

> *Taipei is not my home,*
> *My home doesn't have neon lights.*
> *Lu-kang's dawn, Lu-kang's dusk,*
> *People roaming about in civilisation.*

At the song's end, the singer realizes that Lu-kang too has changed. "The people got what they thought they wanted, but lost what they had," he wails.

In this song, and the very powerful "Masters of the Future", Lo worries about the upcoming, "modern", generation's sense of its past. He sees the young as technologically adept but soulless, floating about ("*p'iao-lai p'iao-ch'u*") without direction.

Lo Ta-yu sings in Mandarin,[42] but a significant number of singers now use Taiwanese. Additionally, much of the power in the writing of Yang Ch'ing-ch'u and other *hsiang-t'u* authors comes from their use of Taiwanese slang. This has even involved creating some new Chinese ideographs. The writers revel in the vulgarity of their characters, something of a slap at Taiwan's mainlander élite. As the use of Taiwanese has been tightly restricted in the broadcast media while Mandarin has been promoted, songs, drama and the printed page have served as media for preserving the dialect.

The young pop singer Lin Ch'iang (Lim Giong) has said, "using Mandarin to express Taiwanese feelings is just wrong . . . Singing in Taiwanese is the best way . . . It's much more direct, and you can sing with a lot of force."[43] The international pop star Teng Li-chun has recorded several sets of melancholy Taiwanese folk songs, in addition to her trademark soft Taiwanese love songs. Of more social interest are the works of Ch'en Ming-chang, in particular the 1989 "Songs of Madness" recording by his Blacklist Workshop. This highly political and inventive "medicine for the age" addresses a number of social issues and many of the selections are performed as Taiwanese rap songs.[44]

The political significance of facility in Taiwanese dialect has

42. He has recently moved to Hong Kong and begun recording in Cantonese. His 1991 recording, "Yuan Hsiang" (Native Place), is mostly sung in Taiwanese.

43. Bruce Einhorn, "Taiwan's Bad Boy", *Far Eastern Economic Review* (28 May 1992), pp. 32–4; p. 32.

44. See the series of articles, "Tsa Lai T'ing Fan-shu-tzu Ch'ang-ke" (Let's Go Hear a Sweet Potato Sing), in *Hsin-hsin-wen* (the Journalist), 199 (31 December 1990–6 January 1991), pp. 24–39, which includes a discussion with Hwang Chun-ming and Lin Hwai-min. Also Hsu Ching-yun and Lin Ching-chieh, "The Songs they are A-Changin' ", *Free China Review*, 42 (3) (March 1992), pp. 46–51.

grown dramatically. Political rallies are now frequently conducted in Taiwanese, and some militant opposition politicians insisted on using it in the second National Assembly convened in 1992. This implies that the "nation" is Taiwan and its lingua franca is not Mandarin. Many up and coming mainlander political figures have been tutored in the dialect, including John Chang (Chang Hsiao-yen), son of the late President Chiang Ching-kuo, who himself said in 1987 that he was a Taiwanese as he had spent nearly forty years there. As Mandarin is the official language of the ROC and the medium of instruction in school, the current necessity to use it in political settings indicates both the shifting balance of power between society and the state, and the new nature of "cultural capital":[45] facility in Mandarin and "Chinese" tradition are no longer as valuable as mastery of Taiwaneseness, starting with language.

Of particular importance is a new interest in Taiwan's local history by scholars, preservationists and collectors. Despite a rich store of primary materials, Chinese academics had generally neglected the island's history. Only in the 1980s was it taught in the universities.[46] Delving into the island's history raises sensitive issues as to how "Chinese" Taiwan is. Can it be taken as a microcosm for all of China, or will in-depth research only reveal its uniqueness?[47] Then there is the formerly taboo subject of the KMT's take-over and the brutal 28 February Incident of 1947 when mainland troops killed unknown thousands of Taiwanese rising up against the corruption of their self-styled liberators. The previous *locus classicus* for this traumatic event was the eyewitness account of the American consular official George Kerr.[48] In the mid-1980s some local scholars began to publish on the Incident, and in 1990 President Li Teng-hui appointed a committee to investigate it. The report was published in 1992 along with an exhaustive study in English co-authored by two scholars from

45. Pierre Bourdieu, "Cultural Reproduction and Social Reproduction", in Jerome Karabel and A.H. Halsey (eds), *Power and Ideology in Education* (New York: Oxford University Press, 1977), pp. 487–511.

46. Yin Chang-i, "Chang-yao Hsien-jen Chi-lang; Chien-li Pen-t'u Shi-hsueh" (Make Known the Patterns of the Predecessors; Establish an Indigenous Historiography) in Hsiao Hsin-huang *et al.* (eds), *T'ai-wan, Tsai Chuan-lie-tian-shang* (Taiwan at the Turning Point) (Taipei: Ta-lu, Lo-ch'eng Publishing Co., 1986), pp. 80–99.

47. See the interesting articles collected in the Government Information Office's monthly *Free China Review*, 42 (3) (March 1992). Also *Chung-kuo Lun-t'an* (China Tribune), 338 (25 October 1989), which also discusses Taiwan historical studies.

48. George H. Kerr, *Formosa Betrayed* (Boston, MA: Houghton-Mifflin, 1965).

Taiwan.[49] In February of that year, Li met with family members
of victims of the massacre. At the time of writing there is a public
call for a commemorative monument, a museum, compensation and
official apologies. Through a public catharsis of this defining event
in modern Taiwan's history, Li hopes to put the tragic past to rest
and enable the citizens to march forward in unity.

Besides the scholarly pursuit, within society there has been a rage for
collecting Taiwanese antiques, including wooden puppets used in once-
popular indigenous puppet plays. The government has become involved
in preserving various folk arts and there is renewed interest in religious
festivals.[50] Professor Hsia Chu-joe of National Taiwan University has
spearheaded a movement to preserve traditional buildings and there
is a sudden interest in archaeology. Taiwanese cuisine has moved from
open markets and alleyways into extremely expensive restaurants
and hotels. Tea shops-cum-art galleries which express a traditional
Taiwanese atmosphere have also mushroomed.

Popular and academic works vary in their attempt either to link
Taiwan with the greater stream of Chinese tradition or to attempt
to sever it. Pai Hsien-yung's pathbreaking James Joyce/Sherwood
Anderson-style short story collection of the early 1970s, *T'ai-pei-jen*
(Taipei Residents), presents vignettes of mainland emigrés in Taiwan
but not of Taiwan. They try in varying degrees to recreate a lifestyle
they had, or thought they had, mellowed by time and distance, on the
mainland. They include emigrés from the very highest élite (Pai's father,
Pai Chung-hsi, was such a person), as well as prostitutes, old soldiers,
petit bourgeois, etc. Lai Sheng-ch'uan's tour-de-force play, *That Night
We Performed Comedians' Dialogues*, links Taiwan and the mainland
through the brilliant device of five crosstalk (*hsiang-sheng*) performances
from different places and times presented in reverse chronological order:
Taipei 1985, Taipei 1963, Chungking 1943, Peking 1925 and Peking
1900. Lai uses a traditional performing art still highly popular on the
mainland but nearly extinct in Taiwan to explore themes of tradition,
history, tastes and so on. The popular and sentimental film, *The Second
Spring of Old Mo*, grew out of the renewed contacts with the mainland
in the mid-1980s. In it, an old soldier learns that the wife he left

49. Lai Tse-han, Ramon H. Myers and Wei Wou, *A Tragic Beginning: The Taiwan
Uprising of February 28, 1947* (Stanford University Press, 1991.)
50. See the special issue of *Free China Review* 40 (4) (April 1990). Emily Martin Ahern
discusses the role of festivals in expressing, obliquely, local political and economic
opposition to the state in "The Thai Ti Kong Festival", in Ahern and Gates (eds), *The
Anthropology of Taiwanese Society*, pp. 397–425.

on the mainland has died; he then marries a young aborigine woman, demonstrating, at last, a commitment to Taiwan. Another film, *Banana Paradise*, follows two footsoldiers from the mainland to Taiwan, tracing their trials and tribulations and then recontact with family in China.

In this context, mention should also be made of Hou Te-chien's dirge-like "Descendants of the Dragon". Without mentioning Taiwan, this song explicitly links all Chinese with the motherland through such lyrics as:

> *In the far off east there is a river,*
> *Its name is the Yangtze River.*
> *In the far off east there is a river,*
> *Its name is the Yellow River.*
> *Although I've never seen the beauty of the*
> *Yangtze River, I often journey on its waters in my dreams.*
> *Although I've never heard the strength of the*
> *Yellow River, it surges in my dreams.*
> *In the ancient east there is a dragon,*
> *Its name is China.*
> *In the ancient east there is a people,*
> *They are the descendants of the dragon.*
> *I grew up under the feet of the great dragon;*
> *After growing up, I'm a descendant of the dragon.*
> *Black eyes, black hair, yellow skin; forever*
> *descendants of the dragon.*

When Hou slipped off to the mainland in 1983, his songs were banned in Taiwan but aggressively promoted by the Communists. Egregiously overproduced renditions of "Descendants of the Dragon", sung by basso profundos backed by full orchestra and choir, were broadcast ceaselessly.[51]

As a reaction to the efforts to establish a separate identity, the ROC government relaxed its prohibitions against the works of left-wing Chinese writers from earlier in the century. Thus the works of Pa Chin, Mao Tun, Lu Hsun and so on are now widely available, as are videos from the mainland. Ironically, visiting "the motherland" for many people, Taiwanese and mainlanders, reconfirms their sense of Taiwan's distinctiveness rather than its essential "Chineseness."[52] Intellectuals

---

51. Hou was one of the last to leave T'ien-an-men Square on 4 June 1989. He was subsequently unceremoniously put in the hold of a boat and shipped back to Taiwan.

52. Some evidence is presented in Hu Chang, "Impressions of Mainland China Carried Back by Taiwan Visitors", in Ramon H. Myers (ed.), *Two Societies in Opposition*, pp. 141–55.

have engaged in a debate over the strength of ties to Taiwan (*T'ai-wan-chieh*) versus China as a whole (*Chung-kuo-chieh*) and the concomitant sense of a Taiwan consciousness (*T'ai-wan i-shih*) as opposed to a Chinese consciousness (*Chung-kuo i-shih*).[53]

## Conclusions

Taiwan clearly exists in the shadow of China. As the nature of its existence under ROC control faced unprecedented challenges from external and internal forces from the 1970s onwards, some of its more articulate citizens began to explore, through a variety of media and activities, the essence of Taiwan's identity. Re-establishing contact with the mainland has only intensified this quest: one's sense of self grows out of interaction with others. We have seen that many artists and scholars, in addition to politicians, are trying to articulate the nature of Taiwan's experience, its origins and the influences on it. This naturally involves challenging the legitimate right of the KMT party-state to define the nature of Taiwan's identity and whether or not it has a historical destiny. It is a measure of how inhibited the once unassailable centre has become, as a result of the strengthening of civil society and the changes within the élite itself, that it has given up trying to suppress these challenges and instead has joined in as a competitor. The status of mainland recovery as a national mission has been superseded by a public debate over how to do a better job of managing Taiwan's own affairs, including working out an ideal relationship with the mainland.

It is unclear what percentage of Taiwan's people identify with the emerging "identity" of the island. Many people consume the products but do not necessarily buy the message. Opposition political rallies draw large and enthusiastic crowds, but the electorate appears to draw the line at transforming the call for independence into actual policy.

Both intellectuals trying to establish the distinctiveness of Taiwan and those emphasising its links to China stress that Taiwan has become a modern Chinese society at a great cost not only to the environment, but also to memory and even the soul. Rather than seeing tradition, as embodied in the rhythms of rural life, as a hindrance to modernisation, they argue that forgetting one's past will cause even greater dislocation.

53. Ch'en Ch'i-nan, *Kuan-chien Nien-tai ti T'ai-wan* (Critical years for Taiwan) (Taipei: Yun-ch'en Cultural Co., 1988), pp. 11–18; Chu T'ien-shun (ed.), *Tang-tai T'ai-wan Cheng-chih Yen Chiu*; and Huang Kuang-kuo, " 'T'ai-wan-chieh' yu 'Chung-kuo-chieh': Tui-k'ang yu Ch'u-lu" ("Taiwan Ties" and "China Ties": Confrontation and a Way Out), *Chung-kuo Lun-t'an* (China Tribune), 25 (1), (10 October 1987).

# 8

## POLICY TOWARDS THE CHINESE
## MAINLAND: TAIPEI'S VIEW*

### Ying-jeou Ma

*Relations across the Straits since 1949: a brief review*

In 1949 relations between Taiwan and mainland China entered a
military conflict phase, which lasted for thirty years until 1978. This
period witnessed several important battles such as the battle of Quemoy
(Kinmen) of 1949, and the Quemoy-Matsu Crisis of 1958. After 1958,
while the Communist shelling of Quemoy and Matsu islands continued
on an every-other-day basis, a gradual relaxation of tension quietly
developed. After US President Richard Nixon visited the Chinese
mainland in February 1972 and signed the Shanghai Communiqué with
Peking's Premier, Chou En-lai, propaganda leaflets replaced high explo-
sives as the content of shells flying across the Quemoy Straits. In
view of its forthcoming establishment of diplomatic relations with the
United States and the American termination of its defence treaty with
the Republic of China, Peking decided in December 1978 to adopt
a "peaceful unification" strategy as its fundamental policy towards
Taiwan, and dropped the three-decade-old slogan "liberating Taiwan
by force".

This was followed by the peaceful confrontation phase, which
lasted from 1979 till 1987. On 1 January 1979 Peking stopped shelling
Quemoy and Matsu, and the Standing Committee of the National
People's Congress (NPC) issued a "Letter to Taiwan Compatriots"
which ushered in a period of intensive propaganda offensive against
Taipei. The letter called for an end to military confrontation, for direct
postal, trade and travel links, and for increased interchange across
the Taiwan Straits. The campaign culminated in NPC President Yeh
Chien-ying's "Nine-Point Proposal" of September 1981 and Teng
Hsiao-ping's "one country, two systems" scheme of 1983. Meanwhile,
Taipei responded on the one hand by proposing reunification under

---

* A version of this paper was published in *Issues and Studies*, vol. 28, no. 6 (June 1992).

Table 8.1.

PUBLIC OPINION ON PACE OF EXCHANGES ACROSS TAIWAN STRAITS (%)

| Answer | Dec. 1988[a] | Mar. 1989[a] | June 1989[b] | Oct. 1989[b] | June 1990[c] | Oct. 1990[d] | Jan. 1991[c] | Sept. 1991[c] | Nov. 1991[c] | Feb. 1992[c] | May 1992[a] | June 1992[c] | Sept. 1992[c] |
|---|---|---|---|---|---|---|---|---|---|---|---|---|---|
| Too fast | 16.7 | 16.8 | 13.2 | 10.1 | 12.7 | 19.4 | 13.7 | 12.4 | 9.6 | 6.6 | 14.2 | 15.7 | 19.9 |
| Just right | 38.5 | 43.2 | 51.4 | 58.1 | 51.0 | 44.0 | 48.5 | 41.0 | 49.5 | 50.0 | 48.8 | 44.8 | 50.6 |
| Too slow | 16.7 | 14.6 | 13.8 | 16.5 | 19.4 | 18.9 | 17.3 | 17.2 | 20.1 | 23.9 | 17.2 | 22.0 | 13.6 |
| Other* | 28.2 | 25.5 | 21.6 | 15.3 | 16.8 | 17.7 | 20.5 | 22.4 | 20.9 | 19.5 | 19.8 | 17.5 | 15.9 |

Survey conducted by:
(a) *China Times*; (b) Research, Development and Evaluation Commission, Executive Yuan;
(c) Organising Committee of National Affairs Conference; (d) Mainland Affairs Commission;
(e) Mainland Affairs Council
* "Other" stands for "uncertain", "don't know" and "refuse to answer".
*Survey respondents*: c. 1,000 adults in Taiwan area.

Dr Sun Yat-sen's Three Principles of the People (i.e. nationalism, democracy and social well-being) and rejecting all the overtures of Peking. On the other hand, it quietly embarked on an impressive and far-reaching programme of political democratisation and economic liberalisation which considerably increased its popularity at home and improved its image abroad.

On 2 November 1987 the ROC government began to permit Taiwan residents to visit their relatives on the Chinese mainland, which marked the beginning of the present phase in cross-Straits relations, one that is characterised by people-to-people or unofficial exchanges. The following year, the Kuomintang (KMT) adopted "Current Mainland Policies" at its Thirteenth National Congress. A month later, on 18 August 1988, the Executive Yuan (cabinet) set up an inter-agency task force called the Mainland Affairs Commission to coordinate policies towards the Chinese mainland among the various ministries and councils. While the ROC government has continued to reject Peking's call for direct contact and negotiations, it has gone far beyond permitting family visits by Taiwan residents to the Chinese mainland. Since November 1987 restrictions on travel and trade across the Taiwan Straits have gradually been lifted. As of the end of November 1992, Taiwan residents had made more than 4 million trips to the mainland, while more than 34,000 mainland residents had visited or settled in Taiwan. People on the two sides of the Taiwan Straits exchanged more than 58 million letters in four years and over 27 million phone calls in three years (representing only 40 per cent of telephone demand, however). Indirect trade through Hong Kong reached US$5.8 billion in 1991, nearly a seventy-fold increase since 1979. Indirect investment was estimated to total more than US$4.5 billion at the end of November 1992. In addition, exchanges of books, videos and other media have brought the people of the two sides of the Straits even closer together.

### Peking's current policies towards Taipei

Peking's fundamental positions towards Taipei after 1979 may be summed up in three phases: "one country, two systems" after China's peaceful unification; "two-party negotiations"; and "establishing three direct links". These phases may be broken down into the following policies:

1. *Unification and the use of force.* Peking insists on making no commit-

ment to renounce the use of force against Taiwan in pursuing China's unification.

2. *External relations*. Peking opposes "two China", "one China, one Taiwan", "Taiwan independence", "one country, two governments", or Taipei's "flexible diplomacy". It does all it can to prevent Taipei from establishing diplomatic or official ties with countries that have diplomatic relations with Peking, and from joining any intergovernmental organisations.

3. *Characterization of Peking–Taipei relations*. Peking regards itself as the national government of China while Taiwan is merely a province and the ROC government a "local authority", not even a "political entity". It intends to turn Taiwan into a "special administrative region" (SAR) like Hong Kong after unification. Taiwan as an SAR may keep its current political, social and economic systems and its armed forces, but the latter must follow orders from Peking. Other than international economic contacts, Taiwan will have no diplomatic relations abroad and the national title (Republic of China), flag and emblem will disappear.

4. *CCP–KMT negotiations*. The KMT and the Chinese Communist Party (CCP) should hold direct negotiations on unification, or on bilateral relations, with the participation of representatives from other political parties or groups from the mainland and Taiwan.

5. *Direct transportation links and two-way exchanges*. Transportation authorities of the two sides should start negotiations leading to direct air and sea links and to the establishment of cultural, academic, athletic, scientific and technological exchanges.

6. *Investment and trade*. Peking is anxious to attract more Taiwanese capital and expand exports to Taiwan, using closer economic ties with Taiwan to thwart the latter's "separatist tendencies".

7. *Internal education*. Peking admonishes the mainland people to heighten vigilance against the spread of "admiration for Taiwan" fever, lest it should cause "peaceful evolution" on the Chinese mainland.

## Taipei's current policies towards Peking

Taipei's fundamental positions towards Peking may also be summed up in three phrases: "one China, two areas, two political entities"; "peaceful and democratic unification of China"; and "a three-phase, no time frame approach to unification". The three phases mean unofficial exchanges in the short term, official relations in the medium term, and unification negotiations in the long term. Specifically, Taipei's positions imply the following policies:

1. *Unification and the use of force*. President Li Teng-hui's termination on 1 May 1991 of the Period of National Mobilisation for Suppressing Communist Rebellion signifies the ROC government's determination not to use force in the process of national unification.

2. *External relations*. Under the "one China" principle, Taipei practices "pragmatic diplomacy," that is, creating opportunities to resume suspended diplomatic ties or to establish new ones, and to join or rejoin global or regional inter-governmental organizations.

3. *Characterization of Taipei–Peking relations*. Taipei regards itself as the national government of China while Peking is a "political entity" that controls the Chinese mainland. Taipei proposes the "one country, two areas, two political entities" scheme, a pragmatic characterisation of political reality across the Taiwan Straits, which allows sufficient "creative ambiguity" for both sides to live with each other. For civil matters involving residents of the two areas, rules of conflict of laws should apply.

4. *KMT–CCP negotiations*. Taipei opposes any political negotiation with Peking in the current (first) phase of national unification but supports unofficial, technical consultations between non-official intermediary groups with authorisation from their respective governing authorities. There are two such organisations – the Straits Exchange Foundation for Taipei and the Association for Relations across the Taiwan Straits (ARATS) for Peking. The former was established in February 1991 and the latter in December 1991.

Even when the time is ripe for official contacts between the two sides in the next (second) phase of national unification, party-to-party negotiations may still be inappropriate since the number of political parties in Taiwan has reached seventy-one, none of which can legitimately represent the whole of Taiwan's people. Only the ROC government can do so.

5. *Direct transportation links and two-way exchanges* (see Table 8.2 for public opinion in Taiwan). In the current phase of national unification, trade, postal and transportation links across the Taiwan Straits have to remain indirect. They will become direct in the next phase when mutual trust has been established between the two sides; in other words, when Peking is ready not to deny Taipei's existence as a political entity, not to use force to settle bilateral disputes, and not to interfere with Taipei's conduct of external relations under the "one China, two areas, two political entities" principle, direct links may be established. In the meantime, two-way exchanges have in fact already been permitted, albeit in

Table 8.2.
PUBLIC OPINION ON DIRECT NAVIGATION BETWEEN TAIWAN
AND CHINESE MAINLAND

|  | *Survey conductor* | *Answers* | % | *Note* |
|---|---|---|---|---|
| Aug. 1990 | *United Daily* | Approve<br>Disapprove<br>No opinion | 54.0<br>21.0<br>25.0 | |
| Oct. 1990 | Mainland Affairs Commission | Approve<br>Disapprove<br>No opinion | 16.8<br>66.4<br>16.8 | Under the circumstances that the ROC flag is covered and all documents or publications on board with the ROC title or emblem not permitted |
| Jan. 1991 | Mainland Affairs Council | Approve<br>Disapprove<br>No opinion | 11.9<br>73.6<br>14.4 | |
| April 1991 | *United Daily* | Approve<br>Disapprove<br>No opinion | 68.0<br>16.0<br>15.2 | |
| May 1991 | Mainland Affairs Council | Approve<br>Disapprove<br>No opinion | 76.8<br>12.8<br>10.2 | The Guidelines for National Unification suggests that direct air/sea links and direct trade with the mainland should be permitted only when Peking no longer denies Taiwan's existence as a political entity and rejects it in the international community on the basis of mutual respect |
| June 1991 | *China Times* | Strongly agree<br>Agree<br>Disagree<br>Strongly disagree<br>No opinion | 12.9<br>50.5<br>19.6<br>1.4<br>15.5 | |
| Feb. 1992 | Mainland Affairs Council | Approve<br>Disapprove<br>No opinion | 11.5<br>76.4<br>12.0 | Under the circumstances that the ROC flag is covered and all documents or publications on board with the ROC title or emblem not permitted |

Table 8.2 (cont.)

| | Survey conductor | Answers | % | Note |
|---|---|---|---|---|
| | | Approve | 25.8 | Under the circumstances |
| | | Disapprove | 60.0 | that Peking insists on |
| | | No opinion | 14.2 | making no commitment to renounce the use of force against Taiwan |
| | | Approve | 56.7 | For the sake of national |
| | | Disapprove | 27.2 | welfare and security, |
| | | No opinion | 16.2 | government should maintain indrect navigation |
| June 1992 | Mainland Affairs Council | Approve | 11.8 | Under the circumstances |
| | | Disapprove | 63.0 | that the ROC flag is |
| | | No opinion | 25.2 | covered and all documents or publications on board with the ROC title or emblem not permitted |
| Sept. 1992 | Mainland Affairs Council | Approve | 10.6 | |
| | | Disapprove | 78.6 | |
| | | No opinion | 10.8 | |
| Sept. 1992 | United Daily | Approve | 61 | Do you approve direct |
| | | Disapprove | 22 | navigation with the |
| | | No opinion | 18 | Chinese mainland? |
| | | As soon as possible | 15 | Should we start direct |
| | | Wait for friendly responses | 61 | navigation with the |
| | | Against direct navigation | 4 | Chinese mainland as soon |
| | | Don't know/no opinion | 19 | as possible or wait until Peking makes specific, friendly responses to us? |
| Sept. 1992 | China Times Evening News | Approve | 51.0 | Do you approve direct |
| | | Disapprove | 31.4 | navigation with the |
| | | Other | 17.6 | Chinese mainland? |
| | | Approve | 20.0 | Do you approve direct |
| | | Disapprove | 50.4 | navigation with the |
| | | Other | 28.9 | Chinese mainland if Peking refuses to renounce using force against Taiwan and continues isolating Taiwan internationally? |

Survey respondents: c. 1,000 adults in Taiwan area (except for June 1992: c. 3,000 adults in Taiwan area)

Table 8.3.

PUBLIC OPINION ON WHETHER TO PERMIT DIRECT TRADE WITH,
AND INVESTMENT ON, CHINESE MAINLAND

| | Survey conductor | Answers | % | Note |
|---|---|---|---|---|
| March 1988 | China Times | Approve | 40.7 | |
| | | Disapprove | 33.0 | |
| | | No opinion | 26.2 | |
| Oct. 1988 | United Daily | Permit direct trade | 38.0 | |
| | | Maintain indirect trade | 27.0 | |
| | | Other | 35.0 | |
| April 1990 | Public Opinion Research Foundation | Permit investment completely | 13.9 | |
| | | Permit investment partially | 46.9 | |
| | | Oppose | 8.8 | |
| | | Other | 30.7 | |
| June 1990 | Organising Committee of National Affairs Conference | Permit unconditionally | 11.8 | |
| | | Permit conditionally | 43.7 | |
| | | Maintain *status quo* (indirect) | 30.2 | |
| | | Other | 14.3 | |
| Oct. 1990 | Mainland Affairs Commission | Strongly agree | 29.0 | Would Formosa Plastic Corp. Chairman Y. C. Wang's planned investment in Chinese mainland have negative impact on Taiwan's economy? |
| | | Agree | 49.9 | |
| | | Disagree | 11.7 | |
| | | Strongly disagree | 0.5 | |
| | | No opinion | 8.9 | |
| Oct. 1990 | Mainland Affairs Commission | Strongly agree | 13.3 | For the sake of national security and economic development, government may restrict certain categories of business to invest in Chinese mainland |
| | | Agree | 48.6 | |
| | | Disagree | 20.2 | |
| | | Strongly disagree | 3.5 | |
| | | No opinion | 14.4 | |
| Jan. 1991 | Mainland Affairs Council | Strongly agree | 26.1 | Will it cause damage if the government permits direct |
| | | Agree | 51.7 | |
| | | Disagree | 8.0 | |
| | | Strongly disagree | 0.6 | |

Table 8.3 (*cont.*)

| Survey conductor | Answers | % | Note |
|---|---|---|---|
| | No opinion | 13.6 | trade and investment without any protection to those Taiwan business people and investors? |
| April 1991 *United Daily* Council | Agree/Strongly agree | 63.0 | Government should permit direct trade and investment after bringing an end to the period of National Mobilisation for Suppression of the Communist Rebellion and abrogating the Temporary Provisions (of the ROC Constitution) |
| | Disagree/Strongly disagree | 19.0 | |
| | Other | 18.0 | |
| June 1991 *China Times* | Strongly agree | 11.2 | |
| | Agree | 53.2 | |
| | Disagree | 18.3 | |
| | Strongly disagree | 0.8 | |
| | No opinion | 16.5 | |
| June 1992 Mainland Affairs Council | Agree | 54.4 | Government should permit direct trade and investment after Peking no longer denies Taiwan's status as a political entity and isolates it in the international community |
| | Disagree | 16.2 | |
| | No opinion | 29.4 | |

*Survey respondents*: *c*. 1,000 adults in Taiwan area.

an unbalanced way. While Taipei does not allow mainland residents to enter Taiwan without restrictions, Peking permits relatively more people, but little information, from Taiwan to go to the mainland. Ironically, while Taipei relaxed restrictions on mainland residents' entry into Taiwan after 1990, Peking has prevented an increasing number of scientists, lawyers and journalists from visiting Taiwan after they were given entry permits. Obviously, Peking is more interested in attracting Taiwan's capital than exposing its own élite to the latter's way of life.

6. *Trade and investment* (see Table 8.3 for public opinion in Taiwan). Taipei insists that trade with and investment in the mainland must be conducted indirectly. As of 21 December 1992, Taipei permits the indirect importation from the mainland of 434 items, including medicinal herbs, industrial raw materials and semi-finished goods produced on the mainland. Taipei imposes few restrictions on goods shipped to the mainland via a third place. Meanwhile, Taiwan's companies may invest in 3,764 industrial items on the Chinese mainland through their subsidiaries abroad. By 30 November 1992, 2,714 cases of investment in the mainland had been reported to the Ministry of Economic Affairs. Although only about 50 per cent of the companies have registered, it is an encouraging sign that finally many are willing to cooperate with the government. Specific measures are being taken to assist these companies and to investigate those that have not yet reported.

7. *Internal education.* Few people in Taiwan are interested in living in a Communist society, yet they are fascinated by the mainland's vast land, beautiful scenery, low labour cost, rich natural resources and long cultural tradition. What the ROC government intends to do in such a pluralistic society is to build, with Taiwan's security and the welfare of its 20 million people in mind, a national consensus on orderly exchanges with the mainland to foster mutual understanding. There has been notable progress towards this in the early 1990s.

## Planning for the future

President Li Teng-hui's historic move in terminating the National Mobilisation Period and abolishing the Temporary Provisions of the Constitution, which demonstrated his commitment to constitutional reform as well as to adjusting Taipei's relations with Peking, has not been met by a positive response from Peking in terms of reducing military threat and lessening diplomatic isolation. On the contrary,

Table 8.4.
## PUBLIC OPINION ON TAIWAN INDEPENDENCE MOVEMENT

| | Survey conductor | Taiwan Independence Movement | Would the Chinese Communists use force against Taiwan if Taiwan declares independence? | Change "Republic of China" into "Republic of Taiwan" |
|---|---|---|---|---|
| June 1990 | Public Opinion Research Foundation | Approve 12.5% Disapprove 67.0% | — | — |
| Dec. 1990 | Public Opinion Research Foundation | Approve 12.0% Disapprove 61.7% | Yes: 50.80% | — |
| June 1991 | Public Opinion Research Foundation | Approve 12.7% Disapprove 65.3% | Yes: 58.40% | — |
| Aug. 1991 | United Daily | — | — | Approve 3.0% Disapprove 65.0% No opinion 31.0% |
| Sept. 1991 | China Times | — | — | Approve 6.3% Disapprove 65.0% No opinion 28.7% |
| Sept. 1991 | Mainland Affairs Council | — | Yes: 60.6% | — |
| Nov. 1991 | United Daily | Approve 9.0% Disapprove 64.0% | — | — |

*Survey respondents:* c. 1,000 adults in Taiwan area.

Peking has actually hardened its position and stepped up its campaign against Taipei on the international level. For example, Peking registered a strong protest with Manila in late May 1991 when the latter engaged Taipei in negotiations over fishery disputes. A week later, Taipei's vice-minister for economic affairs was denied entry into the former Soviet Union under pressure from Peking. More recently, Peking has deliberately obstructed Taipei's application for membership of the General Agreement on Tariffs and Trade (GATT) and closed the French consulate general in Canton to show its displeasure over the reported sale by France of Mirage fighter planes to Taipei.

Peking's overweening posture has been badly received in Taipei. To cope with Peking's intransigent attitude and the rising need at home to regulate contacts with the mainland, Taipei has focused on seven policy matters.

*Reorganizing the policy-making apparatus.* On 7 October 1990, the National Unification Council (NUC) was established as a presidential task force with research and consultation functions on broad policy issues. Presided over by President Li himself, the NUC is composed of top officials in the national and local governments, leaders from the ruling KMT, the opposition Democratic Progressive Party (DPP) and other political parties, and prominent figures from the private sector,

Table 8.5.
PUBLIC OPINION ON TAIWAN'S FUTURE

| | Survey conductor | Answers | % | Note |
|---|---|---|---|---|
| June 1990 | *United Daily* | Support unification | 11 | If the Chinese |
| | | Support independence | 42 | Communists continue |
| | (survey respondents: | Other* | 47 | one-party dictatorship |
| | 1,128 adults in the | Support unification | 75 | |
| | Taiwan area) | Support independence | 5 | If the Chinese |
| | | Other* | 20 | Communists practise democracy and freedom |
| Feb. 1992 | Mainland Affairs Council | Strongly agree | 11.6 | If the Chinese |
| | | Agree | 56.1 | Communists practise |
| | (survey respondents: | Disagree | 10.2 | democracy and |
| | 3,022 adults in the | Strongly disagree | 1.1 | freedom, Taiwan |
| | Taiwan area) | No opinion | 10.4 | and the Chinese |
| | | Undecided | 10.6 | mainland should be unified |

* "Other" stands for "uncertain", "don't know" and "refuse to answer".

including the press. In late January 1991, the Mainland Affairs Council (MAC) of the Executive Yuan was formally established to replace the former Mainland Affairs Commission. This is an inter-agency ministerial-level council with broad functions regarding overall planning and coordination of mainland policies. The MAC's members include nineteen ministers, council chairmen and heads of the cabinet agencies. Meanwhile, various government agencies also set up their own mainland affairs task forces to coordinate internal mainland work.

*Negotiating via intermediaries.* The Straits Exchange Foundation (SEF) mentioned above is financed jointly by the government and the private sector, and is authorised under contract to negotiate with its mainland counterpart, ARATS, in handling problems arising from cross-Straits exchanges involving the exercise of governmental authority, problems which government agencies are not supposed to handle directly in the

Table 8.6.

PUBLIC OPINION ON GUIDELINES FOR NATIONAL UNIFICATION

| Questions | Answers | % |
|---|---|---|
| Guidelines for National Unification indicate that the two sides of the Taiwan Straits should be unified under the principles of reason, peace, parity and reciprocity | Strongly agree | 23.2 |
| | Agree | 60.3 |
| | No opinion | 9.4 |
| | Disagree | 5.9 |
| | Strongly disagree | 0.9 |
| Guidelines for National Unification indicate that the timing and manner of China's unification should first respect the rights and interests of the people in the Taiwan area, and protect their security and welfare | Strongly agree | 45.0 |
| | Agree | 49.3 |
| | No opinion | 3.3 |
| | Disagree | 2.0 |
| | Strongly disagree | 0.4 |
| Future relations across Taiwan Straits | Immediate negotiation leading to unification | 6.6 |
| | Maintain *status quo* and begin unification negotiation only when the time is ripe | 82.0 |
| | Permanent separation leading to a new and independent country | 6.4 |
| | Other | 5.0 |

*Date:* May 1991.
*Survey respondents:* 1,230 adults in Taiwan area.
*Survey conductor:* Mainland Affairs Council, the Executive Yuan.

current phase of national unification. In addition, the SEF organises seminars and helps people and organizations from both sides of the Straits with problems regarding family reunions, trade, and cultural exchanges.

In the last two years, the SEF has made several trips to the Chinese mainland to visit Taiwan companies in the coastal provinces and to negotiate with ARATS over non-political subjects like joint anti-crime efforts, document certification and establishment of a registered mail service. Consensus was reached in March 1992 on the latter two subjects but negotiation was stalled when ARATS insisted on inserting a "one China" clause in the preamble of the proposed agreements. SEF firmly objected to this because Taipei and Peking have diametrically opposing interpretations on the meaning of "one China". The negotiations were suspended for seven months before being resumed in late October 1992 in Hong Kong. As more progress on substantive issues was made and pressure for early conclusion began to mount, ARATS finally agreed in November not to insist on that insertion. Barring accidents, chances are good at the time of going to press for signing the two agreements in the first half of 1993. This could clear the way for a meeting between Chairman C.F. Koo of SEF and President Tao-han Wang of ARATS on broad issues of cultural and economic exchanges across the Taiwan Straits, including, among other things, the protection of Taiwan investors in the Chinese Mainland.

*Formulating the guidelines for national unification and planning their implementation* (see Table 8.6 for public opinion). The NUC adopted the "Guidelines for National Unification" on 23 February 1991 which were

Table 8.7.
STATISTICS ON INDIRECT MAIL LINKS BETWEEN TAIWAN AND CHINESE MAINLAND, 30 JUNE 1992 (*no. of letters*)

|  | Outbound (Taiwan to Chinese mainland) | Inbound (Chinese mainland to Taiwan) | Total |
|---|---|---|---|
| November | 484,405 | 757,914 | 1,242,319 |
| Total since 1988 | 24,044,797 | 33,992,828 | 58,037,625 |

*Notes*

1. Daily average in Nov. 1992: Outbound 16,147/Inbound 25,264 per day (26 working days are counted in one month).
2. Mail service from Taiwan to Chinese mainland began on 18 April, 1988. Mail service from Chinese mainland to Taiwan began 19 March, 1988.

*Source*: Dept. of Posts and Telecommunications, Ministry of Communications and Transportation.

approved by President Li on 5 March, and were later adopted by the Executive Yuan Council (Cabinet Meeting). The Guidelines set the goal of China's unification as a free, democratic, and equitably prosperous country, to be achieved through three phases under the principles of reason, peace, parity, and reciprocity. The first phase, or the exchange and reciprocity phase, calls for each side of the Taiwan Straits not to deny the other side's existence as a political entity, to pursue domestic economic and political reforms, to settle all disputes through peaceful means, and to respect each other in the international community. If these goals are met, then the second phase, that of mutual trust and cooperation, will be unfolded. The two sides will then establish official channels of communication, with an exchange of visits by high-level officials. Meanwhile, Taipei will consider assisting Peking in developing the southeastern coastal provinces to narrow the gap in the standard of living between the two societies. When these tasks are accomplished, then the two sides can set up a mechanism jointly in the third phase, that of negotiation and unification, and begin negotiating issues of integration leading to eventual unification.

Now that the Executive Yuan has adopted the Guidelines for National Unification, the related government agencies have made a total of thirty-eight plans to implement the objectives of the first phase.

*Legislating Taiwan–mainland relations.* The Legislative Yuan passed, in July 1992, a "Statute Governing the Relations between the People of the Taiwan Area and the People of the Mainland Area", which came into force with its implementing on 18 September 1992. The bill has ninety-six articles covering civil, criminal and administrative matters

Table 8.8.
STATISTICS ON INDIRECT TELECOMMUNICATIONS BETWEEN
TAIWAN AND CHINESE MAINLAND, 30 JUNE 1992

| | No. in Nov. 1992 | Completion rate (%) | Total (Since 26.6.1989) |
|---|---|---|---|
| Telephone | 1,677,911 | 41.57 | 27,487,437 |
| Telex | 771 | 98.72 | 35,134 |
| Telefax* | 158 | 95.18 | 3,443 |
| Telegraph | 2,543 | 100.00 | 145,663 |
| Total | 1,681,383 | — | 27,671,677 |

*Source*: Dept. of Posts and Telecommunications, Ministry of Communications and Transportation.
* "Telefax" here refers to public telefax. As fax machines are widely used in the private sector, their use is included in the telephone statistics.

and applies conflict-of-laws rules in civil matters. Meanwhile, Article 10 of the Constitutional Amendments adopted by the National Assembly in April 1991 provides the authorisation needed for this unprecedented and complicated bill. The enactment of this statute and dozens of implementary regulations ushers in an era of institutionalisation and rule of law regarding relations across the Taiwan Straits.

*Establishing orderly exchanges.* Cross-Straits exchanges will be promoted in the following areas:

(1) Social exchange: More residents from the Chinese mainland will be allowed to visit Taiwan for family or humanitarian reasons. A quota of 240 was set in January 1992 (raised to 300 for 1993) to permit mainland spouses of Taiwan residents to settle down permanently in Taiwan. Senile and sick Taiwan residents may also bring in their mainland relatives to care for them.

(2) Cultural exchange: Two-way exchanges are being promoted, including those between students of all ages. Yet a two-way information flow must first be guaranteed if mainland people are to understand what the ROC stands for and what Taipei's policies are. Since the abortive Soviet coup in August 1991, Peking has tightened its control over the flow of information and people from Taiwan, making cultural exchange even more difficult.

(3) Economic exchange: An early warning system with computer models is being set up to watch cross-Straits indirect trade, to make sure that it does not unduly affect Taiwan's economic development and international competitiveness. Companies from Taiwan investing on the mainland are encouraged to organise associations to protect their own interests. Plans are also being made to introduce the mainland's industrial technology for commercialisation in Taiwan. It is to be hoped that a sound, mutually beneficial relationship could be forged as a result.

*Building consensus at home.* Consensus must be built in Taiwan among business people, interest groups, the press and politicians, who should understand that the pace of the adjustment of Taipei's relations with Peking must be geared to Peking's seriousness in reducing hostility towards Taipei. Such a consensus is emerging as more and more people in Taiwan begin to appreciate the prudent pace of the ROC government's mainland policy.

*Training Adequate Staff.* As the mainland policy involves a wide range of issues, well-trained planners, analysts and administrators are badly

Table 8.9.
VOLUME OF TRADE BETWEEN TAIWAN AND CHINESE MAINLAND THROUGH HONG KONG
(*Unit: US$1,000*)

| | Import (to Taiwan) | Export (to mainland) | Total | Surplus for Taiwan (deficit for mainland) |
|---|---|---|---|---|
| 1988 | 478,698 | 2,242,218 | 2,720,916 | 1,763,520 |
| Growth rate compared to 1987 | 65.68% | 82.81 | 79.54% | 88.09% |
| 1989 | 586,901 | 2,896,487 | 3,483,388 | 2,309,586 |
| Growth rate compared to 1988 | 22.60% | 29.18% | 28.02% | 30.96% |
| 1990 | 765,000 | 3,278,000 | 4,043,000 | 2,513,000 |
| Growth rate compared to 1989 | 30.41% | 13.18% | 16.08% | 8.80% |
| 1991 | 1,125,950 | 4,667,150 | 5,793,100 | 3,541,200 |
| Growth rate compared to 1990 | 47.11% | 42.36% | 43.26% | 40.92% |
| Sept. 1992 | 81,642 | 527,673 | 609,315 | 446,031 |
| Growth rate compared to May 1991 | −23.29% | 26.26% | 16.21% | 43.20% |
| Jan.–Sept. 1992 | 823,012 | 4,457,091 | 5,280,103 | 3,634,079 |
| Growth rate compared to Jan.–Sept. 1991 | 6.90% | 36.42% | 30.79% | 45.54% |

*Note:* Trade volume across the Taiwan Straits during Jan.–Sept. 1992 is 4.62% of Taiwan's total trade in the period.
*Source:* Customs of Hong Kong government.

needed to formulate and implement sound policies. As of 1991, requirements for a new category of civil servants have been added to the civil service examination. Meanwhile, the Mainland Affairs Council regularly sponsors seminars and symposiums and subsidises research and publications on mainland affairs, thus providing more on-the-job training for government officials.

## Concluding remarks

Communism is collapsing everywhere in the world. Now that the Communist system has been abandoned in the country where it originated, the Chinese Communists' legitimacy has been further undermined. If Peking keeps resisting the global movement towards democracy, it will become the last orphan of the Communist world. People in the ROC on Taiwan would like to see peaceful and democratic changes, not revolutionary chaos, on the Chinese mainland. The present situation there indicates that great changes are inevitable after the aged leaders disappear from the political scene.

In view of Peking's intransigent attitude, the ROC government should (1) stick firmly to the final goal of national unification while pursuing neither immediate unification with nor permanent separation from the mainland; (2) establish order in cross-Straits interchange and prudently manage its pace on the basis of the Guidelines for National Unification; and (3) maintain sufficient defence capability and continue its current "pragmatic diplomacy" to broaden its international relations. Taipei can only deal successfully with Peking from a position of strength, not weakness.

Important progress has been made in the organisation, policy formulation and implementation of mainland affairs. Meanwhile, Peking's willingness to respond to Taipei's call for joint anti-crime efforts, and to set up a counterpart organisation of the SEF, and not to insist on inserting a "one China" clause in technical agreements also demonstrates that it has finally realised that pragmatism ought to be the name of the game across the Taiwan Straits. More planning, coordination, training and public education are needed in the future to forge a broadly based national consensus regarding Taipei's mainland policy. A stable and gradually improving relationship between the two sides of the Taiwan Straits is in the interest of all.

Communist Chinese leaders love to boast that what they practise on the mainland is "socialism with Chinese characteristics". People in the ROC in Taiwan sincerely hope, on the contrary, that there will be more and more Chinese characteristics, and less and less socialism on the Chinese mainland.

# EPILOGUE

Just as the shadow of China has a considerable effect on political life in Taiwan, the shadow of Taiwan is not without influence upon events on the Chinese mainland. Admittedly, the two territories' impact upon each other since 1949 has been lopsided. It could hardly have been otherwise, given the disparity in strength, size and resources, and the harsh reality of history. In 1949 Mao Tse-tung's Communist regime was the rising revolutionary force and Chiang Kai-shek's Kuomintang government was everywhere in retreat. However, as the two territories march into the 1990s the picture has charged. Taiwan is now in the process of a successful transformation from a relatively unimportant authoritarian regime built on a largely agrarian economy to an increasingly democratic state and a major regional economic power house. In the early 1950s Taiwan under the Kuomintang was a negative example to the Communists, and comparisons between the two would have been to the latter's advantage. Now the tables have been turned. Unless the mainland should turn inward again, it can no longer ignore Taiwan's spectacular successes. Increasingly, it will live under the shadow of Taiwan, whether Taiwan continues to stay apart from it or not. The Taiwanese shadow will mainly take the form of setting an example and of being a potential competitor to the PRC.

The Taiwan model is not merely a matter of providing a formula for economic successes, even less for rapid economic development on the basis of authoritarianism. While there is no doubt that Chiang Kai-shek's dictatorship did not prevent an economic miracle in Taiwan, it was not the crucial factor in its occurrence. The most important lesson the PRC can usefully learn from Taiwan is that forces for political changes towards greater freedom, democracy and respect for human rights will follow successful economic development. Taiwan has proved that even a quasi-Leninist party-state can successfully adapt to such changes and go on to win genuine popular support. From a liberal standpoint, the greatest achievement of Taiwan since 1949 was not the economic miracle but the political breakthrough. Never in the history of the Chinese people had a dictatorship voluntarily and peacefully abdicated its near absolute power for what it believed to be the national good—a historic step which Chiang Ching-kuo took in 1986. The greatness of the younger Chiang as a leader lies in his leading Taiwan to an orderly democratic transformation, just before the socio-economic

212

forces produced by the post-1949 developments ripened and forced a potentially disruptive showdown with the regime. One must not forget that Chiang could have ignored the socio-economic undercurrent in 1986 and prepared to resort to repression. His political wisdom and far-sightedness have been rewarded so far by Taiwan's continuous march towards democracy, without damaging either economic prosperity or social stability or the Kuomintang as the leading political party. Taiwan is still a long way from a democracy by North American or West European standards, and the danger of an attempt to restore authoritarianism remains, as long as the armed forces are still subject to the Kuomintang's control through the political officer system. However, the point of no return in developing a brand of democracy was probably reached after the parliamentary elections of December 1991 and particularly those of December 1992. A successful withdrawal of the Kuomintang from the armed forces in due course will be particularly instructive to the PRC, where the armed services too are party rather than national forces. Despite some of the principal differences between Taiwan and the mainland, such as the presence of an inhibited centre and the absence of the ideological strait-jacket of a variant of Communism in the former, there is much for the mainland to learn from Taiwan's experiences as a whole.

Whatever the PRC regime decides to do about the Taiwan model, Taiwan will remain a reality. Its very existence will provide a living model of what the Chinese people can do politically, economically, socially and in any other field. Unlike Hong Kong's successes, which could (though unjustifiably) be dismissed as a special case on the grounds that it is a city-state administered by the British and thus irrelevant for comparison with mother China, Taiwan's achievements cannot be ignored so easily. Nor will the Taiwan model disappear as the Hong Kong model may do after the PRC's take-over in 1997, when the PRC will be able to impose virtually any political model it wishes on Hong Kong. In the long term, the very presence of a prosperous and increasingly democratic Taiwan will set the standard to which the other Chinese, across the Straits, will aspire. The PRC can choose to destroy it or emulate it or cooperate with it, but not to ignore it.

# INDEX